THE *Esquire* WINE & LIQUOR HANDBOOK

Other Avon Books by
ESQUIRE PRESS

BAD NEWS: THE BEST OF ESQUIRE MAGAZINE'S
DUBIOUS ACHIEVEMENTS, 1961–1984

THE *Esquire* WINE & LIQUOR HANDBOOK

DAVID LASKIN
and the Editors of ESQUIRE

AN ESQUIRE PRESS BOOK

 AVON
PUBLISHERS OF BARD, CAMELOT, DISCUS AND FLARE BOOKS

THE ESQUIRE WINE & LIQUOR HANDBOOK is an original publication of Esquire Press/Avon Books. This work has never before appeared in book form.

AVON BOOKS
A division of
The Hearst Corporation
1790 Broadway
New York, New York 10019

Copyright © 1984 by Esquire Press
Published by arrangement with Esquire Associates
Library of Congress Catalog Card Number: 84-45254
ISBN: 0-380-88674-X

First Avon Printing, October, 1984

AVON TRADEMARK REG. U. S. PAT. OFF. AND IN
OTHER COUNTRIES, MARCA REGISTRADA, HECHO EN
U. S. A.

Printed in the U. S. A.

DON 10 9 8 7 6 5 4 3 2 1

Contents

THE *Esquire*
WINE & LIQUOR
HANDBOOK

THE DISCRIMINATING DRINKER

Alcohol, according to most early cultures, was a gift of the gods. While it may have lost some of its divine associations, it still retains the power to bring people together, to make speech flow and friendship flower, to turn a meal into an occasion and an occasion into a festivity. Life is pleasurable enough without drink, but with drink, it's especially agreeable.

Today's discriminating drinkers are overwhelmingly committed to the idea of moderation. We drink less than our fathers and grandfathers did, and we drink a greater variety of beverages. This isn't to say that excess never occurs; it is seen, however, as both unnecessary and unhealthy. Those who enjoy wine, beer, and spirits today drink because it's relaxing, because it's a delightful way to enhance good company and good food, because it's interesting, because it tastes good.

Nearly everything our forefathers drank is available to us still—along with so much more the old-timers never dreamed of. We have a dazzling global range to choose from: fine vodkas from Russia, Poland, and Finland; excellent sparkling wines from France and California; distinctive imported beers from Mexico, China, the Philippines, et cetera, as well as interesting new products from our own microbreweries; dark rums and light rums; rare Highland malt whiskeys, light Canadians, and deep, authoritative Bourbons; traditional cordials like Bénédictine and Grand Marnier as well as the newer cream liqueurs. The list seems endless. And with the greater variety has come a willingness to experiment.

Freed from stodgy conventions of the past, we drink what and when we want to. "Proper" means what suits our sense of style and occasion. If we wish to pour liqueurs over ice, drink champagne for breakfast, or shake a dash of Pernod into a dry martini—that's our business, and our pleasure.

If there is one basic characteristic of today's drinking habits, it is this: a

1

preference for lightness. In drinks, "light" can mean many things: clean and pure tasting, thin in body, low in alcohol and often in calories, pale in color, dry, elegant, refreshing. Brut champagne is light; vintage port is not.

It's difficult to pinpoint precisely when the move to lightness began, but it seems to be an integral part of the modern sensibility that feels at home in uncluttered living spaces, comfortable in clean-lined, unencumbering clothing, and nourished by fresh, simply prepared foods. When vodka, which was practically unknown in this country before the Second World War, took a huge leap in sales during the 1960s and 1970s, it heralded the trend. Soon lighter blends of Scotch and other whiskeys were introduced; a glass of white wine became an acceptable, then a fashionable, and finally an utterly standard round-the-clock drink. But even this wasn't light enough. In the late 1970s, Perrier supplanted white wine as the supreme light drink: Lightness had reached its ultimate.

Luckily, today's enlightened drinkers are not blinded by the light: The appreciation of lightness has by no means stifled the urge to experiment. Americans are inquisitive about mixing new drinks and rediscovering old standbys; we want to try regional beers and imported ales, big French red wines and soft, subtle California whites; we enjoy comparing Cognac and Armagnac, Sherry and Madeira, Scotch and Irish whiskeys; we're finding out how pleasant a glass of chilled vermouth can be before a big meal, or when we might prefer Campari or

Lillet. We quietly acquire knowledge as we travel, drinking the local specialty as we go—be it ouzo in Greece, Calvados in Normandy, tequila in Mexico, aquavit in Sweden, or Anchor Steam Beer in San Francisco. When eating out, we weigh the wine steward's suggestion against our own increasingly informed opinion. When visiting friends, we take an interest in what they're drinking. We're open to the new, and we remember. It's not a matter of crash courses or boning up— it's a matter of attention, instinct, and taste.

Discriminating drinkers are not snobs; but, when only the best will do, they want to know what the best is. They don't wish to squander single-malt Scotch on Rob Roys or vintage Champagne on mimosas. Wine experts used to make a lot of people nervous about choosing the correct label and matching the exact wine to certain foods. Today's enlightened drinkers brush fussiness away. We want to experience both the "fun" wines—like beaujolais, Asti spumanti, and rosés— and more serious wines—like grand cru Bordeaux and German beerenauslesen. It's as pointless to exclude the former from one's table as it is tasteless to treat the latter without a measure of respect.

What it all comes down to is style. Discriminating drinkers don't need to parade expertise or apologize for it, either. They want knowledge to enhance their drinking hours; they want to exercise and refine their taste; they want to be good hosts to their friends. *The Esquire Wine & Liquor Handbook* answers these needs by offering essential guidance to the wide variety of spirits, wines, beers, waters, and mixers available in America today. We begin with a useful section on setting up the home bar; we end with practical and inspirational tips on giving parties. In between, you'll find hundreds of drink ideas and more than 1000 drink recipes—enough to keep you hosting and toasting until the end of time.

What more is there to say, except . . . *Cheers!*

—The editors of *Esquire*

THE BAR AT HOME

1

STOCKING UP

In the beginning was . . . the six-pack of beer. In time was added the jug of California chablis, the fifth of Canadian Club, the quart of vodka, and then—on one gloriously prosperous day—the pint of fine Scotch.

This, we recognize, is how many home bars grow. Rare is the young person who strolls into a liquor store with a pocketful of cash and coolly trades it for a complete set of spirits, liqueurs, and wines. Most home bars start out quite spartan and gradually acquire epicurean trappings. The lists below reflect this natural process of alcoholic evolution.

THE SURVIVAL BAR

The Survival Bar includes the bare minimum you can get away with and still offer some choice of drinks to your guests. One can vary the Survival Bar, of course. Committed wine drinkers may prefer to skip spirits altogether

and put their money instead into several well-chosen wines or aperitifs. The same goes for committed beer drinkers, who pride themselves on a varied selection of domestic and imported bottles while eschewing whiskey and gin. But the Survival Bar we have outlined will allow you to fulfill requests as varied as whiskey on the rocks, vodka martini, Bloody Mary, wine spritzer—in addition to the ubiquitous "glass of wine, please." And, with brandy on hand, you are not caught unprepared when, after dinner, the wine is finished and your guests wish to linger.

1 bottle (750 milliliters or, in old parlance, a "fifth") vodka
1 bottle blended Scotch whiskey
1 bottle Bourbon whiskey
1 small bottle (500 milliliters) dry vermouth
1 large bottle red wine, a French beaujolais or a good California generic red
1 large bottle white wine, a

California chablis or Italian
frascati or soave
1 bottle brandy
1 six-pack beer or ale.

THE BASIC BAR

The Basic Bar includes the standard
wines and spirits for home consumption and entertaining. With these bottles on your shelf, you'll be set to mix
most drinks your intimates request and
quite a few they've never heard of. If
you are building a bar, this is the list
you will want to complete.

1 large bottle (1¾ liter) vodka
1 large bottle American gin
1 large bottle blended Scotch
whiskey
1 large bottle American blended
whiskey or Canadian whiskey
1 bottle Bourbon whiskey
1 large bottle light (Puerto
Rican) rum
1 small bottle dry vermouth
1 small bottle sweet vermouth
1 bottle brandy:
French Cognac and
Armagnac are the superior
brandies for after-dinner
sipping; but prices come down
fairly rapidly for other types,
which are suitable for mixing.
Liqueurs:
Start with one or two half-
bottles of different types; for
example, Kahlúa (coffee-
flavored) and Cointreau
(orange). Other old standbys
include Bénédictine,

Drambuie, Grand Marnier,
amaretto, crème de menthe.
4 or more bottles white wine:
Good to have a lot in reserve,
as this is the drink of choice
for more and more people. A
jug of California chablis or
white table wine and a few
bottles of California
johannisberg riesling or
sauvignon blanc will start you
off. Add Mâcon blanc or a
couple bottles of Loire valley
whites from France; Italian
soave, frascati, or orvieto, and
medium-priced German
whites, perhaps a decent
liebfraumilch.
2 bottles red wine:
A couple of bottles of
beaujolais, chianti, or good
California generic red will do.
2 bottles sparkling wine:
California or Spanish
sparkling wines can be good,
inexpensive, and have just as
many bubbles as French
Champagne.
2 six-packs beer:
Keep a six of your favorite
domestic or imported label on
hand, and a six of light—low-
calorie—beer for the dieters.

STOCKED IN STYLE
If the Basic Bar looks like kid stuff to
you, you may add the items listed below. With these bottles crowding the
bar, you can play wizard, concocting
magic potions for your guests and offer-

ing them their choice of the world's
luxury brandies and liqueurs.

1 bottle Russian or Polish vodka
(keep in freezer for straight
shots)
1 bottle English gin
1 bottle superpremium 12-year-
old blended Scotch whiskey
1 bottle single-malt Scotch
whiskey, preferably from the
Highlands
1 bottle Irish whiskey
1 bottle Tennessee whiskey
1 bottle dark Jamaican rum
1 bottle medium-bodied rum
from Haiti, Trinidad, or
Barbados
1 bottle white or gold tequila
1 bottle V.S.O.P. Cognac
1 bottle V.S.O.P. Armagnac
2 or 3 half-bottles of eau-de-vie
of choice: kirsch, slivovitz,
poire, framboise
4 or 5 liqueurs in half bottles:
Choose from: B & B,
Chartreuse, Irish Mist, Peter
Heering, sambuca, Southern
Comfort, Tía Maria, anisette,
crème de cacao, crème de
cassis, mandarine, peppermint
schnapps, Irish cream liqueur
2 or 3 aperitif wines and bitters:
Dubonnet, Lillet, Campari,
mistelle
1 bottle cream sherry
1 bottle fino sherry (preferably
manzanilla)
1 bottle ruby port
1 bottle tawny port
1 bottle sercial madeira

White wine:
French chablis, sauternes,
graves, burgundy,
chardonnay; German
gewürztraminer; pinot blanc
from some of the better
California wineries; 2 or 3
bottles of German white in
the spätlese and auslese class
Red wine:
A few bottles of good-quality
claret, burgundy, and rhone;
California gamay, pinot noir,
zinfandel, and cabernet
sauvignon; some of the big
Italian reds, such as barolo,
gattinara, barbaresco
Sparkling wine:
Keep a few bottles of real
French Champagne, of the
brut (dry) type on hand, as
well as some of the better
California sparkling wines;
Italian spumante and German
sekt are also nice for variety.

FOR CONNOISSEURS, COLLECTORS, AND COGNOSCENTI

If your sybaritic cravings are still left
unsatisfied, send the butler to lay in
the "necessities" below. Beyond this,
humble planet Earth has naught to offer.

Flavored vodka:
Take your pick of Limonnaya,
Okhotnichya, Starka, or
Pertsovka
Hollands (gin):
The original genever from The

Netherlands, full-flavored, robust, and best straight
Aquavit:
Clear Scandinavian spirit, distilled like gin but with caraway seed instead of juniper
Ultrapremium Scotch:
Whiskey of 20 years or older
Single-malt Scotches:
Complete your collection with the products of the Lowlands, Islay, and Skye
Aged and overproof (130+) rum
Añejo (aged) tequila
Brandy:
Napoleon or Vieille Réserve Cognac and/or Armagnac; Italian grappa and Peruvian pisco for variety
Liqueurs:
Fill out your collection with some of the more exotic fruit and nut flavors; for example: banana, cherry, blackberry, hazelnut, peach, plum, melon, chocolate, coconut, praline, caraway seed, walnut
Aperitifs:
Pernod, Byrrh, St. Raphäel, Punt e Mes
Oloroso and amontillado sherry
Malmsey and verdelho Madeira
Marsala
Málaga
Vintage Port
White wine:
French from Burgundy gundy (Meursault and Montrachet)

and Sauternes (Château d'Yquem); German whites in the beerenauslese and trockenbeerenauslese classes
Red wine:
From France, first-growth Bordeaux reds, such as Château Lafite-Rothschild, Château Mouton-Rothschild, Château Margaux, Château Latour; true Burgundy reds from the Côte de Nuits, especially Chambertin, Romanée-Conti, Clos de Vougeot; from Italy, Brunello di Montalcino, Vino Nobile di Montepulciano, Recioto Amarone della Valpolicella; from Spain, Vega Sicilia; California wines from some of Napa's finer wineries, such as Robert Mondavi, Clos du Val, Stag's Leap, Mayacamas, Beaulieu Vineyards, and Heitz Cellars
Sparkling wine:
Vintage Champagne and cuvée speciale; to your supply of brut add sec, demi-sec, and doux (the sweeter categories) to cover you for any possible festive occasion
Beer:
Beers, ales, stouts, and porters from around the world—but don't keep too much too long, because the life span of all beers is limited.

BOTTLE MEASURES

Traditional Names of Bottles	New Metric Sizes	No. of fluid ounces (U.S. Customary Measure)
Split	187 milliliters (mL)	6.3 ounces (oz)
Tenth	375 milliliters (mL)	12.7 ounces (oz)
Pint	500 milliliters (mL)	16.9 ounces (oz)
Standard Bottle of Wine This size bottle, once called a "fifth" (for ⅕ gallon) is also standard for many liquors and liqueurs	750 milliliters (mL)	25.4 ounces (oz)
Quart	1 liter (L)	33.8 oz or 1 quart (qt) 1.8 oz
Magnum	1.5 liters (L)	50.7 oz or 1.58 qt
Half Gallon	1.75 liters (L)	59.2 oz or 1.85 qt
Double Magnum (or Jeroboam)	3 liters (L)	101.4 oz or 3.17 qt or 0.79 gal

2

BARWARE
AND BAR TIPS

If you were to try to collect all the bar gadgets, glassware, mixers, and drink flavoring ingredients on the market, as interesting a hobby as that might be you'd probably have to build a new wing on your barroom, kitchen, liquor cabinet, or whatever place you keep your drinking supplies. You'd have a Cuisinart for frappés, an electric unit for hot toddies, a special freezer for ultrafrozen untainted ice cubes, special racks for wine, a collection of trays and tongs, bitters, and snifters, and, no doubt, a constant hangover. Fun is fun, but so are funds! Here, then, are some basic lists of bar essentials—barware first, then glassware, and finally mixing ingredients and tips. For those whose imbibing styles have already outdistanced the ordinary, we add in each category a list

of slightly more recherché items that will ease the flow of fine liquor.

BARWARE

FOR THE BASIC BAR

Shot glasses come in a variety of sizes, from three-quarter-ounce (half jigger) to one ounce (pony) to one-and-a-half-ounce (one jigger—the standard measure for many cocktails) to two-ounce size (for a collins, fizz or generous highball). Some shot glasses have lines on the side for measuring. Another popular version is a metal, double-ended variety: The pony is one end, the jigger the other. Professional bartenders often use speed pourers, devices installed in the bottle necks that dole out precise doses without the need for shot glasses.

Long bar spoon is useful both in measuring teaspoonfuls of sugar and in stirring cocktails.

Shot glass

Bar spoon

13

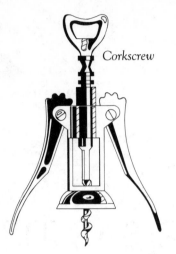

Corkscrew

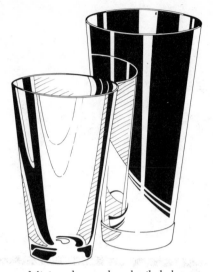

Mixing glass and cocktail shaker

Corkscrew, bottle opener, can opener are essential for wine, bottled beer, canned juices, etc. You can find one tool that performs all three functions. For ease of handling, a wing-type corkscrew is the best; get one with a bottle opener on top.

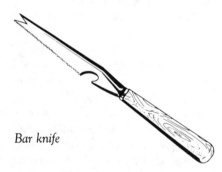

Bar knife

Paring knife for cutting lemon and lime wedges, peels, etc. A special **bar knife** has an opener, and also a two-pronged tip to the blade that is useful for spearing garnishes.

Small cutting board comes in handy at the bar.

Shakers and strainers come in several varieties. An inexpensive and efficient combination used by many bartenders is a simple mixing glass with a larger stainless steel shaker that fits over the glass. You will also need a wire strainer with clips that let it rest tightly on the rim of the mixing glass as you strain the drink into a drinking glass. There are also traditional shakers made of glass or metal that have tightly fitting tops with built-in strainers and a smaller opening for pouring. Still another choice is a mixing glass equipped with a screw top and pouring spout.

Strainer

FOR THE MORE ADVANCED BAR

Ice aids produce ice for drinks in three forms—cubed, crushed, and shaved. Ice cubes (a.k.a. "rocks") can be made in any freezer, but commercially produced cubes are frozen harder and are also free of impurities that your water or the air in your freezer may contain. Ice can be crushed by wrapping cubes in a towel and bashing them with a blunt instrument, such as a mallet, or by attacking a solid large block with an **ice pick.** Less alarming to guests and neighbors is an **ice-crusher:** These can be electric, mechanical, or come as an attachment on a blender. "Shaved" means the ice has been crushed twice. A **vacuum ice bucket** keeps cubes, crushed, or shaved ice from turning to slush and keeps you

from running to the freezer. You can transfer ice with **tongs** or a **scoop.**

A **Champagne bucket** is the most elegant way of chilling and presenting bubbling (or even still) white wines. Fill with cubes, insert bottle—instant class.

A **muddler** is not a boring slob who's always making a mess of things: It is a round-based stick of hardest hardwood used for mashing sugar and bitters in old fashioneds, mint in mint juleps, and for other fruits and herbs. When the recipe tells you to muddle, this is what you do it with.

Champagne bucket

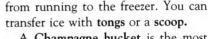

Martini pitcher

Martini pitcher should have a molded lip that holds back the ice while you pour out the drink. Use a glass stirring rod whenever you are stirring seltzer or carbonated mixers because a metal stirrer or spoon may cause the fizz to fizzle.

Lemon/lime squeezer

Lemon-lime squeezer of the one-handed type with built-in strainer is favored by pros, but an electric juicer is neat, clean, and fast enough to keep you away from packaged mixes except in emergencies.

A **blender** adds froth, foam, and body to sours, punches, thick frozen drinks, and potations containing fruit and/or egg.

Funnel aids in pouring into small-necked bottles and decanters, especially when you've already had a few.

Trays will serve if you don't have an official home bar—load a large one with liquor, ice bucket, glasses, gadgets, and carry to wherever the action happens to be.

Dish towels of real linen are best for polishing glasses.

Drink accessories include toothpicks to spear olives, onions, and so on; swizzle sticks and straws for stirring; coasters; cocktail napkins, which add a nice touch and can also double as coasters.

GLASSWARE

Your collection of glassware should obviously suit your own drinking and entertaining style. If you never mix drinks and don't care for brandies and cordials, there's no point in stocking up on stemmed cocktail glasses, snifters, or tiny liqueur glasses. On the other hand, don't throw them out if someone makes you a present: You never know when your tastes (or those of your friends) will change.

As with barware, there is basic glassware you can't do without if you drink at all; and then there is glassware for those who drink a lot of different kinds of drinks and want to serve them in the containers designed to optimize their taste, appearance, and effects. Our own overriding prejudice is for thin, clear crystal glasses: They're light in the hand, they're easy to get one's mouth around, and they permit one to see the often beautiful colors of whatever drink is in them.

THE BAR MINIMUM

If you are possessed of limited means or a utilitarian temper, you can get by with only one variety of all-purpose glass in the home, and this is the **stemmed balloon wine glass** of 9-ounce to 14-ounce capacity. Designed for serving red or white wine, it can be used for almost anything from beer to cocktails to brandy.

NICE TO HAVE ON HAND

Cocktail glasses: Solid stems are not just for show—they keep hands from warming the drinks. The *4½-ounce size* is good for martinis, manhattans and

Balloon wine glass

Martini glass

Sour glass

stingers. The *6-ounce size* will hold frozen daiquiris and cocktails with ice more comfortably. You can interchange **sour glasses** with cocktail glasses. A *Delmonico glass* is about the same size but lacks the stem.

Highball or collins glasses: If you want a highball glass that doubles for Collinses and juleps, get the 14-ounce size with straight sides. The standard highball glass is 8-ounce to 10-ounce.

Rocks glasses *(a.k.a. **old-fashioned glasses**)***:** These hold 6-to-10 ounces for drinks "on the rocks." Best to get them with heavy bottoms, so they'll stand up to your muddling machinations and your heavy-handed friends. Serve straight-liquor drinks in them, too, if you don't want to invest in *whiskey shot glasses.*

Liqueur glasses: Most practical is the two-ounce *pony glass*, which can be

Highball glass

Rocks glass

Pony glass

17

Claret wine glass

Tulip champagne glass

Brandy snifter

used for liqueurs, brandy, and the pousse-café.

Wine glasses: These come in a range of shapes and sizes, each one developed for a particular wine. There's a *claret glass* for the Bordeaux wines; a squat-bowled *Rhine-wine glass* for those particular German wines; *tulips and flutes* for Champagne (wide-mouthed saucers are *not* recommended, as they encourage bubbles to escape); and long-stemmed *white-wine glasses* that taper inward toward the mouth. Avoid wine glasses that hold less than 6½ ounces: They're too small for swirling, an essential process in proper appreciation of the bouquet.

SPLENDOR IN THE GLASS

Brandy snifters: Supply the brandy experience to your nose as well as your mouth. Choose 3-ounce, 6-ounce, or 12-ounce sizes. Any bigger than that and you might feel you're drinking from a goldfish bowl.

Beer vessels: Include the traditional *Pilsner glass* in 10-ounce size, the footed *beer shell* of 16 ounces, the fat, squat *beer goblet*, the sturdy-handled *stein*, and the tall, straight-sided *tankard*, usually of silver or pewter, with a hinged lid.

Sherry and port glasses: Often delicate little 2-ounce affairs, these can be difficult to pour into and bothersome to drink from. You're better off with a 3-to-4½-ounce *dock glass*, which bellies out a bit at the bottom. Useful for madeira, too.

Parfait glasses: These are slim 7½-ounce glasses used for drinks containing fruit or ice cream.

"Hurricane" glasses: Use these large (22-ounce), tall, curved-stem glasses for tropical-fruit drinks.

Irish-coffee glasses: Here's the last word in elegance when serving this and other warming concoctions. Some are simply stemmed heat-proof goblets; others are tall slim glass mugs with

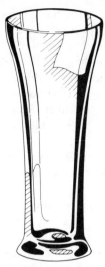

Pilsner glass

Dock glass

Irish coffee glass

handles; still others slip into a kind of wire basket with a handle.

Mugs: These offer an alternative for the hot drink.

Punch cups: Many usually come with a punch bowl. Stay away from those that are too small to hold comfortably.

MIXING SUPPLIES

Even purists of the straight-up school yearn now and then for a mixed drink. Alcohol is not enough: Every home bar needs mixing and flavoring ingredients, as well (see Section Six, chapter 2 for more information on widely used waters and mixers). Perhaps you'll decide against stocking up on passion-fruit nectar, but tonic and soda are essential. The list below reflects what the well-equipped home bartender should have on hand; pick and choose among them.

CARBONATED BEVERAGES

Soda: club soda, salt-free seltzer, or sparkling mineral waters can be used

Tonic water: a.k.a. quinine; a must for summer

Bitter lemon: lemon-flavored tonic water

Cola: many brands available, choose your favorite

Ginger ale: the drier, the better

7-Up: a favorite lemon-flavored soda for mixing

In all cases, small bottles are best unless you're having a party; then, buy the quart or liter size.

FRUITS AND JUICES

Lemons and limes: for fresh juice, and for peels and wedges

Oranges: for fresh juice, and for garnishes

Grapefruit juice: fresh or frozen; not as commonly called for as orange juice, but good to have on hand

Rose's lime juice: the best-known

brand of sweetened lime syrup; not a substitute for fresh lime juice

Sweet-and-sour: a lemon-and-sugar mixture that is prepared and sold under a variety of names, it is also easy to prepare and store at home, as follows:

Using a blender or a quart jar with a tight-fitting cap, pour in 12 ounces lemon juice, 18 ounces distilled water, ¼ cup sugar, the white of 1 egg; blend or shake until light and frothy. Keeps in refrigerator for about 10 days. Always reblend or shake before each use.

Tomato juice: either in small cans or in a jar that can be stored in the refrigerator after opening; **V-8** juice is a popular substitute, and prepared Bloody Mary mix can be bought in cans

Pineapples and pineapple juice: crushed pineapple, pineapple juice, and sliced fresh pineapple garnishes are commonly used in tropical drinks

OTHER MIXABLES

Sugar syrup: superfine sugar can sweeten most drinks, but occasionally a recipe calls for sugar syrup (sometimes called simple syrup), which you can make in advance, as follows:

Dissolve 2 cups sugar in 1 cup water in a saucepan; simmer about 10 minutes; pour into jar and cool; cover and refrigerate until needed.

Grenadine: sweet cherry-red syrup from pomegranate pulp; a requisite for making a tequila sunrise; keeps forever without spoiling

Falernum: a syrup flavored with lime and ginger, made in the Caribbean, used primarily in sweet tropical drinks and containing little alcohol

Orgeat: an almond syrup for flavoring mai tais and other tropical drinks

Cream: added to many after-dinner-drink recipes; unless specified, either heavy or light cream can be added, as you prefer

Eggs: egg whites are used in many cocktail mixes; whole eggs, in eggnogs and other drinks

Water: keep bottled spring water on hand if your tap water is heavily chlorinated or has harsh-tasting minerals

Tea and coffee: tea is often combined with spirits for both hot and cold drinks; coffee, for hot after-dinner potions

Bouillon: for both hot and cold drinks, such as the Bull Shot

Coconut cream: an ingredient of piña coladas and other tropical drinks

Orange-flower water: a solution of water and neroli oil used to flavor drinks like the Ramos Gin Fizz

Bitters: a dash can enliven many a drink.

Bitters are made from a variety of herbs, barks, roots, seeds, and flowers incorporated into an alcohol base. The *flavoring* bitters, of which Angostura from Trinidad is the best-known example, should not be confused with Campari and Fernet Branca, which are *beverage* bitters—for drinking. Because Angostura is so popular, drink recipes often call for it. If the recipe doesn't specify, however, some other flavoring bitters are: Abbott's

Aged Bitters from Baltimore, Peychaud's Bitters from New Orleans, and various orange bitters made primarily in Britain from the peels of Seville oranges. For true enthusiasts, there are bitters bottles with a special cap through which you shake a pre-measured dash.

Tabasco and Worcestershire: where would the Bloody Mary be without a dash of these hot sauces? The first is made from red-hot peppers; the second, from soy, vinegar, and spices.

GARNISHES

In addition to fruit wedges and slices, there are other garnishes commonly called for. The most popular are listed below.

Cocktail onions: come in jars and can be kept refrigerated for some time

Olives: get small, green, pitted ones, either plain or stuffed with pimentos, and keep tightly covered in refrigerator

Maraschino cherries: most commonly used are the red variety, but they also come in green

Fresh mint: essential for the mint julep, and nice for other summer coolers

Nutmeg: often ground on top of hot drinks or cream drinks

Cinnamon sticks: as flavorers and stirrers.

TIPS FOR MIXING DRINKS

- Cold drinks should always be mixed in *chilled* glasses. If space permits, keep glasses in the freezer, standing upside down. You can also pack them with crushed or cubed ice several minutes before mixing the drink.

- Superfine sugar should be used for mixing because it dissolves more readily than either confectioner's sugar or regular table sugar.

- When mixing a drink in a cocktail shaker, use four ice cubes unless the recipe says otherwise.

- Citrus twists should consist of the colored part of the peel, not the white membrane underneath. The standard citrus twist measures about one inch by one-half inch.

- To float cream or a spirit on top of a drink, hold a teaspoon over the drink with its bottom uppermost. Slowly pour the cream or spirit over the rounded back of the spoon until it spreads evenly over the surface of the drink.

- When a recipe calls for soda or club soda, you can also use sparkling water, charged water, sparkling mineral water, or seltzer.

- Drinks containing mixers should be stirred gently, slowly, and as little as possible, so that the carbonation is not dissipated.

- To frost a glass with salt or sugar, first moisten the rim with lime or lemon juice—or whatever fruit juice or liquor is prevalent in the drink—then dip the rim into a bowl of salt or sugar and tap the glass with a spoon to shake off the excess.

- When preparing hot drinks, fill

glass or mug with boiling water. Leave water in for about 30 seconds, then pour it out. If you're using a glass that is not heat-proof, place a metal spoon (preferably silver) in it before pouring in the hot liquid—the spoon will absorb the heat and prevent the glass from breaking.

MEASURES TO REMEMBER

It's important when mixing drinks to measure accurately, especially when you're using a new recipe. Keep in mind these standard measures.

1 pinch	= $\frac{1}{8}$ teaspoonful		
1 dash	= $\frac{1}{6}$ teaspoonful		
1 barspoon	= 1 teaspoonful = $\frac{1}{6}$ fluid ounce =	4.9 milliliters	
	(oz)	(ml)	
1 tablespoonful	= $\frac{1}{2}$ fluid oz = 14.8 ml		
1 pony	= 1 fluid oz = 29.6 ml		
1 jigger	= $1\frac{1}{2}$ fluid oz = 44.4 ml		
1 shot*	= $1\frac{1}{2}$ fluid oz		
8 tablespoons	= $\frac{1}{2}$ cup = 4 fluid oz		
8 tablespoonfuls	= $\frac{1}{2}$ cup = 4 fluid oz =	118.4 ml	
1 cup	= $\frac{1}{2}$ pint = 8 fluid oz =	236.8 ml	
2 cups	= 1 pint = 16 fluid oz =	0.46 liters (l)	
4 cups	= 1 quart = 32 fluid oz =	0.946 l	
16 cups	= 4 quarts = 1 fluid gallon =	3.8 l	

*A proper shot is a full $1\frac{1}{2}$ ounces; shot *glasses* come in sizes from $\frac{3}{4}$ to $1\frac{1}{2}$ ounces, often with lines etched to indicate other measures.

SPIRITS

Liquor, alcohol, spirits, booze —by whatever name you call it, in essence it's all the same thing: Essence. Spirits are essences—the condensed vapors that rise off a fermenting liquid when it is boiled. Distillation, the process basic to the production of all liquors, occurs for the simple reason that alcohol becomes gas at a lower boiling point than water. The Arabs, who gave us the word *alcohol,* were pioneers in perfecting the distillation technique, although they were more interested in making perfumes and trying to convert base metals to gold than in creating potable beverages. The Europeans learned the process from the Arabs, and they too hoped that the alcohol that ran off the primitive stills would work wonders. They called it *aqua vitae*—water of life—and today we are still discovering just how life-enhancing these liquids can be.

A few other facts to consider before plunging into the different categories of liquors:

• *Proof* refers to the alcoholic content of a spirit, and in the United States the number designating the proof is double that of the percentage of alcohol. An "overproof" spirit is a spirit of more than 100 proof (and therefore more than 50 percent alcohol).

• Alcohol is the only food taken into the body without being affected by the digestive system: It enters the bloodstream unchanged and travels quickly to the brain.

• Contrary to myth, alcohol is not a stimulant but a depressant. It doesn't warm you up, either, but has the opposite effect—which is why so much rum and gin is drunk in the tropics.

• The key word in the enjoyment of spirits is *moderation.* You can also protect yourself against the evil effects of too much aqua vitae by coating the stomach walls beforehand with food, preferably the fat of milk. There are many highly touted "cures" for a hangover, but the most reliable still seem to be rest and time.

So, properly forewarned, you are now ready to sample the wondrous variety of the world's spirits.

1

VODKA

Vodka is spirits pure and simple, neither flavored nor aged. By United States law, it must be colorless, odorless, and tasteless; and this quality (or absence of qualities) makes vodka the most mixable of spirits. It takes on the flavor of whatever you pour into a glass with it, and it cuts the viscosity of fruit juices and liqueurs without dampening their taste. In addition, the aftereffects of vodka are substantially less irksome than those of any other kind of alcoholic drink. These factors alone may explain vodka's meteoric rise from obscurity before the Second World War to its current status as America's largest-selling spirit. Various legends surround the early history of vodka in the U.S.A. One attributes its first success to one Jack Morgan of Hollywood's Cock 'n' Bull Restaurant. The story goes that, just after the war, Mr. Morgan mixed vodka and ginger beer, added half a lime, and poured the concoction into a copper mug. He called it a *Moscow Mule,* and the stuff threw the country for a loop.

The origins of vodka are buried under even more historical claptrap and bring in the further complication of international disputes between the Russians and the Poles. Both lay claim to the invention of vodka as their own (dating it back anywhere from six hundred to a thousand years ago), and both insist the word for this spirit is a diminutive of their own term for *water.* Whoever is right, there is no doubt that both the Russians and the Poles have perfected the art of vodka-making, and between them they distill the finest "little water" in the world.

Contrary to popular belief, vodka is *not* made from potatoes, although it can be and has been. These days, vodka is produced primarily from grain—usually wheat, corn, or rye. The grain is crushed and mixed with water to produce the mash, which is then injected with yeast so that it will ferment. It is put through a continuous still (as opposed to a pot still) to obtain the purest possible grain neutral spirit—just about pure alcohol, running off at about 190 proof.

Various filtering processes have been invented to purify this clear spirit even more, although state-of-the-art American distilling techniques have made this unnecessary. Some Russian vodka is still filtered through quartz sand and a special charcoal made from birch trees. The resulting ultrapure substance is then reduced with water to 80 proof or 100 proof and bottled without aging.

Since all U.S. vodkas must conform to government requirement that the spirit be "without any distinctive character, completely without aroma, entirely colorless and tasteless," there tends to be very little difference between brands. Therefore, when you buy an American vodka your main consideration should be price. You may be tempted by a classy package or ad, but the contents of the bottle is what counts—and even laboratory analysis hasn't turned up many differences.

Russian and Polish vodkas, however, are a different breed—more sophisticated, cleaner, more refined. Russia's Stolichnaya, available for several years now in this country, is the preferred brand of many a serious vodka drinker. It has a slight silkiness of body and faint sweetness of taste. Store the bottle in the refrigerator, or even the freezer (where the liquor will thicken slightly), and serve Stoli neat in thin, chilled liqueur glasses. (Legend has it that Peter the Great took his vodka frigid and neat, with a grinding of fresh pepper.) Poland exports a brand known as Wyborowa, which is distilled from rye and has a nice little tang. Don't waste these fine imported vodkas by mixing them: Their distinctiveness is of the subtle sort that gets lost in a Bloody Mary or a Cape Codder.

Vodka makers have introduced a new twist in the old spirit with *flavored* vodkas. Perhaps the most unusual are Zubrovka (U.S.S.R.) and Zubrowka (Poland)—vodkas steeped with buffalo grass. Bottled with a blade of the grass suspended in the liquor, these vodkas are as fresh and fragrant as new-mown hay. Unfortunately, neither is available at present in the U.S. because of a technical violation of government regulations; but the situation may change. Meanwhile, seekers of a new taste experience in vodka may hunt down Limonnaya, a lemon-flavored vodka; Okhotnichya, the "hunter's vodka" flavored with meadow grasses and heath honey; and the hot and spicy Pertsovka, which, in a Bloody Mary, will take care of the seasoning all by itself.

Its extreme mixability makes vodka a year-round spirit, showing up in tonics during the summer, in Black Russians on long winter nights, in the faintly heretical vodka martini after a hard day in any season, and, of course, in the Bloody Mary, the ubiquitous brunch and lunchtime favorite.

Vodka Recipes

See Section One for information on barware, mixing supplies, and mixing tips. For conversion to metric or other measurements, refer to tables on pages 11 and 22.

FIVE VODKA STANDARDS

BLOODY MARY
In a well-chilled shaker, combine 1½ ounces vodka, 3 ounces tomato juice, ½ ounce lemon juice, 2 dashes of Worcestershire sauce and one or two of Tabasco, a heaping teaspoonful of horseradish from which the liquid has been squeezed, and salt and pepper to taste. Shake hard and pour into an iceless collins glass or oversized wine glass. Garnish with celery stalk.

The Bloody Mary may also be shaken with ice and strained into the glass, or mixed in the glass and served on the rocks.

VODKA COLLINS
Fill a collins glass with ice and pour in 1 ounce vodka and 2 ounces sweet-and-sour. Stir, fill with soda, and stir again one or two turns. (Sweet-and-sour is described in Section One, chapter 2.)

SCREWDRIVER
Fill an old-fashioned or rocks glass with ice. Pour in 1½ ounces vodka and 4 ounces orange juice. Stir, and garnish with orange slice, if you like.

BLACK RUSSIAN
Shake 3 ounces vodka with 1 ounce Kahlúa (or other coffee liqueur) and ice

in a cocktail shaker. Strain into cocktail glass.

VODKA MARTINI
Shake 1½ ounces vodka and ½ ounce dry vermouth with ice in a cocktail shaker. Strain into a cocktail glass. Garnish with grapefruit peel. As with the true gin martini, the vodka martini may be made as dry as you like by decreasing the vermouth to as little as one drop. It can also be made by pouring vodka and vermouth over ice in a rocks glass. For a vodka Gibson, garnish with a couple of cocktail onions.

OTHER VODKA DRINKS

VODKA GIMLET
Fill a rocks glass with ice and pour in 1½ ounces vodka and ½ ounce Rose's lime juice. Stir, and garnish with lime slice.

CZAR PETER'S PREFERENCE
Chill a bottle of Stolichnaya and a pony glass in the freezer for an hour or so. Pour 2 ounces of the chilled vodka into the chilled glass and top with freshly ground pepper.

TAWNY RUSSIAN
In a rocks glass half-filled with ice cubes, stir 1 ounce amaretto and 1 ounce vodka.

29

BLACK MARBLE
Pour 3 ounces Russian or Polish vodka over ice in a rocks glass. Garnish with a black olive and a thin slice of orange.

MIDNIGHT SUN
Stir 2½ ounces vodka, ½ ounce grenadine, and 3 ice cubes slowly in a mixing glass. Strain into cocktail glass and garnish with lemon wedge.

HAYRIDE
Shake 1½ ounces vodka, 1 dash grenadine, 4 ounces orange juice, and 3 ice cubes in cocktail shaker. Strain into a rocks glass half filled with ice. Garnish with orange slice.

HIGH ROLLER
Shake 1½ ounces vodka, ¾ ounces Grand Marnier, and 4 ounces orange juice with ice in a shaker. Strain into a rocks glass and shake drops of grenadine on the surface.

HARVEY WALLBANGER
Fill collins glass with ice. Pour in 1 ounce vodka, then fill almost to top with orange juice. Stir well, and add ½ ounce Galliano liqueur.

EGGHEAD
Combine in blender (at medium speed) 1½ ounces vodka, 4 ounces orange juice, 1 egg, 3 ice cubes. Pour over a couple of ice cubes in rocks glass.

SALTY DOG
Dip rim of 10-ounce glass into lemon juice, then into crystal salt. Put some ice cubes in the glass with 2 ounces vodka. Fill with grapefruit juice, stir lightly.

SALT LICK
Frost rim of large wine glass with salt, as for Salty Dog. Fill glass with ice and pour over it 1½ ounces vodka, 2 ounces bitter lemon soda, 2 ounces grapefruit juice. Stir for one or two turns.

CAPE CODDER
Fill rocks glass with ice and add 1½ ounces vodka, 3 ounces cranberry juice, a dash of lime juice. Stir slowly.

For cranberry juice, 1 ounce cranberry liqueur can be substituted. You can sweeten a Cape Codder by adding a splash of Rose's lime juice instead of the fresh lime juice.

CAPE GRAPE
Fill a highball glass half full of ice. Add 1½ ounces vodka, 4 ounces grapefruit juice, 1 ounce cranberry liqueur, and stir slowly. Twist a strip of grapefruit peel over the drink, then drop it in as garnish.

VODKA REFRESHER
Pack an 8-ounce glass with crushed ice and add 3 ounces vodka. Put in freezer. Just before serving, add Cranapple juice or equal parts of cranberry and apple juices to fill.

Another mixer to try: freshly squeezed juice of the tangelo—a cross between a tangerine and a grapefruit.

DAISY BUCHANAN'S SEABREEZE
Fill a highball glass with ice and add 1 ounce vodka, 1 ounce grapefruit juice, 3 ounces cranberry juice. Stir.

CARMEN MIRANDA

Into a blender, put 1 ounce vodka, 1 ounce golden rum, 2 teaspoonfuls lime juice, 1 teaspoonful Falernum syrup, about half a banana (peeled and sliced), and 3 ounces crushed ice. Blend at medium speed for 15 seconds. Strain into rocks glass.

PEACHADILLY

Combine in blender 1½ ounces vodka, ½ peeled fresh peach (or canned, if necessary), ½ ounce lemon juice, ½ ounce peach preserve, and 4 ounces crushed ice. Blend at medium speed until just about smooth. Pour into large wine glass.

PRICKLY APRICOT

Fill collins glass with ice. Add 2 ounces vodka and 4½ ounces apricot nectar. Fill to the top with ginger ale. Stir well.

BRUNCH COCKTAIL

Moisten rim of cocktail glass with strawberry liqueur, sugar-frost rim, and set glass aside. Shake 1½ ounces vodka and ½ ounce light rum with ice cubes in cocktail shaker. Strain into the prepared glass and drop in a whole, stemmed strawberry.

PEAR IDYLL

Put three ice cubes in a highball glass and add 2 ounces vodka and 4½ ounces pear nectar. Top up with 7-Up. Stir well.

GORKI PARK

Put into a blender 2½ ounces vodka, 1 teaspoonful grenadine, 3 large fresh strawberries, 1 dash orange bitters, 3 ounces crushed ice. Blend at medium speed for 10 seconds. Strain into a cocktail glass and garnish with half a strawberry.

APPLE COOLER

Fill highball glass with ice. Pour in 2 ounces vodka, then unsweetened apple juice nearly to the top. Add dash of calvados.

PETER'S PIECE

Pour 1 ounce Peter Heering, 1½ ounces vodka, ½ ounce orange juice, and 3 ounces crushed ice into cocktail shaker. Shake hard. Strain into cocktail glass.

SECOND COMING

Pour 2½ ounces 100-proof vodka, ½ ounce brandy, and ½ ounce cherry brandy into cocktail shaker. Add ice cubes and shake hard. Strain into rocks glass half filled with ice.

ST. PATRICK'S DAY DELIGHT

Put 1½ ounces vodka, ¾ ounce melon liqueur, and 3 ice cubes into cocktail shaker and shake hard. Fill a rocks glass half full of crushed ice and strain drink into it. Garnish with green maraschino cherry.

SOLIDARITY

Pour 2 ounces Polish vodka, ½ ounce Polish blackberry brandy, ½ ounce slivovitz, 2 dashes orange bitters into cocktail shaker. Add 4 ice cubes and shake hard. Strain into cocktail glass.

DARK EYES

Pour 2 teaspoonfuls blackberry brandy, 1½ ounces vodka, and 2 teaspoonfuls lime juice over ice cubes in a cocktail shaker and shake hard. Strain into brandy snifter. Garnish with slice of lime.

SHELBY'S CYCLONE
Mix with ice in a rocks glass 1 ounce vodka, 1 ounce melon liqueur, ½ ounce pineapple juice, ½ ounce soda, and a squeeze of lime. Garnish with lemon wedge.

KANGAROO
Pour into rocks glass 2 ounces vodka, ¾ ounce dry vermouth, 4 ounces crushed ice. Twist lemon peel above the glass, then toss in.

KANGAROO II
Follow recipe above for Kangaroo, but add ½ ounce kiwi fruit liqueur.

ODESSA FILE
Pour 2 ounces 100-proof vodka, 1 ounce dry vermouth, and 1 teaspoonful kümmel over ice cubes in a cocktail shaker. Shake hard. Strain into cocktail glass.

ROSY TICKLE
Pour 1½ ounces vodka, 1½ teaspoonfuls kümmel, and 1½ teaspoonfuls Rose's lime juice over 2 ounces crushed ice in a cocktail shaker. Shake hard. Strain into cocktail glass.

SAILING AWAY IN STYLE
Into a cocktail shaker pour 1½ ounces Grand Marnier, 3 ounces vodka, ½ ounce peppermint schnapps. Add 3 ice cubes and shake hard. Strain into ice-filled rocks glass and garnish with sprig of mint.

OLD PALE
Mix 1 ounce peppermint schnapps, 1½ ounces vodka, and 1 teaspoonful strawberry liqueur in mixing glass. Pour (unstrained) into cocktail glass.

ICEBERG
Shake together 2 ounces vodka and 1 teaspoonful Pernod in a cocktail shaker with ice. Strain into cocktail glass.

GODMOTHER
Pour 1½ ounces of vodka and ½ ounce amaretto into rocks glass filled with ice. Stir.

GREEN DRAGON
Pour 1½ ounces vodka and ½ ounce green crème de menthe into rocks glass filled with ice. Stir.

RUSSIAN NAIL
Pour 1 ounce vodka and ¾ ounce Drambuie into rocks glass filled with ice. Stir. Twist lemon peel above the drink, then toss in.

KAMAKAZI
Pour into cocktail glass 1½ ounces vodka and the juice from one lime wedge. Add a dash of Cointreau and stir.

GYPSY MOTH
Pour 1½ ounces vodka, ½ ounce Bénédictine, 1 teaspoonful lemon juice, 1 teaspoonful orange juice into cocktail shaker with 4 ice cubes and shake hard. Strain into cocktail glass. Garnish with slice of orange.

RUBINO

Over 3 ice cubes in mixing glass, pour 1 ounce vodka, 1 ounce red Dubonnet, and ½ ounce Campari and stir thoroughly. Strain into rocks glass filled with ice.

PAPARAZZI

Mix 1½ ounces vodka with ¼ ounce Campari. Serve with a lemon twist in a chilled cocktail glass.

MR. LUCKY

Pour 1 ounce vodka, 1 ounce white port, 1 dash Angostura bitters into cocktail shaker and shake hard with 4 ice cubes. Strain into cocktail glass. Squeeze strip of lemon peel over drink and toss in.

CZARINA

In mixing glass, mix ½ ounce vodka, ¼ ounce dry vermouth, ¼ ounce apricot brandy, 1 dash Angostura bitters, and 4 ice cubes. Strain into cocktail glass.

CZAR

Pour 1 ounce vodka, 1 ounce Grand Marnier, ½ ounce lime juice, and 1 dash orange bitters over 4 ice cubes in cocktail shaker. Shake hard. Strain into large wine glass and top with 3 ounces dry sparkling wine.

WHITE RUSSIAN

Pour 1½ ounces vodka and ½ ounce Kahlúa into rocks glass filled with ice. Stir. Float heavy cream on top.

WHITE SPIDER

Pour 1½ ounces vodka and ½ ounce white crème de menthe into rocks glass filled with ice. Stir.

FAN-TAN

Pour 1 ounce vodka, ½ ounce gold rum, ¾ ounce coffee liqueur, and 2 ounces milk into rocks glass filled with ice. Stir.

POLAR BEAR

Pour 1 ounce vodka, 1 ounce dark crème de cacao, and ½ ounce heavy cream into rocks glass filled with ice. Stir.

KRETCHMA

Pour 1 ounce vodka, 1 ounce white crème de cacao, 2 teaspoonfuls lemon juice, 2 dashes grenadine into cocktail shaker with 4 ice cubes and shake hard. Strain into rocks glass half filled with ice.

CREAMY MIMI

Pour 1 ounce vodka, 1 ounce sweet vermouth, 1 ounce heavy cream, 2 teaspoonfuls triple sec, 2 teaspoonfuls white crème de cacao, and 3 ounces crushed ice into cocktail shaker. Shake hard. Strain into rocks glass.

NINOTCHKA

Pour 1½ ounces vodka, 1 teaspoonful lemon juice, 2 teaspoonfuls white crème de cacao over ice cubes in a cocktail shaker. Shake hard. Strain into cocktail glass.

THE KISS

Pour 1½ ounces vodka, ¾ ounce chocolate cherry liqueur, and ¾ ounce heavy cream into cocktail shaker. Add ice cubes and shake hard. Strain into cocktail glass and garnish with fresh strawberry.

FOGGY DAWN

Place 1 ounce vodka, ½ ounce grenadine, 4 ounces milk and a few ice cubes in cocktail shaker and shake hard. Strain into rocks glass. Garnish with maraschino cherry.

PEACHES 'N' CREAM

Blend in blender until smooth 1 ounce vodka, 4 fresh peaches (peeled, pitted, and sliced). Add 2 large scoops vanilla ice cream and blend until mixed well. Pour into large wine glass; top with fresh whipped cream.

GORILLA PUNCH

In a mixing glass combine 1 ounce vodka, ½ ounce blue curaçao, 2 ounces orange juice, 2 ounces pineapple juice, and 4 ice cubes. Mix, then strain into a collins glass filled with ice. Garnish with cherry.

CHI CHI

Pour 1 ounce vodka, 1 ounce cream of coconut, 2 ounces pineapple juice over ice cubes in mixing glass. Stir, and strain into collins glass filled with ice. Garnish with a long spear of pineapple.

THE BULLSHOT

Pour 1½ ounces vodka, 4 ounces beef bouillon, and 1 dash each of Worcestershire, A-1, and Tabasco sauces, and a dash of Angostura bitters into mixing glass. Stir thoroughly. Pour over ice in highball glass, garnish with lemon wedge, and sprinkle with celery salt.

THE BLOOD SHOT

Pour 1½ ounces vodka, 1½ ounces beef bouillon, and 1½ ounces tomato juice into mixing glass and stir well. Add dashes of Tabasco and Worcestershire, and salt and pepper to taste. Pour over ice in highball glass.

You can substitute clam juice for the beef bouillon and V-8 juice for the tomato juice.

CLAMDIGGER

Pour 1½ ounces vodka, 3 ounces tomato juice, 3 ounces clam juice, 1 dash each Tabasco and Worcestershire sauces, and a touch of horseradish in mixing glass and stir thoroughly. Pour into highball glass half filled with ice. Squeeze strip of lemon peel over drink, then toss it in.

BUGS BUNNY

Fill a highball glass with ice and pour in 1½ ounces vodka, 3 ounces carrot juice, ½ ounce lemon juice, Worcestershire and Tabasco to taste, and a bit of horseradish. Stir.

BLOOD-AND-THUNDER MARY

Pour into well-chilled cocktail shaker 1 ounce vodka, 1 ounce beer, 4 teaspoonfuls celery salt, a dash of garlic powder, salt and pepper to taste, 1 teaspoonful Worcestershire, 1 teaspoonful bouillon, 5 ounces tomato juice, and ¼ ounce lemon juice. Shake with ice, and pour into collins glass.

CREOLE MARY

To the basic Blood Mary recipe, add a mixture of pickled okra, chopped celery, and jalapeño peppers to taste.

BLOODY MARY SOUP

Heat in a saucepan 6 ounces of thin (not cream) tomato soup and ½ ounce lemon juice, with salt, pepper, Worcestershire, and Tabasco to taste. Before it boils, remove pan from flame and stir in 3 ounces vodka. Pour into preheated mug and garnish, if you like, with sour cream and chopped chives.

PRAIRIE OYSTER

Separate the yolk from a raw egg and set aside. Pour 2 ounces vodka, 2 ounces tomato juice, 1 teaspoonful lemon juice, 2 dashes Worcestershire sauce, with salt and pepper to taste, into mixing glass and stir well. Now carefully ease the egg yolk into the bottom of a large wine glass so that it doesn't break open. Pour mixture over yolk.

PURPLE PASSION

Five minutes before mixing, put a small cluster of grapes in the freezer so they will develop a frost. Fill a tall highball glass with ice and pour in 1½ ounces vodka, 3 ounces grapefruit juice, 3 ounces grape juice. Stir one or two turns. Get grapes from freezer and lower gently into the drink.

WHITE RIOT

Pour 1½ ounces vodka over ice in large wine glass, top up with sparkling white grape juice. Garnish with wedge of lime.

YELLOW FEVER

Fill highball glass with ice and pour in 1½ ounces vodka, 6 ounces lemonade. Stir. Garnish with slice of lemon.

BULL FROG

Fill highball glass with ice and pour in 1½ ounces vodka, 6 ounces limeade. Stir. Garnish with slice of lime.

TWISTER

Fill highball glass with ice and pour in 2 ounces vodka and ½ ounce fresh lime juice. Top with 7-Up.

MALINKY MALCHIK

Fill highball glass with ice and pour in 1½ ounces vodka, ½ ounce crème de cassis, 2 teaspoonfuls lemon juice. Stir, and top with ginger ale.

SPECIAL HOUSE FIZZ

Pour into cocktail shaker 1½ ounces vodka, 1½ ounces framboise, and a splash each of orange, lime, and pineapple juices. Shake, then top with sparkling wine. Serve over ice in highball glass.

PALM BEACH DELIGHT

Fill a collins glass with ice and pour in 2½ ounces vodka and 3 ounces grape juice; top with 7-Up. Garnish with lemon slice.

2

GIN

Gin, that most identifiably English of spirits, was originated by a Dutchman and takes its name from a French word. Unlike vodka and scotch, gin did not evolve over long centuries of folk manufacture. It was invented in Holland in the mid-16th century for medicinal purposes. Credit for this liquor goes to Franciscus de la Boe (alias Dr. Sylvius), a chemist at the University of Leiden, who redistilled a neutral spirit with juniper berries and thus obtained what he hoped would be a cure-all. He called his medicine *genièvre* (the French word for *juniper*) and sold it through apothecary shops. The Dutch took to the delightful medicine at once, changed its name to *genever*, and soon found that it cured even what didn't ail them.

Now, how did gin travel the route from Dutch medicine to English cheer? Legend has it that the first Britons to sample gin were the one thousand horsemen and five thousand foot soldiers Queen Elizabeth sent to the Low Countries in 1585 to fight Philip of Spain. The British legions returned home amazed and impressed by the "Dutch courage" of their comrades-in-arms; they spread the good word all through the sceptered isle and, before you could say "juniper berry," *genièvre/genever* had a new name and a new country of enthusiasts.

Since then, gin has had its ups and downs in reputation and in fashion. During the 18th century, gin-drinking spread like the plague among the English lower classes, contributing to the squalor and misery depicted by Hogarth in *Gin Lane*, one of his famous engravings. "Drunk for a penny, dead drunk for tuppence, clean straw for nothing" was a slogan of the day—and it probably says a lot about the quality of the gin. Gin sunk to another low in the United States during Prohibition, when "bathtub gin" was often as foul tasting as it was dangerous.

But gin came back, and came back in style. The dry martini, subject of endless dispute as to proportions and origins, was *the* drink of sophistication from the 1920s onward, and it still provides one of the most pleasant and rapid ways to unwind. One thinks of Winston Churchill, who liked his martini so dry that he reputedly merely waved the vermouth bottle over his glass of gin. One conjures up an image of well-born young people in tennis whites sipping gin-and-tonics on a summer evening. No doubt about it—gin has class.

The gin that the English developed is basically pure, though diluted, grain alcohol (about 75 percent corn, 15 percent malted barley, and 10 percent other grains) that is then *redistilled* with or through juniper berries and a marvelous mixture of what distillers call *botanicals*. These flavoring agents can include cassia bark, coriander seed, angelica root, aniseed, both sweet and bitter orange peels, bitter almonds, fennel, and orrisroot. The juniper berries and botanicals are usually placed in a cylindrical tray (called a *berryhead*) that sits on the still, although some distillers mix the flavoring agents in with the spirit and distill the whole mash. Each distillery has its own secret formula of ingredients, and that's why each gin has its own subtle distinctiveness of flavor and fragrance.

Most of the gin produced in England and America now is called *london dry*. The term no longer refers to the place of origin but to the clean, light, unsweet style of the liquor that was perfected in England in the late 19th century. There is, however, another type of gin called *hollands, schiedam,* or *genever*—a product, not surprisingly, of the Netherlands and much closer in concept to the original gins. Hollands gin is very full-flavored and full-bodied, with a robust, almost rooty flavor that results from the greater proportion of barley in the grain formula and the low proof at which it is distilled. The pronounced flavor of hollands makes it unsuitable for mixing in cocktails. The Dutch down it neat and cold, the perfect accompaniment to Dutch herring.

English and American gins, while both carrying the term *london dry* (or *extra dry, very dry,* etc.) on the label, do have certain differences. The British distill their gin from base spirits of slightly lower proofs and, in some cases, higher barley content. Thus their gins retain more character and body than ours. Popular British brands include Beefeater (the leading import to the U.S.A.), Bombay, Plymouth, and Tanqueray. Hiram Walker, Gordon's, Gilbey's, and Fleischmann's are all popular American brands.

Whereas gin is not ordinarily aged—and, in fact, U.S. regulations permit no age claims to be printed on the label—some U.S. producers do market a product called *golden gin* that has been aged in wood for short periods, hence its pale golden color.

Ever since cocktails became popular early in this century, gin has been one of the ingredients preferred to give them their kick. Perhaps no cocktail has spawned more legends or inspired more debate than the dry martini. Neither its origin nor the correct way of mixing one up has yet been established definitively, and probably never will be. John Doxat, who wrote a book on the subject called *Stirred, Not Shaken*—

The Dry Martini, stated that the drink was invented around 1910 for John D. Rockefeller at New York's Knickerbocker Hotel by a barman named Martini. Others give credit to Jerry Thomas, one of the all-time-great bartenders and a pioneer in the field of mixed drinks. Since its invention, the dry martini has been getting drier (20-to-1 gin to vermouth is standard at many bars today) and more complex (people are throwing in everything from sake to Chanel No. 5). Even at the more traditional 3-to-1 or 4-to-1 proportions, the martini packs enough potency to command considerable respect; if you hear yourself ordering a third, look out!

Gin Recipes

See Section One for information on barware, mixing supplies, and mixing tips. For conversion to metric or other measurements, refer to tables on pages 11 and 22.

SEVEN GIN STANDARDS

THE DRY MARTINI
Stir 1½ ounces london dry gin with ½ ounce dry vermouth in a mixing glass with ice cubes for not more than 30 seconds. Strain into cocktail glass. Twist a strip of lemon above the drink to release a drop of oil, then garnish with an olive. For a drier dry martini, use less vermouth: Proportions of gin to vermouth may be 8 or 12, or even 20, to 1.

GIBSON
Follow recipe for dry martini and substitute 2 or 3 cocktail onions for the olive. Lemon peel optional.

THE GIMLET
Shake 1½ ounces dry gin with ½ ounce Rose's lime juice in cocktail shaker and strain into cocktail glass. Splash of club soda optional.

GIN RICKEY
Pour 2 ounces gin and 1 teaspoonful grenadine into a rocks glass. Squeeze in juice of half a lime and top with soda water. Garnish with the squeezed-out lime.

TOM COLLINS
In a mixing glass, stir 3 ounces gin, 1½ ounces lemon juice, and 1 teaspoonful superfine sugar until sugar dissolves. Pour into highball glass, top with club soda, and garnish with a wedge of orange.

GIN AND TONIC
Pour 2 ounces gin into highball glass filled with ice cubes. Squeeze wedge of lemon or lime over glass, then drop it in. Fill glass to top with tonic water.

GIN FIZZ
Pour 1½ ounces lemon juice into highball glass. Add 1 teaspoonful superfine sugar and stir until sugar dissolves. Add crushed ice and pour 3 ounces gin over it. Put glass in freezer for a minute or so, then, just before serving, fill glass with club soda and garnish with twist of lemon.

GIN COCKTAILS WITH APERITIFS AND BITTERS

ALTHEA GIBSON
Follow recipe for dry martini, but garnish with black olive only.

PERNOD MARTINI
Stir together 1 ounce gin, ½ teaspoonful Pernod, ½ ounce dry vermouth, and ice cubes. Strain liquid into cocktail glass. Garnish with cocktail onion, if you like.

MERRY WIDOW

In a cocktail shaker, shake 1 ounce gin, 1 ounce dry vermouth, 2 dashes Bénédictine, 2 dashes Pernod, 1 dash Angostura bitters, and ice cubes. Strain into cocktail glass and garnish with lemon peel.

ROSE COCKTAIL

Shake 2 ounces gin, ½ ounce dry vermouth, 1 teaspoonful lime juice, 3 dashes grenadine, and ice cubes in cocktail shaker. Sugar-frost rim of cocktail glass, if you wish. Strain into glass.

ALLIES

Shake 1 ounce gin, 1 ounce dry vermouth, and 2 dashes kümmel in cocktail shaker with ice cubes. Strain into cocktail glass.

ALMOND COCKTAIL

Pour 2 ounces gin, 1 ounce dry vermouth, and ½ ounce amaretto in mixing glass and stir. Strain into rocks glass filled with ice cubes.

MANHATTAN SOUTH

Pour into mixing glass: 1 ounce gin, ½ ounce dry vermouth, ½ ounce Southern Comfort, 1 dash Angostura bitters; add ice cubes. Stir. Strain into cocktail glass.

CARUSO

Stir in mixing glass ½ ounce gin, ½ ounce dry vermouth, ½ ounce crème de menthe, and ice cubes. Strain into cocktail glass.

MELANCHOLY BABY

Shake 1 ounce gin, ½ ounce dry vermouth, and ½ ounce melon liqueur with ice cubes in a cocktail shaker. Half fill cocktail glass with crushed ice. Strain ingredients into glass.

VOILÀ

Shake 1½ ounces gin, ½ ounce dry vermouth, 3-to-4 dashes Angostura bitters, 2 dashes maraschino liqueur, and ice cubes in cocktail shaker. Strain into cocktail glass.

FIBBER MCGEE

Pour 1½ ounces gin, 1 ounce grapefruit juice, 1 ounce sweet vermouth, and 2 dashes Angostura bitters in cocktail shaker with ice cubes. Shake well and strain into cocktail glass. Twist strip of lemon peel above drink to release one drop of oil; toss peel in.

BRONX COCKTAIL

Shake 2 ounces gin, ½ ounce orange juice, and 2 teaspoonfuls dry vermouth in cocktail shaker with ice cubes. Strain into cocktail glass.

BRONX SILVER

Follow recipe for bronx cocktail, but add 1 egg white to cocktail shaker.

BRONX GOLDEN

Follow recipe for bronx cocktail, but add one egg yolk to cocktail shaker.

MOTHER-OF-PEARL

Pour 1½ ounces gin, ½ ounce dry vermouth, 1 teaspoonful Pernod, and 2 teaspoonfuls white crème de menthe into cocktail shaker with ice cubes. Shake well. Strain into cocktail glass.

BLUE MOON

Shake 1½ ounces gin, ½ ounce dry vermouth, 1 teaspoonful blue curaçao, 1 dash Angostura bitters, and ice cubes in cocktail shaker. Strain into cocktail glass.

ROLLS-ROYCE

Put 1 ounce gin, ½ ounce each sweet vermouth and dry vermouth, and 1 teaspoonful Bénédictine in cocktail shaker with ice cubes. Shake. Strain into cocktail glass.

PERFECT COCKTAIL

Shake 1 ounce gin, 1 ounce dry vermouth, and 1 ounce sweet vermouth in cocktail shaker with ice cubes. Strain into cocktail glass.

PERFECT STRAWBERRY

Shake 1½ ounces gin, ½ ounce each sweet vermouth and dry vermouth, 2 dashes strawberry liqueur, and ice cubes in cocktail shaker. Strain into cocktail glass and drop in two strawberries as garnish.

BITTERSWEET

Shake 1½ ounces gin, 1 ounce sweet vermouth, and 2 dashes Angostura bitters with ice cubes in cocktail shaker. Strain into cocktail glass.

CAMPOBELLO

Shake 1½ ounces gin, 1 ounce sweet vermouth, 1 ounce Campari, and ice cubes in cocktail shaker. Strain into cocktail glass.

THE ENGLISH

Stir 1½ ounces london dry gin with a dash of orange bitters in cocktail glass.

Fill glass with ice cubes and squeeze over it a drop of oil from a sliver of lemon peel.

THE ENGLISH II

Shake in a cocktail shaker 1½ ounces gin, 2 dashes orange bitters, ½ ounce lime juice, 1 teaspoonful superfine sugar, and ice cubes. Strain into cocktail glass.

DERBY

In a cocktail shaker, shake 1½ ounces gin, 2 or 3 dashes peach bitters, and ice cubes. Place 3 more ice cubes in a rocks glass; strain mixture into glass. Garnish with sprig of mint.

ORANGE GIMLET

Put into cocktail shaker 1½ ounces gin, 1 ounce Lillet, 2 dashes orange bitters, and ice cubes. Strain into cocktail glass.

FERNET BRANCA COCKTAIL

Shake 1 ounce gin, ½ ounce sweet bitters, ½ ounce Fernet Branca, and ice cubes in cocktail shaker. Strain into cocktail glass.

NAPOLEON

Shake together 2½ ounces gin, 3 drops Fernet Branca bitters, 3 drops Dubonnet, and 3 drops curaçao with ice cubes in cocktail shaker. Strain into cocktail glass.

OPERA

Pour in mixing glass 1½ ounces gin and ½ ounce each Dubonnet and maraschino liqueur. Stir. Strain into cocktail glass. Garnish with twist of orange.

OPERA II
Shake in cocktail shaker 1 ounce gin, 1 ounce Dubonnet, 1 ounce Grand Marnier, and ½ ounce orange juice. Strain into cocktail glass.

BIRTHDAY COOLER
Pour into mixing glass 1½ ounces gin and 2 ounces Pernod or Ricard. Stir. Strain into rocks glass filled with cracked ice.

RUBY SLIPPERS
In cocktail shaker, shake 2 ounces gin, 1 ounce port wine, ½ ounce lime juice, 1 teaspoonful grenadine, and ice cubes. Strain into cocktail glass.

WATERLOO
Stir 1½ ounces gin and ½ ounce port wine with ice cubes in mixing glass. Strain into cocktail glass and garnish with lemon twist.

SEVILLE
Shake 1½ ounces gin, ½ ounce sherry, ½ ounce orange juice, and ice cubes in cocktail shaker. Strain into cocktail glass. Squeeze lemon wedge above glass, then drop it in.

GIN COCKTAILS WITH OTHER SPIRITS

GOLDEN DROP
Pour 1½ ounces gin into rocks glass filled with ice. Shake two drops Scotch whiskey on top. Garnish with lemon twist.

GIN DAIQUIRI
Shake 1½ ounces gin, ¾ ounce golden rum, 2 teaspoonfuls lime juice, and 1 teaspoonful superfine sugar in cocktail shaker with ice cubes. Strain into cocktail glass.

GIN JAMAICA
Shake 1 ounce gin, ½ ounce gold Jamaican rum, ½ ounce pineapple juice, ½ ounce lime juice, and ice cubes in cocktail shaker. Strain into cocktail glass.

GIN COCKTAILS WITH LIQUEURS

NAVY BLAZER
In mixing glass, stir 2½ ounces gin, ½ ounce blue curaçao, and 1 dash orange bitters. Strain into rocks glass filled with cracked ice. Add splash of club soda if desired.

BLUE RIBBON
Stir in a mixing glass 1½ ounces gin, 1 ounce white curaçao, and ½ ounce blue curaçao. Strain into rocks glass filled with cracked ice. Splash of club soda optional.

CHERRY HILL BOY
Shake 1 ounce gin, ½ ounce kirsch, ½ ounce cherry liqueur, and crushed ice in cocktail shaker. Pour, unstrained, into cocktail glass.

CHERRY HILL BOY II
Shake 1½ ounces gin, ½ ounce cherry liqueur, 1 teaspoonful maraschino liqueur, and 2 teaspoonfuls lemon juice with ice cubes in cocktail shaker. Strain into cocktail glass and drop in a maraschino cherry, if desired.

SINGAPORE GIN SLING

Pour 3 ounces lemon juice into mixing glass. Add 1 heaping teaspoonful of superfine sugar and stir until it dissolves. Add 2 ounces gin, ½ ounce Cointreau, and ½ ounce cherry brandy and stir again. Strain into highball glass filled with ice cubes. Top with club soda. Stir again 1 or 2 turns; garnish with lemon peel.

CHERRY CRUSTA

Moisten rim of cocktail glass with lime juice and dip it in sugar bowl to frost rim. Set glass aside. In cocktail shaker, shake 2 ounces gin, 1 ounce brandy, 2 teaspoonfuls lime juice, and ice cubes. Strain into the prepared glass.

FALLEN ANGEL

Shake 2½ ounces gin, 2½ ounces lemon juice, 2 dashes crème de menthe, and 1 dash Angostura bitters with ice cubes in cocktail shaker. Strain into rocks glass.

TROPICAL GIN STINGER

Pour 1 ounce gin, 1 ounce crème de menthe, and 2 ounces fresh pineapple juice into cocktail shaker and shake. Strain into rocks glass half filled with cracked ice.

APRICOCKTAIL

Shake 1½ ounces gin, 2 dashes apricot brandy, 1 dash grenadine, ½ ounce lime juice, and ice cubes in cocktail shaker. Strain into cocktail glass.

APRICOCKTAIL II

Shake 1 ounce gin, 1 ounce apricot brandy, 1 ounce orange juice, and ice cubes in cocktail shaker. Strain into

cocktail glass. Optional garnish: a sprinkle of shredded coconut.

WHITE HEATHER

Shake 1 ounce gin, ½ ounce Cointreau, ½ ounce pineapple juice, and ½ ounce dry vermouth in cocktail shaker with ice cubes. Strain into rocks glass half filled with ice cubes.

WHITE HEATHER CRUSTA

Moisten rim of cocktail glass with Cointreau and sugar-frost rim. Pour into cocktail shaker 1½ ounces gin, 1 ounce Cointreau, 1 teaspoonful each lemon juice and lime juice, and ice. Shake, then strain into prepared glass.

MISSISSIPPI MULE

Shake 1½ ounces gin, 1 ounce crème de cassis, ½ ounce lemon juice, and 1 dash Angostura bitters in cocktail shaker with ice cubes. Strain into cocktail glass; garnish with lemon wedge.

DEMPSEY

Pour 1½ ounces gin, 1½ ounces calvados, 2 dashes grenadine, and 2 dashes Angostura bitters in cocktail shaker. Shake. Strain into rocks glass filled with crushed ice.

ACE OF SPADES

Shake 1½ ounces gin, 1 tablespoonful blackberry liqueur, 1 teaspoonful lime juice, and ice cubes in cocktail shaker. Strain into cocktail glass.

ALASKA

Combine 1½ ounces gin, 1 ounce yellow Chartreuse, and cracked ice in cocktail shaker. Shake, then strain into cocktail glass; garnish with lemon wedge.

EMERALD ISLE

Shake 1½ ounces gin, ½ ounce green crème de menthe, and 2 dashes Angostura bitters with ice cubes in cocktail shaker. Strain into cocktail glass.

LEAP YEAR COCKTAIL

Shake with ice in cocktail shaker 1½ ounces gin, ½ ounce Grand Marnier, ½ ounce sweet vermouth, and 1 teaspoonful lemon juice. Strain into cocktail glass; garnish with lemon peel

GIN COCKTAILS WITH CREAM, HONEY, OR EGG

SNOWBALL

Shake with ice cubes in cocktail shaker 1 ounce gin, 2 teaspoonfuls white crème de menthe, 2 teaspoonfuls sambuca, and 2 teaspoonfuls cream. Strain into cocktail glass.

UNION JACK

Shake in cocktail shaker 1½ ounces gin, 1 ounce sloe gin, 2 teaspoonfuls cream, and 1 teaspoonful grenadine, with ice cubes. Strain into cocktail glass.

VELVET KISS

Combine 1 ounce gin, ½ ounce crème de banane, ½ ounce pineapple juice, and 1 ounce heavy cream in cocktail shaker. Add ice cubes and shake. Strain into cocktail glass.

ALEXANDER'S SISTER'S COCKTAIL

Shake 1 ounce gin, 1 ounce crème de menthe, and 1 ounce heavy cream with crushed ice in cocktail shaker. Strain into cocktail glass. Dust with nutmeg, if desired.

GIN ZOOM

Into 1 tablespoonful boiling water in a bowl, stir 1 teaspoonful honey until dissolved. Pour mixture into shaker, and add 1 tablespoonful light cream, 2½ ounces gin, and ice cubes. Shake, then strain into cocktail glass.

HELLO HONEY

Shake 1½ ounces gin, 1 teaspoonful honey, ½ teaspoonful lemon juice, and ice cubes in cocktail shaker. Strain into cocktail glass.

PINK LADY

Shake together in cocktail shaker 1½ ounces gin, 1 teaspoonful grenadine, 1 teaspoonful sweet cream, and 1 egg white. Strain into cocktail glass filled with cracked ice.

PINK LADY II

Shake 1½ ounces gin, 1 teaspoonful strawberry liqueur, 1 teaspoonful lemon juice, 1 teaspoonful sweet cream, and 1 egg white in cocktail shaker. Strain into cocktail glass filled with cracked ice.

SKINNY LADY

Shake well 2 ounces gin, ½ teaspoonful grenadine, and 1 egg white with ice cubes in cocktail shaker. Strain into cocktail glass.

PINK PANTHER

In cocktail shaker with ice cubes, shake ¾ ounces gin, ¾ ounces dry vermouth, 1 egg white, 1 ounce orange juice, and ½ ounce crème de cassis. Strain into cocktail glass.

SAMBUCA SHAKE
Put 2½ ounces gin, 1 tablespoonful sambuca, 1 egg white, and ½ ounce heavy cream with ice cubes in cocktail shaker. Half fill rocks glass halfway with crushed ice. Shake, then strain ingredients into glass.

BOXCAR
Shake in cocktail shaker 1½ ounces gin, 1½ ounces Cointreau, 1 teaspoonful lime juice, 1 egg white, and ice cubes. Moisten rim of sour-style glass with Cointreau and sugar-frost it. Strain mixture into glass.

SPOLETO SPECIAL
Shake 1 ounce gin, ½ ounce dry vermouth, ½ ounce orange juice, and 1 egg white with ice cubes in cocktail shaker. Strain into cocktail glass and dust with nutmeg.

GIN COCKTAILS WITH FRUIT JUICES

PAPAYA SPLENDOR
Into a rocks glass filled with cracked ice, pour 2 ounces gin and ½ ounce lemon juice. Top with papaya nectar (available canned) and stir gently. Garnish with lemon slice.

PINEAPPLE GIMLET
Put into mixing glass 1½ ounces gin, ½ ounce lime juice, and ice cubes. Stir, then pour into rocks glass. Top with pineapple juice.

SALTY DOG
Frost the rim of a rocks glass with salt and drop into it 3 or 4 ice cubes. Pour 2 ounces gin over the ice, fill with grapefruit juice, and stir. Can also be made with vodka.

ORANGE BLOSSOM
Shake 1½ ounces gin, 1 ounce orange juice, and cracked ice in a cocktail shaker. Strain into cocktail glass.

BITTER BLOSSOM
In cocktail shaker, shake 1½ ounces gin, 1 ounce orange juice, and 2 dashes orange bitters with ice cubes. Strain into cocktail glass.

GINNY-GIN, SOUTHERN STYLE
Shake 1 ounce gin, 1½ ounces Southern Comfort, 1 teaspoonful lemon juice, 1 teaspoonful grapefruit juice, and ice cubes in cocktail shaker. Strain into rocks glass filled with ice.

GIN FIX
Dissolve 1 teaspoonful superfine sugar in 1 teaspoonful water in the bottom of a rocks glass. Add 2 ounces lime juice, 2½ ounces gin, crushed ice, and stir.

MONKEY GLAND
To 1½ ounces gin, 1½ ounces orange juice, and ice cubes in cocktail shaker, add 3-to-4 drops Bénédictine, and 3-to-4 drops grenadine. Shake, and strain into cocktail glass.

GIN SUNSET
Shake 1 ounce gin, ½ ounce orange juice, ½ ounce lemon juice, 2 dashes grenadine, and ice cubes in cocktail shaker. Strain into cocktail glass.

DIXIE COCKTAIL

Put 1 ounce gin, 1½ ounces orange juice, 2 teaspoonfuls dry vermouth, 2 teaspoonfuls Pernod, and ice cubes in cocktail shaker. Shake, then strain into rocks glass half filled with ice cubes.

THE RED EYE

Put as much ice as you like in a wine glass and pour in 2 ounces gin. Nearly fill glass with tomato juice, squeeze in juice of half a lemon, and add salt and freshly ground pepper to taste. Stir.

COLE PORTER

Blend thoroughly (in a blender) 3 Italian plum tomatoes (canned), 1½ ounces gin, 1 dash Angostura bitters, 1 dash Worcestershire sauce, and ice cubes. Pour into rocks glass.

GIN FIZZES AND SWIZZLES

(See page 40 for the classic Gin Fizz, a gin standard.)

ORANGE FIZZ

Shake 2½ ounces gin, 1½ ounces orange juice, ½ ounce lemon juice, 2 teaspoonfuls triple sec, 1 teaspoonful superfine sugar, 2 dashes orange bitters, and ice cubes in cocktail shaker. Strain into highball glass. Top with club soda, or add more ice cubes and just a splash of club soda, as desired. Garnish with orange wedge.

NEW ORLEANS FIZZ

Moisten rim of highball glass with lemon juice and dip into sugar to sugar-frost it. Set it aside. In cocktail shaker, shake 2 ounces gin, 1 ounce sweet cream, 1 lightly beaten egg white, 1 ounce lime juice, ½ ounce lemon juice, 3 dashes orange-flower water, and cracked ice. Pour mixture into prepared glass.

RAMOS GIN FIZZ

Lightly beat one egg white and pour into cocktail shaker. Shake it with 3 ounces gin, 1½ teaspoonfuls superfine sugar, ½ ounce each lemon juice and lime juice, 1 ounce heavy cream, 3 drops orange-flower water, and cracked ice. Strain into highball glass filled with ice cubes. Top with splash of club soda.

SPECIAL ALTA MIRA RAMOS FIZZ

Lightly beat one whole egg, then shake it in cocktail shaker with 1½ ounces gin, 1 drop orange-flower water, 1 drop orange curaçao, 1½ ounces sweet-and-sour mix, 1 dash cream, and 1 ounce orange juice. Serve it up in a highball glass.

GIN SWIZZLE

Shake in cocktail shaker with ice cubes 2½ ounces gin, 1 tablespoonful lime juice, and 1 teaspoonful Angostura bitters. Pour into highball glass. Top with club soda, or add more ice and just a splash of club soda, as desired.

INVISIBLE MAN

Stir in mixing glass 2 ounces gin, ½ ounce brandy, ½ ounce triple sec, 2 dashes orange juice, and ice cubes. Pour into highball glass and top with ginger ale.

Q.E. 2

Shake 1½ ounces gin, 2 teaspoonfuls Campari, ½ ounce orange juice, and ice cubes in cocktail shaker. Strain into highball glass filled with ice cubes. Top glass up with chilled club soda.

GIN DAISY

Shake 1½ ounces gin, ½ teaspoonful sugar, juice of ½ lemon, and 1 tea- spoonful grenadine with cracked ice in cocktail shaker. Strain into highball glass, top with club soda, and garnish with wedge of lemon.

GIN GINGER

Combine in mixing glass 1½ ounces gin, 2 ounces orange juice, 4 ounces ginger ale, and 3 or 4 ice cubes. Pour into highball glass and top with ginger ale.

3

WHISKEY

A sage of yesteryear has written of whiskey: "It sloweth age; it strengtheneth youth; it helpeth digestion; it cutteth phlegm; it abandoneth melancholy; it relisheth the heart; it lighteneth the mind and it quickeneth the spirit; it keepeth and preserveth the teeth from chattering and the throat from rattling."

What more can one ask?

This miraculous spirit is derived from the fermenting and distilling of grain. Whiskey originated, most authorities agree, with the Celts in the British Isles sometime between the 10th century and the 15th; and there is no doubt that *whiskey* is a watered-down version of a Celtic word. But here agreement ends. Even spellings differ: The American and the Irish spirits are called *whiskey*; the Scottish and the Canadian are known as *whisky*. The Irish claim whiskey as their own, from *uisgebetha*, the spirit said to have been invented by St. Patrick while resting from his snake-chasing labors. The Scots hotly deny this, insisting that word and drink come from their *uisegebah*. In any case, both words mean "water of life"—a good indication of the esteem in which these peoples held their spirits. Scots and Irish may argue about whiskey till the crack of doom; odds are they'll be quaffing it in quantities till then, too.

SCOTCH

There is a certain mystery surrounding Scotch whiskey that the Scots have done their best to guard and perpetuate. Is it the combination of sea air and heather that makes this whiskey so fine? Is it the mountain water? The bumps and dents on the venerable pot still? Some say that Scotland itself is the secret, mystical ingredient. Whatever the explanation, Scotch whiskey is distinctive, special, and inimitable. On this score, the drinkers of the world take their hats off to the Scots.

One of the secrets of this spirit lies

in the malting process, the first and crucial stage in the production of Scotch. Malt is sprouted grain, an ingredient that must be added to the mash of all grain alcohols because it converts their starches to fermentable sugars. In Scotch-making, the malt is barley, preferably barley grown in the soil of Scotland. Once it has sprouted to about three quarters of an inch, the malt is put into a kiln and dried slowly over a peat fire. This is a key element in the flavor of the liquor. The oily, acrid smoke that peat gives off penetrates the barley malt so deeply that its flavor shows up in the distilled spirit. When Scotch drinkers speak of the "smoky" flavor they so relish, this is what they mean.

Water is almost as important as malting in achieving a fine Scotch whiskey. The best water for Scotch supposedly must rise through a red granite formation and pass over moors that are lush with peat and thick with heather. The waters of Loch Katrine reputedly satisfy these requirements more deliciously than any other.

Traditions are fiercely clung to in Scotland, and in making Scotch the time-honored pot still, made of copper, is preferred to the "newfangled" continuous still (new in 1830, when it was patented by Aeneas Coffey). The liquor runs through two different types of pot still and then into previously used oak casks (old sherry casks, or *butts*, are considered the best) for aging. Scottish law requires a minimum of three years in the barrel, although seven-to-ten years yields better results. Fifteen years is generally too long.

Unblended, this malt whiskey has a dense taste that most American drinkers would find unfamiliar and overpowering. But, thanks to Coffey's more efficient continuous still, distillers have been able to step up their production of the blander grain whiskey. These are made from a variety of grains, with small amounts of malted and unmalted barley—none of it dried over peat smoke.

It was an Edinburgh wholesaler named Andrew Usher who came up with the idea of mixing malt whiskey with grain whiskey to create the first blended Scotch whiskey sometime in the 1850s. This lighter, less smokily pungent liquor is the "Scotch" that caught on in England, and from there its fame spread to the rest of the world. Nowadays, most blended Scotch is a mixture of several kinds of malt and grain whiskey—as many as 50 different ones can go into a blend—with as much as 80 percent grain whiskey in the mixture. Blended Scotch is fine for everyday use in cocktails, highballs and mists, or over ice; however, single-malt Scotches, each the unblended product of a single distillery, are worth acquiring a taste for.

On first sip, the uninitiated may find the single-malt whisky fiery, harsh, overwhelming; but, like many of life's finer things, these pure whiskies in time educate and elevate the drinker to their level. Good Scotch does not burn or sting, but provides an insistent, comfortable heat.

There are four major malt-whisky producing regions in Scotland—the Highlands, Islay, Campbelltown, and the Lowlands—each with its distinctive liquor. The malts distilled in the Highlands are generally acknowledged to be the best; certainly they are the most popular. The Glenlivet, Glenfiddich, Glen Grant, Glenmorangie, and Cardhu are Highland malt whiskies to look for. Elegance, light fragrance, and smoothness are the keynotes of their taste; and they are best enjoyed neat, with a splash of cold water, or on ice. For the most part, malt whiskies are not used in mixed drinks. Many prefer to sip them after dinner, like a liqueur.

IRISH

The Irish have been distilling their own whiskey a lot longer than they have been planting potatoes, and no one would deny that the Irish have a certain authority and expertise in matters of alcohol. Why, then, is Scotch so much more popular than Irish? The answer certainly does not lie in the flavor, for Irish whiskey is a smooth, well-rounded, clean-tasting liquor, a bit more robust and full-bodied than Scotch, more delicate on the tongue and paler in the glass. It is most assuredly *not* distilled from potatoes.

In fact, Irish is made from the same grains as Scotch—malted and unmalted barley. The major difference in production comes with the drying of the barley malt: The Irish use coal instead of peat, and they shield the malt from the smoke, thus keeping out the smoky flavor so prized by the Scots.

Traditionally, Irish whiskey is triple-distilled in pot stills. Until recently, most Irish was straight pot-still whiskey; but today, in response to the public's yen for lighter-tasting spirits, most

of the available brands are blends of malt and low-key grain whiskeys. The Irish generally age whiskey longer than the Scots do, usually between five and eight years.

If you feel too weak of heart and timid of palate to take your Irish neat, add a splash of water or an ice cube or two. Irish coffee is also a fine and respectable way to enjoy this product of the Emerald Isle. Sip and savor it, feel its glow—and before you know it, you'll be speaking with a brogue.

BOURBON

Bourbon used to have an image as the liquor of hillbillies and boors; this, emphatically, is undeserved and of late has been replaced by an aura of chic. True Bourbon, as any devotee will tell you, retains the character that's been blended out of Scotch. For those who like the taste of whiskey, and like it with class, Kentucky Bourbon straight up is the drink of choice.

Bourbon is an American liquor born and bred, our most eminent contribution to the world of spirits. One version has it that its origin coincides precisely with that of the United States: In 1789, the year George Washington took office as President, Bourbon whiskey first flowed off the still of one Reverend Elijah Craig of Georgetown, Bourbon County, Kentucky—hence the name.

Bourbon is made from corn: At least 51 percent of the mash must be corn, along with rye and barley. Bourbon's distinctive taste derives from the limestone-flavored sweet water found abundantly in Kentucky and from the charred-oak barrels in which it is aged. Most of this whiskey is made by the "sweet-mash" process, in which yeast is added to start fermentation. The more celebrated "sour-mash" process, wherein fermentation is spurred by the residue of a previous fermentation, is slower and costlier; but it does produce a finer whiskey—full in flavor and fragrance, and more expensive.

Bourbon is a straight—that is, unblended—whiskey and is bottled at anywhere from 80 proof to 114 proof. Two of the simplest ways to savor this spirit are neat and with spring water; the mint julep is one of the most pleasant ways. Bourbon is also served on the rocks, or it can be used in any standard whiskey cocktail.

TENNESSEE

Tennessee whiskey is not a bourbon, although the two are often confused. And with good reason: They have basic similarities in ingredients, production, and flavor. Tennessee whiskey is made in the same way as sour-mash Bourbon, with one extra step added: Right after distillation, the liquor is filtered through charcoal from hard Tennessee maple trees. Tennessee whiskey, reasonably enough, may be produced only in Tennessee. Jack Daniel's is the top-selling Tennessee whiskey by far, and it also outsells most Bourbons.

RYE

Rye whiskey, distilled and aged like Bourbon whiskey but from a mash containing 51 percent rye grain, used to be quite popular in the United States but is now something of a specialty item. Many drinkers, particularly in the Northeast, still use the term *rye* when what they really mean is *blended whiskey*. The two categories are distinct; indeed, true rye has a full-bodied, robust flavor with a noticeable whiskey tang that would knock the socks off drinkers accustomed to the blander blended whiskeys.

BLENDED WHISKEYS

By government regulation, a U.S. blended whiskey must contain at least 20 percent straight whiskey; the rest is usually unaged grain neutral spirits (virtually pure alcohol with little or no flavor). Premium blends, valued for their lightness and balance, may be composed from as many as 75 different whiskeys and neutral spirits.

Blended whiskeys moved into prominence during the Second World War, when distillers used them as a way of stretching their supplies of aged straight whiskeys. But the category has declined in recent years, as whiskey drinkers in search of lightness have turned more to Canadian whiskeys.

CANADIAN

The Canadians, eager to prove to the world that there's more to North American whiskey than Kentucky Bourbon and Tennessee whiskey, have perfected a singularly light-bodied, silken-smooth spirit, at once crisper and less assertive than U.S. whiskey. Canadian is the ideal whiskey for mixing: It's got the force to stand up to water, the feistiness to enliven soda, and the heartiness to accompany even the sweet carbonation of 7-Up and ginger ale.

Like U.S. whiskeys, Canadian is made primarily from corn, rye, and malted barley, and it is distilled by a process similar to that used in making Bourbon except that a sweet mash is always used. The Canadian government, however, sets no requirements about proof restrictions, distillation techniques, or grain proportions on their native distillers. Official control is limited to labeling. For this reason the Canadians have had a freer hand in developing their own styles, methods, and formulas, with the result that there is a good deal of variation among brands. All, however, share the lightness that is the main characteristic of Canadian whiskey, and all are blends.

By law, Canadian whiskey must be aged at least three years, but six-or-eight years is more common. Because of its agreeableness to all kinds of mixing, it has the distinction of being the only whiskey that is appropriate for warm weather. Likewise, Canadian is the perfect introduction to whiskey for the hesitant or the uninitiated.

Whiskey Recipes

See Section One for information on barware, mixing supplies, and mixing tips. For conversion to metric or other measurements, refer to tables on pages 11 and 22.

SIX WHISKEY STANDARDS

(See pages 60, 63, and 65 for Scotch, Irish, and Bourbon standards.)

THE WHISKEY SOUR
Pour 1 ounce lemon juice, 1 teaspoonful sugar, and 3 ounces rye whiskey over ice in mixing glass. Stir. Strain into sour glass, or into rocks glass with ice cubes, and serve ungarnished. Sour ingredients can also be shaken with cracked ice in a cocktail shaker.

THE OLD-FASHIONED
Put one small sugar cube into the bottom of an old-fashioned or rocks glass, add 1 dash bitters and ½ ounce water, and muddle it all together. Pour in 1½ ounces American blended whiskey, then add ice cubes. Garnish with a twist of lemon and a cherry. A splash of club soda is optional; so is a dash of curaçao.

THE MANHATTAN
In a mixing glass, combine 2 ounces rye or blended whiskey, ½ ounce sweet vermouth, and 1 dash bitters. Add ice cubes, stir, and then strain into cocktail glass. One can also mix ingredients in a rocks glass, add ice, and stir.

JOHN COLLINS
Fill collins glass with ice and add 1 ounce whiskey and 2 ounces sweet-

and-sour. Stir well. Top with soda, stir again one or two turns, and garnish with cherry.

WHISKEY HIGHBALL
Fill highball glass with ice, add 1 ounce whiskey, and top with soda or ginger ale. Stir.

WHISKEY AND WATER
Fill highball glass with ice, add 1 ounce whiskey, and top with water. Stir.

SIMPLE WHISKEY COCKTAILS

WHISKEY SMASH
Put 1 cube sugar, 1 ounce water, and several mint sprigs in the bottom of an old-fashioned glass and muddle. Add ice cubes and pour in 1½ ounces whiskey. Stir. Garnish with sprigs of mint, and serve with soda on the side.

MAPLE LEAF
Pour 1 ounce whiskey (preferably canadian), ¼ ounce lemon juice, and 1 teaspoonful maple syrup over ice in a cocktail shaker. Shake, then strain into cocktail glass.

NEW YORK COCKTAIL
Shake 2½ ounces whiskey, ½ teaspoonful superfine sugar, 1 dash grenadine, and 2 teaspoonfuls lime juice with ice in cocktail shaker. Strain into

cocktail glass. Twist strip of orange peel above drink, then toss it in.

GLOOM LIFTER
Pour 2 ounces whiskey, ½ ounce lemon juice, ¼ ounce sugar syrup, and ½ egg white over ice in cocktail shaker and shake hard. Strain into rocks glass.

DINAH
Put 2½ ounces whiskey, ½ ounce lemon juice, ½ teaspoonful superfine sugar, and ice in a cocktail shaker and shake hard. Strain into cocktail glass.

WARD EIGHT
Squeeze juice of ¼ lemon and ¼ orange over ice in cocktail shaker. Add 1 teaspoonful grenadine and 3 ounces rye whiskey. Shake hard, and strain into cocktail glass.

COMMODORE
Shake 1 ounce rye whiskey, ¼ ounce lime juice, 2 dashes orange bitters, and a pinch of sugar in cocktail shaker with ice. Strain into cocktail glass.

WHISKEY COCKTAILS WITH APERITIFS

DRY MANHATTAN
In a mixing glass, mix 2 ounces whiskey, ¼ ounce dry vermouth, and 1 dash bitters. Add ice cubes, stir, then strain into cocktail glass. A dry manhattan can also be mixed over ice in a rocks glass.

MEDIUM MANHATTAN
In a mixing glass, mix 2 ounces whiskey, 2 teaspoonfuls sweet vermouth, 2 teaspoonfuls dry vermouth, and 1 dash bitters. Add ice, stir, and strain into cocktail glass. Alternatively, mix ingredients with ice in rocks glass.

SWEET MANHATTAN
In a mixing glass, combine 2 ounces whiskey, ¾ ounce sweet vermouth, and 1 dash bitters. Add ice cubes, stir, then strain into cocktail glass. Or mix ingredients over ice in a rocks glass.

PERFECT MANHATTAN
Put in a mixing glass 2 ounces whiskey, ¼ ounce dry vermouth, ¼ ounce sweet vermouth, and 1 dash bitters. Add ice cubes, stir, then strain into cocktail glass. The drink can also be mixed over ice in a rocks glass.

DUBONNET MANHATTAN
Shake 1 ounce Dubonnet and 1 ounce whiskey with ice in cocktail shaker. Strain into cocktail glass and garnish with maraschino cherry.

ALGONQUIN
Using cocktail shaker, shake 1½ ounces whiskey, 1 ounce dry vermouth, and 1 ounce pineapple juice with ice. Strain into cocktail glass.

WHEELER DEALER
Shake 1½ ounces whiskey, 1 ounce dry vermouth, and 1 teaspoonful raspberry liqueur with ice in cocktail shaker. Strain into cocktail glass.

HORSE CAR
Stir—in mixing glass with ice—1 ounce each sweet vermouth, dry vermouth, and whiskey. Add 2 dashes Angostura bitters, stir again, and strain

into rocks glass filled with ice cubes. Garnish with orange peel.

SOUL KISS

In mixing glass with ice, stir together 1 ounce whiskey, 1 ounce dry vermouth, ½ ounce orange juice, ½ ounce Dubonnet. Strain into rocks glass filled with ice; garnish with orange wedge.

ORIENTAL

Shake 1 ounce rye whiskey, ¼ ounce sweet vermouth, ¼ ounce Cointreau, ½ ounce lime juice with ice in cocktail shaker. Strain into cocktail glass.

BROOKLYN

Fill rocks glass with ice and pour in 1 ounce rye whiskey, 1 ounce sweet vermouth, 1 dash Amer Picon orange bitters, and 1 dash maraschino liqueur. Stir.

CAJUN WHISKEY I

Shake with ice 1½ ounces whiskey, 1 ounce sweet vermouth, and 2 dashes Amer Picon orange bitters. Strain into cocktail glass. Garnish with maraschino cherry if desired.

CAJUN WHISKEY II

Follow recipe for Cajun Whiskey I, but add ½ egg white to cocktail shaker and use sour glass instead of cocktail glass.

WHISKEY COCKTAILS WITH OTHER SPIRITS

HARRITY I

Stir 1 ounce each whiskey and gin in mixing glass with ice and a dash or two of Angostura bitters. Strain into cocktail glass.

STICK SHIFT

In mixing glass, stir together 1 ounce whiskey, 1 ounce gin, 1 ounce sweet vermouth, and ice. Strain into cocktail glass.

DOUBLE STANDARD

Pour 1 ounce gin, 1 ounce whiskey, 2 teaspoonfuls lemon juice, ½ teaspoonful superfine sugar, and ½ teaspoonful grenadine into cocktail shaker. Add ice and shake hard. Strain into sour glass.

WHISKEY COCKTAILS WITH LIQUEURS

RATTLESNAKE

Shake together 2 ounces whiskey, 1 teaspoonful lemon juice, 1 teaspoonful Falernum syrup, 1 egg white, and 1 dash Pernod in cocktail shaker with ice. Strain into sour glass.

CHAPEL HILL COCKTAIL

Pour 2 ounces whiskey, ¾ ounce triple sec, ½ ounce lemon juice over ice in cocktail shaker. Shake hard. Strain into cocktail glass; garnish with slice of orange.

SLOW-TALKING DIXIE GAL

Shake together 1½ ounces whiskey, ½ ounce sloe gin, 1 teaspoonful lemon juice, and ½ teaspoonful sugar syrup with ice in cocktail shaker. Strain into cocktail glass.

NORTHERN LIGHT

Pour 1 ounce whiskey (preferably canadian), ½ ounce dry vermouth, ½ ounce Grand Marnier, and ½ ounce cranberry liqueur over ice in cocktail shaker. Shake hard. Strain into cocktail glass.

THE LADY WORE RED

Shake together 1½ ounces whiskey, 2 teaspoonfuls kirsch, 2 teaspoonfuls cherry liqueur, and 3 ounces crushed ice in cocktail shaker. Strain into cocktail glass.

CANADA COCKTAIL

Shake 1½ ounces whiskey (preferably canadian), ½ ounce Cointreau, 2 dashes Angostura bitters, and 1 teaspoonful sugar with ice in cocktail shaker. Strain into cocktail glass.

BENT NAIL

Pour 1½ ounces whiskey (preferably canadian), ½ ounce Drambuie, 1 teaspoonful kirsch, and 3 ounces crushed ice into cocktail shaker. Shake hard. Strain into cocktail glass.

APPLE-PIE-EYED

Shake 1½ ounces whiskey, ½ ounce applejack, ½ ounce lemon juice, 1 teaspoonful sugar syrup in cocktail shaker with ice. Strain into cocktail glass.

LADY DAY

Pour 1½ ounces whiskey, 2 teaspoonfuls banana liqueur, 1 teaspoonful lemon juice, and 1 teaspoonful orange juice over ice in cocktail shaker. Shake hard. Strain into cocktail glass.

FRISCO TROLLEY

Pour over ice in cocktail shaker 1½ ounces whiskey, ½ ounce Bénédictine, and 2 teaspoonfuls lemon juice and shake hard. Strain into cocktail glass.

CANADIAN BLACKBERRY

Shake 1½ ounces canadian whiskey, ½ ounce blackberry brandy, 1 teaspoonful each lemon juice and orange juice with ice cubes in cocktail shaker. Strain into rocks glass filled with ice cubes.

CANADIAN CRANBERRY

Follow recipe for Canadian Blackberry, but substitute ½ ounce cranberry liqueur for the blackberry liqueur.

PREAKNESS

Pour 2½ ounces whiskey, ½ teaspoonful sweet vermouth, ½ teaspoonful Bénédictine, 1 dash Angostura bitters over ice in mixing glass. Stir a couple of turns. Strain into cocktail glass.

WHISKEY BASH

Pour 1½ ounces whiskey and 1 ounce anisette over ice in cocktail shaker and shake hard. Strain into cocktail glass and garnish with cherry, if desired.

PEPPERED WHISKEY

Fill rocks glass with ice and pour in 2 ounces whiskey (preferably canadian) and 1 ounce peppermint schnapps. Stir one or two turns. Twist a strip of lemon peel over drink, then toss it in.

DEAR JOHN

Pour 1½ ounces whiskey, ½ ounce

Southern Comfort, 1 teaspoonful orgeat syrup, 2 teaspoonfuls lime juice over ice in cocktail shaker. Shake hard. Strain into cocktail glass; garnish with half a strawberry.

THE BUSY BEE

Shake together 1½ ounces whiskey (preferably canadian), 1 ounce orange juice, and 1 teaspoonful yellow Chartreuse with ice in cocktail shaker. Strain into cocktail glass.

WHISKEY DRINKS WITH FRUIT JUICES

PALM READER

Pour 1½ ounces whiskey, 1 ounce orange juice, and ½ ounce golden rum over ice in mixing glass. Mix, then strain into cocktail glass.

WHISKEY, HONEY?

Pour 1½ ounces whiskey, ½ ounce grapefruit juice, and 2 teaspoonfuls honey over ice in cocktail shaker and shake hard. Strain into cocktail glass.

ORANGE QUENCHER

Fill rocks glass with ice and pour in 1½ ounces whiskey, ½ ounce curaçao, 2 ounces orange juice, and ½ ounce pineapple juice. Stir.

BLENDED BLESSINGS

Pour 1 ounce Southern Comfort, 2 ounces whiskey, 1 ounce orange juice, ¾ ounce dry vermouth, 1 ounce lemon juice, ¼ of a fresh peach (peeled), and 4 ounces crushed ice into blender. Blend for about half a minute. Strain into highball glass filled with crushed

ice. Garnish with half a lemon slice and half an orange slice.

WHITE SHADOW

Pour 1 ounce whiskey, 1 ounce Pernod, and 1 ounce heavy cream over ice in cocktail shaker and shake hard. Fill rocks glass with ice and strain drink over it. Sprinkle with nutmeg.

LIP BALM

Pour 1½ ounces whiskey, ½ ounce dark rum, 1 teaspoonful coconut cream, and 1 dash white crème de cacao over ice in cocktail shaker. Shake hard. Strain into cocktail glass.

DAIRY KING

Pour 1½ ounces whiskey (preferably canadian), 1 ounce Grand Marnier, 1 teaspoonful lemon juice, 1 teaspoonful heavy cream, and 1 egg over ice in cocktail shaker. Shake hard. Strain into sour glass and sprinkle with nutmeg.

SHAKE HANDS

Pour 1½ ounces whiskey (preferably canadian), ½ ounce Irish Mist, and ½ ounce heavy cream over ice in cocktail shaker. Shake hard. Strain into cocktail glass and sprinkle with nutmeg.

HALIFAX

Shake 1½ ounces whiskey (preferably canadian), ½ ounce amaretto, and ½ ounce heavy cream with ice in cocktail shaker. Strain into cocktail glass.

MINT MIST

Crush 3 sprigs fresh mint with 2 ounces whiskey and 1 teaspoonful crème de menthe in the bottom of a highball glass. Add ice. Fill glass up with soda; garnish with sprig of mint.

WHISKEY HURRICANE

Shake with ice ½ ounce each gin, whiskey, and crème de menthe and 1 ounce lemon juice. Strain into chilled cocktail glass.

COWBOY

Shake 1 ounce rye whiskey and ½ ounce cream with crushed ice in cocktail shaker and strain into cocktail glass.

PINEAPPLE CREAMER

Using a blender, blend 1½ ounces whiskey, ½ ounce grenadine, 1 ounce pineapple juice, ½ ounce lemon juice, and 2 ice cubes for 15 seconds. Add 1 ounce heavy cream, then blend again until frothy. Pour into cocktail glass and garnish, if desired, with sprig of mint.

BENSON COLLINS

Fill highball glass with cracked ice and pour over it 1½ ounces whiskey and 4 dashes white crème de menthe. Top with 7-Up and stir lightly. Garnish with slice of orange.

7 & 7

Fill highball glass with ice, then pour in 1 ounce whiskey—Seagrams 7 Crown makes it a genuine 7 & 7—then top with 7-Up. Stir.

WHISKEY HIGHBALLS

PRESBYTERIAN

Fill highball glass with ice and pour in 1 ounce whiskey. Then bring halfway to the top with soda; complete filling with ginger ale. Stir, and garnish with twist of lemon.

WILD HORSE'S NECK

Carefully peel a lemon completely in such a way that the peel remains in one continuous strip, forming a spiral. Fill highball glass with ice, arranging peel so that it hangs from the rim all the way down the glass. Pour in 1½ ounces whiskey and top with ginger ale.

CABLEGRAM

Dissolve 1 teaspoonful superfine sugar in 1 ounce lemon juice in the bottom of a highball glass. Pour in 2 ounces whiskey, stir, then fill glass almost to the top with ice. Top with ginger ale.

BOSTON SOUR

Pour 1 teaspoonful superfine sugar, 1¼ ounces lemon juice, 1 egg white, and 2 ounces whiskey over ice in cocktail shaker. Shake hard. Strain into collins glass, add a few ice cubes, then top with soda. Garnish with slice of lemon and maraschino cherry.

BLACKBERRY FIZZLE

Shake 1½ ounces whiskey, ½ ounce blackberry brandy, ½ teaspoonful sugar, and ½ ounce lemon juice with ice in cocktail shaker. Strain into highball glass almost filled with crushed ice. Top with soda; garnish with slice of lemon.

TOKYO FIZZ

Pour 2 ounces whiskey, ¾ ounce port, 1 teaspoonful lemon juice, 1 teaspoonful sugar syrup, and ice into cocktail shaker and shake hard. Strain into sour glass half filled with ice. Top with soda and garnish with spear of pineapple.

ASSASSINO
Pour 2 ounces whiskey, 1 ounce dry vermouth, and 1 ounce pineapple juice over ice in cocktail shaker and shake hard. Strain into collins glass half filled with ice; top with soda. Shake a drop or two of Sambuca Romana on top.

BRASSY BLONDE
Fill collins glass most of the way up with ice and pour in 1½ ounces whiskey, 1½ ounces grapefruit juice, 1 teaspoonful strawberry liqueur. Stir once or twice, top with soda, and stir again.

SUNDOWNER
Fill highball glass with ice, then pour in 1½ ounces whiskey and ½ ounce brandy. Top with tonic water and garnish with wedge of lemon.

SIX SCOTCH STANDARDS

ROB ROY
Fill old-fashioned or rocks glass with ice and pour in ¼ ounce sweet vermouth and 1½ ounces Scotch whiskey. Stir. Garnish with cherry. Can also be made by shaking with ice in cocktail shaker and straining into cocktail glass.

SCOTCH SOUR
Pour 1 ounce lemon juice, 1 teaspoonful sugar, and 3 ounces scotch over ice in mixing glass. Strain into sour glass, or into rocks glass with ice cubes, and serve ungarnished. Ingredients can also be shaken with cracked ice in a cocktail shaker.

SCOTCH AND SODA
Fill rocks glass with ice and pour in 1½ ounces scotch and 3 ounces soda.

SCOTCH OLD-FASHIONED
Pour 1½ ounces scotch and 1 dash Angostura bitters over ice in rocks glass and stir. Add 1 orange slice and 1 cherry. Rub twist of lemon around rim of glass and toss in.

RUSTY NAIL
Fill rocks glass with ice and pour in 1½ ounces scotch and 1½ ounces Drambuie. Stir gently.

SCOTCH MIST
Fill rocks glass with crushed ice and pour in 2 ounces blended or single-malt Scotch. Squeeze strip of lemon peel above drink, then drop it in.

OTHER SCOTCH COCKTAILS

DRY ROB ROY
Fill rocks glass with ice and pour in 1½ ounces scotch, ¼ ounce dry vermouth, and 1 dash Drambuie or Bénédictine. Stir.

ALPINE ROB ROY
Fill rocks glass with ice and pour in 2½ ounces single-malt Scotch, ½ ounce dry vermouth, and ½ ounce Fior d'Alpe Isolabella.

AULD NEW YORK

Stir 2 ounces scotch, 1 teaspoonful lime juice, and 1 teaspoonful sugar with ice in mixing glass. Strain into cocktail glass. Squeeze a strip of lemon peel above drink and toss in.

AFFINITY

In mixing glass, stir 2 ounces scotch, 1 ounce sweet vermouth, and 2 dashes Angostura bitters with ice. Strain into cocktail glass.

BOBBY BURNS

Stir 1½ ounces scotch, ½ ounce dry vermouth, ½ ounce sweet vermouth, and 1 dash Bénédictine with ice in mixing glass. Strain into cocktail glass.

IRON LADY

Pour 1½ ounces scotch, ½ ounce dry vermouth, ½ ounce port, and 1 dash orange bitters over ice in mixing glass. Stir. Strain into cocktail glass.

BARBICAN

Shake 2 ounces scotch, ½ ounce Drambuie, and ½ ounce passion-fruit juice with ice in cocktail shaker. Strain into cocktail glass.

BALMORAL

Pour 1¼ ounces gin, 1¼ ounces scotch, and ½ ounce anisette over ice in cocktail shaker. Shake hard. Strain into cocktail glass.

KERRY BLUE

Pour 1½ ounces scotch, 1 dash orange bitters, 1 dash dry vermouth, and ½ ounce blue curaçao over ice in cocktail shaker and shake hard. Strain into cocktail glass.

SCOTCH EGG

In cocktail shaker, combine 1½ ounces scotch, 1 egg, 1 teaspoonful Falernum syrup, and 1 teaspoon curaçao. Add ice and shake hard. Strain into cocktail glass.

LOCH NESS MONSTER

Pour 1½ ounces scotch and 1 teaspoonful peppermint schnapps over ice in cocktail shaker and shake hard. Strain into rocks glass and top with soda. If possible, cut a twig of scotch pine and use as garnish.

RED FIZZ

Pour 2 ounces scotch, 2 ounces dry red wine, 2 teaspoonfuls lemon juice and 1 teaspoonful sugar syrup over ice in cocktail shaker. Shake hard. Pour, without straining, into rocks glass and add 2 ounces soda. Garnish with slice of pineapple.

BARBARY COAST

Put 1 ounce scotch, 1 ounce gin, 1 ounce light rum, ¾ ounce white crème de cacao, and ice into cocktail shaker and shake hard. Strain into rocks glass half filled with ice.

GATHERING OF THE CLANS

Dissolve 1 teaspoonful superfine sugar and 2 teaspoonfuls water in mixing glass; then add 1 teaspoonful lemon juice and 2 ounces scotch; stir. Strain into cocktail glass filled with crushed ice; add 2 or 3 dashes triple sec on top.

SWEET PEAT

Stir ¾ ounce scotch, ½ ounce Cherry Marnier, ¾ ounce sweet vermouth, and ½ ounce orange juice in mixing glass with ice. Strain into cocktail glass.

SPANISH PASSION

Pour 1 ounce scotch, 1 ounce dry sherry, 2 teaspoonfuls lemon juice, and 2 teaspoonfuls passion-fruit syrup over ice in cocktail shaker. Shake hard, then strain into cocktail glass.

MIAMI BEACH

Stir 1½ ounces scotch, 1½ ounces dry vermouth, and 1 ounce grapefruit juice with ice in mixing glass. Strain into cocktail glass.

SCOTCH DRINKS WITH MILK OR CREAM, AND HOT SCOTCH DRINKS

HIGHLAND FLING

Pour 2 ounces scotch, 3 ounces milk, and 1 teaspoonful superfine sugar over ice in cocktail shaker and shake hard. Strain into rocks glass and sprinkle top with nutmeg.

MARLON BRANDO

Fill rocks glass with ice and pour in 1½ ounces Scotch and ½ ounce amaretto. Stir. Float heavy cream on top.

ATHOLL BROSE

Mix 2 ounces scotch, 1 ounce cream, and 1 ounce honey in warmed rocks glass. Allow to cool. Do not add ice. Stir with spoon before serving.

AULD MAN'S MILK

Beat an egg lightly and pour into cocktail shaker. Add 2 ounces scotch, 7 ounces cream, and 1 teaspoonful sugar.

Shake hard with cracked ice. Strain into highball glass. Sprinkle top with nutmeg.

HOT SCOTCH TODDY

Heat ¾ cup water, ¾ ounce sugar, 1 slice lemon with 2 cloves stuck in it, and a piece of stick cinnamon in a small saucepan over moderately high heat. Stir until mixture boils, then add 1½ ounces scotch, remove from heat, and pour into mug.

SCOTCH COFFEE

Pour 2 ounces scotch and 2 teaspoonfuls sugar into bottom of mug or heatproof glass. Nearly fill mug with hot strong black coffee and stir well. Pour lightly whipped cream over back of a spoon, so that it floats on surface of drink.

SCOTCH HIGHBALLS

BANNOCKBURN

Stir 2 ounces scotch, 4 ounces tomato juice, dash of Tabasco, dash Worcestershire sauce, and ¼ ounce lemon juice with ice in mixing glass. Strain into rocks glass, or else into ice-filled highball glass.

PLANTATION SCOTCH PUNCH

Pour 2 ounces pineapple juice, 1½ ounces scotch, 1 ounce grenadine, 1 ounce sweet-and-sour, and 1 dash bitters into cocktail shaker. Shake hard. Pour into highball glass filled with ice. Garnish with slice of orange or pineapple.

JOE COLLINS

Fill collins glass with ice and pour in 1 ounce scotch and 2 ounces sweet-and-sour; stir well. Top with soda, stir again 2 turns, and garnish, if you like, with a maraschino cherry.

BUTTERSCOTCH COLLINS

Dissolve 1 teaspoonful sugar in a little water and pour over ice in collins glass. Now add 1½ ounces scotch, ½ ounce Drambuie, and the juice of half a lemon. Top with soda; stir lightly. Garnish with orange slice and cherry.

GOLDENBERG'S FOLLY

Fill highball glass with ice and pour in 1½ ounces scotch. Top off with cola.

HIGHLAND COOLER

Shake ½ ounce lemon juice, 1 teaspoonful sugar, 1½ ounces scotch, and 2 dashes bitters in cocktail shaker. Pour over ice in a collins glass. Top with ginger ale.

PURPLE HEATHER

Fill highball glass with ice and pour in 1½ ounces scotch and ½ ounce crème de cassis. Top with soda and stir.

TWO IRISH WHISKEY STANDARDS

IRISH COFFEE

Pour 3 ounces Irish whiskey into heatproof glass or mug and add 1 teaspoonful sugar. Fill almost to top with strong black coffee and stir thoroughly. Top with whipped cream, or carefully pour heavy cream over back of a spoon so as to float it on the surface. Optional garnish: a cinnamon stick.

IRISH WHISKEY SOUR

Shake 3 ounces Irish whiskey, 1½ ounces lemon juice, and 1½ teaspoonfuls sugar with ice in cocktail shaker. Strain into cocktail glass and garnish with orange slice.

OTHER IRISH WHISKEY COCKTAILS

IRISH STINGER

Stir with ice in mixing glass 1½ ounces irish, 1½ ounces sweet vermouth, and 1 ounce green Chartreuse. Strain into cocktail glass.

IRISH PERFECT MANHATTAN

Stir with ice in mixing glass 3 ounces irish, ½ ounce sweet vermouth, ½ ounce dry vermouth. Strain into cocktail glass; garnish with sprig of mint.

COMMANDO FIX

Fill sour glass with crushed ice and pour in 2 ounces irish, ¼ ounce Cointreau, ½ ounce lime juice. Stir a few turns; add 1 or 2 dashes raspberry liqueur on top.

BRAINSTORM

Fill old-fashioned or rocks glass with ice and add 2 ounces irish, 1 teaspoonful Bénédictine, and 1 teaspoonful dry vermouth. Stir a few times. Squeeze a strip of lemon peel above the drink and toss in.

BLACK THORN

Pour 1 ounce irish, ½ ounce dry vermouth, 2 dashes Angostura bitters, and 2 dashes Pernod over ice in cocktail shaker. Shake hard. Strain into cocktail glass.

SERPENT'S TOOTH

Pour 1 ounce irish, 2 ounces sweet vermouth, 1 ounce lemon juice, ½ ounce kümmel, and 1 dash Angostura bitters over ice in cocktail shaker. Shake hard. Strain into cocktail glass.

FIVE-LEAF CLOVER

Stir with ice in mixing glass 1 ounce irish, 1 ounce dry vermouth, 1 teaspoonful green Chartreuse, and 1 teaspoonful green crème de menthe. Strain into cocktail glass; garnish with green olive.

IRISH BROGUE

Fill rocks glass with ice and pour in 1½ ounces Irish whiskey and ½ ounce Irish Mist. Stir.

HUDSON'S STING

Pour 2 ounces Irish whiskey, 1 ounce Irish Mist, and 1 ounce peppermint schnapps over ice in cocktail shaker. Shake hard, then strain into cocktail glass.

GREEN DEVIL

Pour 2 ounces irish, 2 ounces clam juice, 2 dashes green crème de menthe, and ½ teaspoonful lemon juice over ice in cocktail shaker. Shake hard. Strain into sour glass.

MINGLING OF THE CLANS

Stir 1¼ ounces Irish whiskey, 1 ounce Scotch whiskey, 2 teaspoonfuls lemon juice, and 3 dashes orange bitters in

mixing glass with ice. Strain into cocktail glass.

THE RED DEVIL

Stir with ice in mixing glass 2 ounces irish, ½ ounce clam juice, 2½ ounces tomato juice, 2 dashes Worcestershire sauce, 1 pinch pepper, and ¼ ounce lime juice. Strain into large wine glass, over ice if you like.

IRISH WHISKEY HIGHBALLS

IRISH HIGHBALL

Partially fill highball glass with crushed ice (about ¾ way up) and add 2 ounces irish. Squeeze lemon peel over drink, then toss it in. Top with ginger ale.

LACE-CURTAIN COOLER

Half fill a highball glass with ice, then pour in 1½ ounces Irish whiskey, 1 ounce dry sherry, ½ ounce crème de noyaux, and ½ ounce lemon juice. Stir one or two turns. Top with soda.

BLACK AND TAN

Pour 1½ ounces Irish whiskey, 1 ounce dark Jamaican rum, ½ ounce lime juice, ½ ounce orange juice, and ½ teaspoonful superfine sugar over ice in cocktail shaker. Shake hard. Strain into collins glass half filled with ice and top up with ginger ale.

IRISH SPRING

Fill collins glass with ice, then pour in 1 ounce irish, ½ ounce peach brandy, 1 ounce orange juice, 1 ounce sweet-and-sour. Stir well; garnish with orange slice and cherry.

SIX BOURBON STANDARDS

BOURBON AND BRANCH

Pour 1½ ounces sour-mash Bourbon whiskey over ice cubes in highball glass. Fill to top with spring water and stir gently.

BOURBON OLD-FASHIONED

Put 1 teaspoonful sugar, 2 dashes bitters, and 1 teaspoonful water in rocks glass. Muddle to dissolve sugar. Put 1 ice cube in glass. Pour in 3 ounces bourbon to fill glass and stir once. Twist lemon strip over glass to release a drop of oil, then toss it in as garnish.

MINT JULEP

With a pestle or spoon, crush well 6 fresh mint leaves with 1 teaspoon superfine sugar in the bottom of a highball glass. Pour in 4 ounces bourbon and pack glass with crushed ice. Put in freezer for ½ hour. Before serving, garnish with fresh mint sprigs and add a straw for sipping.

SAZERAC

Pour 2 ounces bourbon in mixing glass, add 1 teaspoonful sugar and 2 dashes Angostura bitters. Stir to dissolve sugar. Put 3 dashes Pernod in rocks glass, then strain in the mixing-glass mixture. Add ice cubes.

BOURBON AND GINGER

Pour 2 ounces bourbon in rocks glass. Fill glass with ice. Top with ginger ale.

BOURBON TODDY

Into a heavy mug put 1 teaspoonful sugar, 3 whole cloves, a 1-inch stick of cinnamon, a thin slice of lemon. Add 1 ounce boiling water, stir and let stand briefly. Pour in 1½ ounces bourbon and 4 more ounces hot water. Stir again. Sprinkle nutmeg on top.

OTHER BOURBON COCKTAILS

MASHED BOURBON OLD-FASHIONED

Put 1 maraschino cherry, 1 piece of orange, 1 teaspoonful sugar, 2 dashes Angostura bitters, and a dash of soda into a rocks glass. Mash. Pack glass with ice and pour in Bourbon whiskey to fill glass.

SPARKLING JULEP

Put 6 ounces crushed ice into highball glass and set aside. In mixing glass, muddle 3 mint sprigs, 1 teaspoonful superfine sugar, and 1 teaspoonful water. Add 3 ounces bourbon. Stir, then strain into the prepared glass of ice. Top with sparkling white wine. Garnish with mint sprig.

MACHO KAMACHO

Pour into mixing glass 2 ounces bourbon, 2 dashes peach bitters, and a couple of ice cubes. Fill a rocks glass with ice cubes and strain the mixture over the rocks. Drop in one red grape.

THE CRANBOURBON

Shake together 2 ounces bourbon, one dash Angostura bitters, ½ ounce lemon juice, and 1 teaspoonful sugar. Strain into rocks glass filled with ice cubes. Top with cranberry juice.

SUMMER SOUR

Pour into mixing glass 1 ounce fresh lemon juice, 1 teaspoonful sugar, and 2 ounces bourbon. Stir until sugar dissolves. Strain into rocks glass filled with ice cubes. Top with splash of soda.

STONE AGE SOUR

Stir in mixing glass 1½ ounces bourbon, ½ ounce lemon juice, 3 or 4 dashes peppermint schnapps, and ice cubes. Strain into sour glass containing about an inch of crushed ice.

VIA CONDOTTI

Stir in mixing glass 2 ounces bourbon, ½ ounce sweet vermouth, ½ ounce Fernet Branca, and ice cubes. Strain into cocktail glass.

VIA CONDOTTI II

Follow recipe for Via Condotti, but add 2 dashes anisette liqueur to mixing glass.

AS THE CROW FLIES

Shake 1 ounce bourbon, ½ ounce lemon juice, and a dash of grenadine with ice cubes in cocktail shaker. Strain into cocktail glass.

THE LAURA

Pour into mixing glass 1½ ounces bourbon, 1 ounce sweet vermouth, and ½ ounce each dry vermouth, Campari, and Galliano. Mix well; strain into cocktail glass. Garnish with cherry.

RICHELIEU

Shake in cocktail shaker 1 ounce Dubonnet, 1 teaspoonful Vieille Cure liqueur, 2 ounces bourbon, and ice cubes. Strain into cocktail glass. Twist lemon peel to release one drop of oil into drink and toss the peel in, too.

D.C. SHUTTLE

Stir in mixing glass ½ ounce bourbon, ¼ ounce dry vermouth, ½ ounce orange curaçao, a dash of grenadine, and ice cubes. Strain into cocktail glass holding one inch of crushed ice.

SISTERS COCKTAIL

Shake with ice cubes 1½ ounces bourbon, 1½ ounces brandy, 1 teaspoonful lemon juice, 1 teaspoonful Grand Marnier. Strain into cocktail glass.

BOURBON AFTERSHAVE

In cocktail shaker with ice cubes, shake 1½ ounces bourbon, ½ ounce applejack, and a dash of peppermint schnapps. Strain into cocktail glass. Squeeze slender wedge of lime over glass and stir once.

BEDTIME

Shake 2½ ounces bourbon, ½ ounce Bénédictine, and ice cubes in cocktail shaker. Strain into cocktail glass.

GOLDWASSER MANHATTAN

Shake, in cocktail shaker with ice cubes, 3 ounces bourbon and a dash of Angostura bitters. Strain into cocktail glass. Then slightly shake a bottle of goldwasser to stir up the gold flecks, top up the cocktail glass with the liqueur, and stir gently.

HATS OFF

In mixing glass, stir 1½ ounces bourbon, ½ ounce peppermint schnapps, and ice cubes. Strain into rocks glass filled with ice.

SCARLET RIBBON
Shake in cocktail shaker 1½ ounces bourbon, ½ ounce cranberry juice, 1 ounce grapefruit juice, ½ teaspoonful orgeat syrup, and ice cubes. Strain into cocktail glass.

TRIPLE THREAT
Shake in cocktail shaker 1½ ounces bourbon, 1 ounce raspberry liqueur, ½ ounce triple sec, 1 teaspoonful orgeat syrup, and ice cubes. Strain into cocktail glass.

BIG BOY NOW
Stir in mixing glass 1½ ounces bourbon, 1 teaspoonful cherry brandy, and 1 teaspoonful lemon juice. Pour over rocks glass half filled with ice.

TURKEY SHOOTER
Shake, in cocktail shaker, ¾ ounce bourbon, ¼ ounce white crème de menthe, and ice cubes. Strain into brandy snifter.

BOURBON DAISY
Shake in cocktail shaker 1½ ounces bourbon and ½ ounce each lemon juice, grenadine, and Southern Comfort. Strain into cocktail glass half filled with ice cubes. Top with club soda and garnish with a pineapple spear.

BOURBON COWBOY
In mixing glass with ice cubes, stir 1½ ounces bourbon, ½ ounce lime juice, and ½ ounce triple sec. Strain into rocks glass half filled with ice cubes.

BALTIMORE ORIOLE
Shake with ice cubes in cocktail shaker 1½ ounces bourbon, ½ ounce Cointreau, and 1 ounce orange juice. Strain into rocks glass half filled with ice cubes. Twist peel of lemon over glass to release a drop of oil and toss the peel in, too.

SLOW BIRD
Stir, in mixing glass, 1½ ounces bourbon, ½ ounce sloe gin, ½ ounce lemon juice, 1 teaspoonful superfine sugar, and ice cubes. Strain into cocktail glass.

BOURBON DRINKS WITH MILK, CREAM, OR EGG

BOURBON MILK PUNCH
Pour into cocktail shaker 1½ ounces bourbon, 3 ounces milk, 1 teaspoonful superfine sugar, 1 dash vanilla extract, and ice cubes. Shake well. Strain into rocks glass and sprinkle grated nutmeg on top.

KENTUCKY GENT
Put in blender 2 scoops ice cream, 1 ounce peppermint schnapps, 1½ ounces Bourbon whiskey, and a little cracked ice. Blend at medium speed until smooth. Pour into brandy snifter.

SHORT AND BUBBLY
Shake, in cocktail shaker, 2 ounces bourbon, 1½ ounces cream, and ice cubes. Strain into cocktail glass and top up with soda.

PHASE I
Pour 1 ounce bourbon and ½ teaspoon-

ful superfine sugar into rocks glass and stir until sugar dissolves. Add 3 ice cubes and top with milk. Stir gently.

PHASE II

Shake with ice in cocktail shaker 1½ ounces bourbon, 1 ounce rum, and ½ ounce heavy cream. Strain into cocktail glass. Sprinkle cinnamon on top.

BOURBON FOR BREAKFAST

Using a blender at medium speed for 20 seconds, blend 1 egg white, 1½ ounces bourbon, ½ ounce curaçao, and 2 dashes grenadine. Strain into sour or rocks glass half filled with ice cubes.

NOCTURNAL

Shake well in cocktail shaker 2 ounces bourbon, 1 ounce dark crème de cacao, ½ ounce heavy cream, and ice cubes. Strain into rocks glass holding about an inch of crushed ice. Garnish with blanched almonds.

BOURBON DRINKS WITH FRUIT JUICES

FRIDAY THE THIRTEENTH

In rocks glass half filled with ice cubes, gently stir 1½ ounces bourbon, 1½ ounces orange juice, and 2 dashes gold rum.

DEATH VALLEY VULTURE

Shake with ice cubes in cocktail shaker 3 ounces bourbon and 1½ ounces orange juice. Strain into cocktail glass containing about an inch of ice. Garnish with slice of lime.

THAT OLD DEVIL MOON

Shake 1½ ounces bourbon, 1 ounce Cointreau, and 3 ounces orange juice with ice cubes in cocktail shaker. Strain into rocks glass filled with ice cubes. Float grenadine on top.

KENTUCKY COOLER

Shake with ice in cocktail shaker ½ ounce rum, 1½ ounces bourbon, ¼ ounce each orange juice and lemon juice, and 1 dash grenadine. Strain into cocktail glass.

MASON-DIXIE

Pour ½ inch rum into cocktail glass. Then in cocktail shaker shake 1 ounce bourbon, ½ ounce each white crème de cacao and white crème de menthe, 1 ounce light rum, and ice cubes. Strain onto the rum in the cocktail glass.

BOURBON BOUNCE

Pour into highball glass half full of ice 2 ounces bourbon, 1 ounce triple sec, and ½ ounce lemon juice. Stir. Fill almost to the top with orange juice; stir again. Float a little ginger ale on top.

WATERMELON

Fill highball glass with ice cubes. Pour in 2 ounces Southern Comfort; fill to top with pineapple juice. Stir. Add a splash of grenadine.

LONG HOT NIGHT

Put about 4 ice cubes in highball glass. Pour in 2½ ounces bourbon and stir. Add 3 ounces each pineapple juice and cranberry juice; stir again.

CENTRAL AIR
Shake in cocktail shaker with ice cubes ½ ounce Southern Comfort, 1½ ounces bourbon, 2 teaspoonfuls lemon juice, and 1 teaspoonful superfine sugar. Pour into highball glass half filled with ice cubes. Garnish with peach slice.

BOURBON HIGHBALLS

TALL AND GALLANT
Pour into mixing glass 1½ ounces bourbon, 1 ounce lemon juice, ½ ounce Galliano liqueur, 1 teaspoonful orgeat syrup, and ice cubes. Stir well. Fill highball glass halfway with ice cubes. Strain drink into glass. Top with ginger ale.

BOURBON ICED TEA
Pour into highball glass filled with ice cubes 1 ounce Southern Comfort, 1 ounce bourbon, 3 ounces chilled tea, ½ ounce lemon juice, and ½ ounce sugar syrup. Stir with vigor. Top with club soda; garnish with lemon wedge.

BOURBON HIGH
Pour into highball glass filled with ice 1 ounce bourbon. Add ginger ale to the top.

NEW YORK TO L.A.
Into a highball glass half full of ice cubes, pour 1 ounce bourbon, 1 ounce brandy, and 2 teaspoonsful triple sec. Stir. Top glass up with ginger ale.

SOUTHERN PRESBYTERIAN
Half fill a highball glass with ice cubes. Pour in 3 ounces bourbon; add equal parts club soda and ginger ale to fill glass.

4

TEQUILA

Although Mexicans have been enjoying tequila for centuries, this potent spirit has only recently shaken off its sinister reputation here in the States and gained widespread popularity. In fact, tequila was the fastest-growing seller in spirits during the 1970s, as vodka had been in the 1960s. Even so, certain misconceptions about tequila linger on, and these should be disposed of at once.

Tequila does not derive from the same plant as mescaline, nor does it induce hallucinations, nor is it the Mexican equivalent of rotgut. Far from any of those things. Good tequila has a tart, biting taste that leaves the tongue clean, tingling, and refreshed. Tequila does pack a wallop, but it's not as likely to leave you with a hangover as the mellower grain spirits are.

Distilled from the fermented juice of the blue agave plant (which the Aztecs called *mezcal*, a plant totally different from the mescal cactus—but hence the confusion with the word *mescaline*),

real Tequila is produced only in the small region of Mexico around the town of Tequila in the state of Jalisco. It is the most distinguished member of a family of agave-based alcoholic beverages that includes pulque, a crude, milky brew, and mezcal, a distilled spirit with a flavor like kerosene spiced with hot peppers. Tequila is a form of mezcal, but it's the classiest and most refined of mezcals, the "cognac" of the line. Tequila must be distilled at least twice, and the better tequilas, known as *añejo*, require a year's aging in wood; routinely the añejos get three years. Gold tequila has been aged in used oak barrels, from which it acquires its pale straw-gold color. The unaged tequilas are known as *white* or *silver*, and they are somewhat harsher.

Now, the question is: Should you drink your tequila straight, mix it in cocktails, or down it the Mexican way—with a lick of salt and a bite of lime wedge? Good añejos, if you can find them, should be drunk straight. Jose Cuervo Especial is a fine añejo, widely available. Herradura Añejo and Sauza Three Generations are harder to find in the United States, but worth the search. These fine Tequilas are dry and light, with just a hint of sharpness, reminiscent of Armagnac. They are intensely aromatic and benefit from being served in snifters.

Inexpensive young tequilas, like Cuervo white or Pepe Lopez, are best suited for the salt-and-lime method, which the Mexicans call *los tres cuates* (the three pals). Or mix them in tequila sours, sunrises, or margaritas. A word of warning about the margarita: Like the dry martini, this drink goes down easy and is wickedly powerful. Drink three of them, and you may forget your name! Many who enjoy sipping their tequila neat chase it down with sangrita, a hot, tongue-tingling tomato-and-orange-juice mixture.

Tequila Recipes

See Section One for information on barware, mixing supplies, and mixing tips. For conversion to metric or other measurements, refer to tables on pages 11 and 22.

THREE TEQUILA STANDARDS

THE MARGARITA
Moisten the rim of a cocktail glass with the rind of a lemon or lime and then dip it in coarse-ground salt to coat it; set glass aside. Pour 1½ ounces tequila, ½ ounce triple sec, and ½ ounce lime juice or lemon juice over crushed ice in cocktail shaker; shake hard. Strain into the salt-frosted glass.

TEQUILA SUNRISE
Fill collins glass with ice; pour in 1 ounce tequila and top with orange juice. Stir thoroughly, then add ½ ounce grenadine. Stir again a few turns.

LOS TRES CUATES
Cut a lime into wedges, stand a salt shaker on the bar in front of you, then pour 1½ ounces tequila into shot glass. Lick the indentation between thumb and index finger on your left hand and sprinkle liberally with salt from shaker. Take the shot glass firmly in left hand and the lime wedge in right hand. Lick the salt, down the shot and bite into lime wedge.

OTHER TEQUILA DRINKS

FUZZY MOTHER
Pour 1½ ounces gold tequila into pony glass. Top with 151-proof rum. Ignite.

TEQUILA CHASED WITH SANGRITA
To prepare sangrita: Combine in a blender 1 cup tomato juice, 3 ounces fresh orange juice, 1½ ounces lime juice, ¼ teaspoonful Worcestershire sauce, ¼ teaspoonful Tabasco sauce, dash of allspice, pinch of salt, pinch of pepper, and some fine-chopped onion. Blend thoroughly. (You can also do this in a shaker.)

Now fill one shot glass with tequila and another with sangrita. Take alternate sips from each.

SANGRITA HIGHBALL
Fill highball glass with ice; pour in 2 ounces tequila and 4 ounces sangrita (see above). Stir.

FROZEN STRAWBERRY MARGARITA
Blend together 3 ounces crushed ice, 1½ ounces tequila, 1½ ounces sweet-and-sour, and ½ cup frozen strawberries (in blender) until smooth. Salt-frost a large cocktail glass (as described in recipe for standard margarita) and pour in the blended mixture.

GRAND MARGARITA
Salt-frost rim of cocktail glass and set aside. Pour 1½ ounces tequila, ½ ounce Grand Marnier, and ½ ounce lime juice or lemon juice over crushed ice in cocktail shaker. Shake hard; strain into the prepared glass.

GOLDEN MARGARITA
Shake together 2 ounces golden tequila, 1 ounce curaçao, ¾ ounce lime juice, and 2 ounces crushed ice. Pour without straining into rocks glass. Garnish with slice or wedge of lime.

TEQUILA SUNSET
Fill collins glass with ice. Pour in 1 ounce tequila, then fill nearly to the top with equal parts orange juice and pineapple juice. Stir well. Top with ½ ounce blackberry brandy. Stir again, if you want, one or two turns.

BLACK BULL
Fill rocks glass with ice, then add 2 ounces tequila and ½ ounce coffee liqueur. Stir.

WHITE BULL
Fill rocks glass with ice. Pour in 2 ounces tequila and ½ ounce coffee liqueur. Float heavy cream on top and stir.

PANTHER
Into rocks glass filled with ice, pour 1½ ounces tequila and ½ ounce sweet-and-sour. Stir.

PINEAPPLE PANTHER
Shake together 1½ ounces of tequila, 1 ounce pineapple juice, and 1 dash grenadine, with ice, in cocktail shaker. Strain into cocktail glass.

MALIBU WAVE
Blend together until smooth 3 ounces crushed ice, 1 ounce tequila, ½ ounce triple sec, ½ teaspoonful blue curaçao, and 1½ ounces sweet-and-sour in blender. Strain into cocktail glass. Garnish with lime wedge.

TEQUILA MANHATTAN
In mixing glass, stir together with ice 1½ ounces tequila, ½ ounce (or less) dry vermouth, a dash of orange bitters. Strain into cocktail glass.

MEXITINI
Stir together in mixing glass 1½ ounces tequila, ½ ounce (or less) dry vermouth, a dash of Pernod, with ice. Strain into cocktail glass.

FIESTA TIME
Pour 1 ounce tequila, 2 ounces St. Raphaël aperitif wine, 2 teaspoonfuls lime juice, and 4 ounces crushed ice into cocktail shaker. Shake hard. Strain into cocktail glass. Garnish with maraschino cherries—one red and one green, if you have both kinds.

ROSITA
Fill rocks glass with ice and pour in 1½ ounces gold tequila, ¾ ounce dry vermouth, ¾ ounce sweet vermouth, and 1½ ounces Campari. Stir one or two turns. Twist a strip of lemon peel above the glass, then toss in.

GORDITA
Fill rocks glass with ice and pour in 2

ounces añejo tequila. Add as much soda as you want, and garnish with large strip of orange peel. Stir a couple turns.

SPANISH MOSS

Pour 1½ ounces tequila and 1 ounce coffee liqueur over ice in cocktail shaker; shake hard. Strain into cocktail glass. Float a few drops of green crème de menthe on the surface.

MOCKINGBIRD

Pour 1½ ounces tequila, 2 teaspoonfuls white crème de menthe, and 1 ounce lime juice over ice in cocktail shaker. Shake hard. Strain into cocktail glass.

COMPADRE

Pour 1 ounce tequila, ⅓ ounce grenadine, ¼ teaspoon maraschino liqueur, and 2 dashes Angostura bitters over crushed ice in cocktail shaker. Shake hard. Strain into cocktail glass.

HAND GRENADE

In mixing glass, pour 3 ounces cranberry juice and 1 ounce tequila over ice; stir. Strain into cocktail glass; twist a strip of orange peel over the drink, then toss in.

BANANA BOAT

Blend together until smooth 1½ ounces tequila, ½ ounce banana liqueur, 1 ounce lime juice, and 2 ounces crushed ice in blender. Pour into sour glass.

VIVA VILLA

In a blender, mix together 2 ounces tequila, 1 ounce grape juice, ½ ounce Cointreau, 1 teaspoonful grenadine, and 3 ounces crushed ice at low speed for 20 seconds. Strain into sour glass.

SNAKE RIVER STINGER

Pour into mixing glass 1 ounce gold tequila, ½ teaspoonful Pernod, ½ teaspoonful white crème de menthe, and 1 ounce crushed ice. Stir; strain into shot glass.

OVER, UNDER INDIAN LEGBREAKER

Fill highball glass with ice cubes and pour in 1 ounce tequila, ½ ounce 151-proof rum, 4 ounces sweet-and-sour, and ¼ ounce grenadine. Stir. Garnish with orange slice and cherry.

TIJUANA BLUE SCREW

Fill highball glass with ice, then pour in 1½ ounces tequila and 4 ounces orange juice. Float a dash of blue curacao on the surface.

BLOODY MARIA

Fill highball glass with ice and add 1½ ounces tequila; top with bloody-mary mix (tomato juice, Worcestershire, Tabasco, horseradish, salt, and pepper to taste). Stir. Garnish with celery stick, lime wedge or both.

TEQUILA BLOODY BULL

Into highball glass filled with ice, pour 1½ ounces tequila, 3 ounces tomato juice, 3 ounces bouillon, and Tabasco, Worcestershire, salt, and pepper to taste. Stir.

SILK STOCKINGS

Blend together until smooth 1½

ounces tequila, 2 ounces evaporated milk, 1 ounce white crème de cacao, 1 teaspoonful grenadine, and 4 ounces crushed ice, using a blender. Pour into large wine glass, sprinkle ground cinnamon on top, and garnish, if desired, with maraschino cherry.

CHARRO

Shake together 4 ounces crushed ice, 1 ounce tequila, 1⅓ ounces evaporated milk, and ⅔ ounce strong coffee in cocktail shaker. Strain into rocks glass half filled with ice cubes.

TOREADOR

Shake together 1½ ounces tequila, ½ ounce white crème de cacao, ½ ounce cream, and 2 ounces crushed ice in cocktail shaker. Strain into cocktail glass. Top off with a dollop of fresh whipped cream, then sprinkle on a bit of cocoa.

RED TURTLE

Fill collins glass with ice. Pour in 3 ounces tequila, 3 ounces crème de noyaux and the juice of two limes. Top with orange juice.

FREDDY FUDPUCKER

Fill highball glass with ice and pour in 2 ounces tequila and 4 ounces orange juice. Top with a splash of Galliano liqueur, and mix.

TROPICAL NIGHT

Fill highball glass nearly to the top with ice cubes and pour in 1½ ounces gold tequila, ½ ounce grenadine, 3 ounces orange juice, and 1 teaspoonful lemon juice. Stir. Garnish with slice of orange and maraschino cherry.

LONG, TALL SENORITA

Fill highball glass with crushed ice and pour in 1½ ounces tequila, 1 teaspoonful grenadine, generous dash of crème de cassis, and ½ ounce lime juice; top with soda. Stir one or two turns.

CONCHITA

Fill highball glass with ice cubes and pour in 1½ ounces tequila and ½ teaspoonful lemon juice. Top with grapefruit juice; stir thoroughly.

BIG BERTHA

Fill highball glass with ice cubes and pour in 1½ ounces tequila, 1½ teaspoonfuls superfine sugar, ½ ounce lemon juice or lime juice, a splash of dry red wine. Stir. Twist strip of lemon peel over drink to release the oil, then toss into glass.

TEQUILA AND TONIC

Fill highball glass nearly to the top with ice, pour in 2 ounces tequila and ½ ounce lime juice or lemon juice. Top with tonic water and stir. Twist a strip of lemon or lime peel above the drink and toss it in.

TEQUILA JULEP

Muddle six or seven mint leaves with 1 teaspoonful superfine sugar in the bottom of a highball glass. Fill glass with ice, then pour in 1½ ounces tequila. Top with soda and stir. Garnish with sprig of mint.

EVITA

Pack highball glass with crushed ice, then pour in 3 ounces tequila and place in freezer. When ready to serve, remove glass from freezer and fill to top with bitter lemon. Garnish with lemon wedge.

TEQUILA AND COLA

Fill highball glass with ice and pour in 1 ounce lemon juice and 1½ ounces tequila; top up with cola. Stir. Twist a strip of lemon peel above drink, then toss it into the glass.

RALLY IN THE PLAZA

Fill collins glass about halfway with crushed ice. Pour in 2 ounces tequila, ½ ounce grenadine, 1 ounce lemon juice, 1 ounce pineapple juice, and 1 ounce orange juice, then fill to top with ginger ale.

TEQUILA COLLINS

Almost fill a collins glass with crushed ice, then pour in 1½ ounces tequila, 1 ounce sugar syrup, and 1 ounce lime juice or lemon juice; top up with soda. Stir. Garnish with orange slice and cherry.

TAXCO FIZZ

Pour 2 ounces tequila, 1 ounce lime juice, 1 teaspoonful superfine sugar, 2 dashes orange bitters, and 1 egg white over crushed ice in cocktail shaker; shake hard. Pour into collins glass and top with soda.

5

RUM

Rum—fortifier of the British Navy, firewater of pirates, barter for slaves, and (some say) a prime mover in the American Revolution—has chalked up quite a bit of history in the three hundred years it's been around. The range of character in the liquor itself is just as extraordinary, covering the spectrum from almost tasteless and colorless to rich and pungent and dark as mahogany. What all rums have in common is sugarcane.

In order to make this spirit, sugarcane in some form—usually molasses—must be fermented and distilled. It was Columbus who first brought sugarcane from the Canary Islands to the islands of the West Indies, where it flourished. The Spanish settlers who followed brought with them the art of distilling—and rum was born. To this day, nearly all the world's rum is produced on the islands of the Caribbean Sea.

While each island distills its own distinctive style of rum, there are two major subdivisions: light-bodied and full-bodied. Light-bodied rums originate primarily from the Spanish-speaking islands, with Puerto Rico setting the standard with its clean, muted spirits. The English-speaking islands, most notably Jamaica, produce the denser, richer, dark rums. Rums from the French-speaking islands fall somewhere in between, although they tend to be closer to the full-bodied Jamaican rums.

Differences in color, texture, and flavor derive from differences in methods of manufacture. The light-bodied rums go through a continuous still, where they pick up fewer congeners (impurities that nevertheless contribute to flavor), and they are aged for shorter periods of time, often no more than a year. The full-bodied dark rums are produced, like single-malt Scotch whiskies, in traditional, slower, pot stills; in Jamaica, the molasses is reinforced with "dunder," the residue of a previous distillation, and this imparts an even more pungent, rummy flavor.

Full-bodied rums are aged between five and eight years, and sometimes even longer. Rums acquire some color during aging, though frequently distillers add caramel for a darker shade.

Puerto Rican rums are excellent for mixing with soda, tonic water, or the complicated fruity ingredients of many tropical confections like the piña colada, the daiquiri, the mai tai, and the zombie. Although all Puerto Rican rums fall into the light-bodied category, there are three shades of lightness: white, gold, and añejo. White rums, preferred in the United States, can often be quite close to vodka in taste (or lack of taste), whereas the gold rums are a bit fuller and more aromatic. Añejos are essentially gold rums, selected for their fullness of flavor and aged for a period ranging from four to six years or longer; they have enough character to stand by themselves, and should be served either neat or on the rocks.

Dark, full-bodied, Jamican-style rums have become more popular in the last few years as drinkers have discovered the potency and intricacy of their flavors. Myers's and Appleton of Jamaica, Mount Gay of Barbados, and Saint James of Martinique all make rums with the class and bravado of fine whiskey. And, like whiskey, these dark rums are best appreciated straight or simply on ice. A drinker new to full-bodied rum may be tempted, on first sip, to describe the taste as sweet; but it's not: This is the flavor of the molasses coming through. On longer acquaintance, the subtleties of both taste and fragrance in dark rums become apparent.

Other interesting rums include the smooth, deeply colored Demerara from Guyana (also available in a 151-proof variety); Rhum Barbancourt from Haiti, with a complex, brandylike style; and arrack, an entirely different style of rum, at once light and fragrant, especially notable in Batavia Arak from Indonesia.

Rum Recipes

See Section One for information on barware, mixing supplies, and mixing tips. For conversion to metric or other measurements, refer to tables on pages 11 and 22.

SIX RUM STANDARDS

DAIQUIRI
Into a cocktail shaker one-quarter full of ice, pour the juice of half a lime, 2 ounces light rum, and 1 teaspoonful superfine sugar. Shake hard. Strain into cocktail glass.

PIÑA COLADA
Pour over 4 ounces of shaved ice in blender 2 ounces gold rum, 3 ounces crushed pineapple (or unsweetened pineapple juice), and 1¼ ounces cream of coconut. Blend until smooth. Strain into highball glass filled with ice cubes. For variety, top with a dash of cherry brandy and garnish with slice of orange.

MAI TAI
Pour 1 ounce lime juice, ¾ ounce curaçao, 3 dashes orgeat syrup, and 2 ounces rum over 4 ice cubes in cocktail shaker; shake hard. Fill highball glass with ice, then strain in the blended liquid. Garnish with spear of fresh pineapple and a sprig of mint.

ZOMBIE
In mixing glass one quarter filled with ice, stir 1 ounce light rum, ½ ounce crème de noyaux (almond), ½ ounce triple sec, 1½ ounces sweet-and-sour, and 1½ ounces orange juice. Strain into collins glass half filled with ice. Top with ½ ounce 151-proof rum; garnish with maraschino cherry.

RUM AND TONIC
Pour 3 ounces rum into highball glass; add a squeeze of lime and a slice of lime. Fill with ice cubes and top up with tonic.

CUBA LIBRE
Pour the juice of half a large lime into a highball glass and toss in a slice of lime peel. Add 1½ ounces gold rum and 2 or 3 ice cubes; fill up with cola.

DAIQUIRI VARIATIONS

FROZEN DAIQUIRI
Put juice of half a lime, 2 ounces light rum, and 1 teaspoonful superfine sugar into blender with 4 ounces shaved ice. Blend, and pour into cocktail glass. Add ⅓ cup sliced strawberries to the mix before blending and you'll have a Frozen Strawberry Daiquiri.

DAIQUIRI FRAPPÉ
Pour the juice of half a lime, 2 ounces rum, 1 (scant) teaspoonful orgeat syrup, and 3 drops triple sec over 6 ounces crushed ice in blender. Blend at high speed while counting to 15. Spoon into cocktail glass.

STRAWBERRY DAIQUIRI

Pour 2 ounces rum, 1 ounce triple sec, 2 ounces lemon juice, 3 teaspoonfuls sugar, 1 dash orange curaçao over a 6-ounce scoop of strawberry ice cream in a blender. Blend at medium speed until smooth. Pour into wine glass.

THE CITY LIGHTS DAIQUIRI

Blend together $\frac{1}{2}$ cup fresh strawberries, $1\frac{1}{2}$ ounces light rum, 4 ounces crushed ice, $\frac{1}{2}$ ounce sugar, 1 teaspoonful grenadine, and 1 dash lemon juice in blender at medium speed until smooth. Pour into wine glass; garnish with ripe strawberries.

DAIQUIRI BLOSSOM

Pour 1 ounce orange juice, 1 ounce light rum, and 1 dash maraschino over ice in cocktail shaker and shake hard. Strain into cocktail glass.

FROZEN BANANA DAIQUIRI

Blend together until smooth 4 ounces crushed ice, 1 ounce light rum, $1\frac{1}{2}$ ounces sweet-and-sour, and $\frac{1}{2}$ medium ripe banana. Pour into cocktail glass.

FROZEN PEACH DAIQUIRI

Blend together 4 ounces crushed ice, 1 ounce light rum, $1\frac{1}{2}$ ounces sweet-and-sour, $\frac{1}{4}$ cup fresh or frozen peaches. Pour into cocktail glass.

FROZEN MINT DAIQUIRI

Blend together $2\frac{1}{2}$ ounces light rum, 2 teaspoonfuls lime juice, 1 teaspoonful superfine sugar, 6 mint leaves, and 6 ounces crushed ice. Blend until smooth. Pour into large wine glass.

CHERRY RUM DAIQUIRI

Pour $\frac{1}{2}$ ounce cherry liqueur, $1\frac{1}{2}$ ounces light rum, 1 teaspoonful lemon juice, and 2 drops kirsch over 4 ounces crushed ice in cocktail shaker. Shake hard. Strain into cocktail glass.

PINEAPPLE DAIQUIRI

Blend together 1 teaspoonful superfine sugar, 2 chunks pineapple, 2 ounces light rum, and 4 ounces crushed ice until smooth. Pour from blender, unstrained, into cocktail glass.

THE DERBY DAIQUIRI

Stir together 6 ounces light rum, $1\frac{1}{2}$ ounces lime juice, $4\frac{1}{2}$ ounces orange juice, and $1\frac{1}{2}$ ounces sugar syrup. Pour over ice in rocks glass. Garnish with lime wedge.

KEY LIME DAIQUIRI

Pour $1\frac{1}{4}$ ounces rum and $\frac{1}{2}$ ounce lime juice over ice in cocktail shaker; shake hard. Strain over ice in rocks glass. Garnish with lime wedge, strawberries, whipped cream, and a graham cracker or butter cookie.

APPLE DAIQUIRI

Pour $\frac{1}{2}$ ounce apple juice, $\frac{1}{2}$ ounce lime juice, $1\frac{1}{2}$ ounces light rum, and 1 scant teaspoonful superfine sugar over 4 ounces shaved ice in cocktail shaker. Shake hard. Strain into cocktail glass.

PIÑA COLADA VARIATIONS

LIGHT IN THE PLAZA

Blend together $1\frac{1}{2}$ ounces light rum, $1\frac{1}{2}$ ounces amaretto, and $1\frac{1}{2}$ ounces piña colada mix (or 1 ounce pineapple juice and ½ ounce cream of coconut) in a blender with 6 ounces crushed ice until thick and creamy. Pour into highball glass and top with a dollop of whipped cream and a dash of grenadine. Garnish, if you like, with maraschino cherry.

SWISS TREAT

Stir in mixing glass 1 ounce rum and 1 ounce piña colada mix (or ⅔ ounce pineapple juice and ⅓ ounce cream of coconut). Add a dash of crème de almond (noyaux) and 1 dash of crème de banane. Pour into cocktail glass.

TROPICAL BOG

Pour 1½ ounces light rum, 2 ounces pineapple juice, ½ ounce cream of coconut, ½ ounce white crème de cacao, and 1¼ ounces light cream over 3 ice cubes in cocktail shaker. Shake hard. Strain into highball glass half filled with ice, pour in 1¼ ounces cranberry juice, and stir gently.

INDIAN PAINTBRUSH

Pour 2½ ounces gold rum, 5 ounces piña colada mix, ½ ounce crushed fresh or thawed frozen strawberries, and 6 ounces crushed ice into blender. Blend until smooth. Pour into large brandy snifter and garnish with 1 fresh strawberry and 1 chunk pineapple.

BRUISED BANANA

In a mixing glass, stir ¾ ounce dark rum, ¾ ounce light rum, and ¾ ounce crème de banane. Add a splash of half-and-half (cream) and 4½ ounces piña colada mix (or 3¼ ounces pineapple

juice and 1¼ ounces cream of coconut). Pour into a 22-ounce hurricane glass filled with crushed ice, and stir. Float a dash of 151-proof rum on top.

PIÑA MONTANA

Stir together in a blender 1½ ounces light rum with 1½ ounces piña colada mix (or 1 ounce pineapple juice and ½ ounce cream of coconut). Add a dollop of vanilla ice cream. Blend, then pour into large wine glass. Garnish with slices of orange and pineapple.

RON COCO

Obtain 1 whole coconut in its husk. Poke holes in its eyes, drain off coconut "milk" and save it. Remove top quarter of coconut. Shake together 1½ ounces light rum, 1 ounce apricot brandy, ¾ ounce cream of coconut, and 2 ounces of the coconut milk with 6 ounces crushed ice. Pour mixture into the coconut, and sprinkle top with some shredded coconut taken from top quarter. Use a straw for drinking.

OTHER RUM DRINKS WITH FRUIT JUICES

AUNT AGATHA

Pour 4 ounces orange juice and 2 ounces light rum over ice in rocks glass; stir gently. Float a few dots of Angostura bitters on the surface of the drink. Garnish with slice of orange.

GILDED CAGE

Pour 1½ ounces orange juice, 2 ounces gold rum, 2 teaspoonfuls light rum, 2 teaspoonfuls Falernum, and 2 dashes lemon juice over ice in cocktail shaker. Shake hard. Strain into cocktail glass.

FALERNUM SOUR

Pour 1½ ounces light rum, ½ ounce Falernum syrup, and 1 ounce lemon juice over 3 ice cubes in cocktail shaker and shake hard. Strain over ice in rocks glass, top with soda, and garnish with slice of orange.

KING ARTHUR'S COOLER

Mix together 1 ounce rum, 1 ounce lemon juice, and 2 ounces orange juice. Pour mixture into hurricane glass full of crushed ice. Garnish with slice of orange or a cherry.

RUM FOR YOUR MONEY

Mix together 1 ounce light rum, 2 ounces orange juice, and 2 ounces sweet-and-sour with ice in mixing glass. Strain into cocktail glass.

THE ISLE OF PINES

Pour 4 ounces light rum into rocks glass (over ice if desired); add 1 dash grapefruit juice and a squeeze of lime.

MONKEY WRENCH

Pour 3 ounces light rum over ice in rocks glass; add 4 ounces grapefruit juice. Stir.

RUM SURPRISE

Dissolve 1 teaspoonful superfine sugar in 3 ounces light rum in the bottom of a highball glass. Pack glass with crushed ice and put in freezer. Just before serving, pour in grapefruit juice to fill.

CREOLE WOMAN

Fill rocks glass with ice and add 1½ ounces light rum, 2 dashes Tabasco sauce, 1 teaspoonful lime juice, and 3 ounces beef bouillon. Stir. Sprinkle top with celery salt and garnish with spear of cucumber.

CAIPIRINHA

Drop 2 or 3 lime quarters into a highball glass; mash them with a dash of sugar. Add 3 ounces rum (preferably Brazilian) and fill glass with ice. Stir.

CUBA LIBRE COCKTAIL

Shake 1½ ounces dark rum and ½ ounce overproof (more than 100 proof) rum with ice in cocktail shaker. Add ½ ounce cola, ½ ounce lime juice, and 2 teaspoonfuls superfine sugar; stir until sugar is dissolved. Strain into cocktail glass.

BACARDI COCKTAIL

Pour 1 teaspoonful lime juice, 2 dashes grenadine, and 1½ ounces light rum (preferably Bacardi) over ice in cocktail shaker. Shake hard. Strain into cocktail glass.

TALL, DARK AND HANDSOME

Half fill collins glass with ice, then pour in 2 ounces dark rum, 2 teaspoonfuls Falernum syrup, 3 dashes Angostura bitters, and ½ ounce lime juice. Stir. Fill glass to the top with ice, and garnish with slice of lime.

TWISTED CANE

Pour 2 teaspoonfuls lime juice, ½ teaspoonful orgeat syrup, 1½ ounces light rum, and 2 dashes Grand Marnier over ice in cocktail shaker. Shake hard. Strain into cocktail glass.

BROWN DERBY

Pour ½ ounce lime juice, 1 teaspoonful maple syrup, and 1½ ounces dark rum over ice in cocktail shaker and shake hard. Strain into rocks glass filled with ice. Garnish with slice of lime.

POOLSIDE COOLER

Pour 3 ounces dark rum, 6 ounces crushed pineapple, ½ teaspoon super-fine sugar, and 4 ounces crushed ice into blender. Blend at high speed for half a minute. Pour—unstrained—over ice in collins glass. Garnish with sprig of mint.

XXX–HARRY'S SPECIAL

Pour 4 ounces orange juice over ice in highball glass; add 2 ounces pineapple juice, 2 ounces light rum, and 2 ounces dark rum. Stir and garnish with sprig of mint.

NEPTUNE'S MONSOON

In a 20-ounce brandy snifter, combine 3 ounces light rum, 3 ounces 151-proof rum, the juice of two limes, 2 ounces Hawaiian Punch (preferably made from the frozen concentrate), and 6 ounces pineapple juice.

ROYAL NAVY ROUSER

Pour into a cocktail shaker 1 ounce cream of coconut, 4 ounces pineapple juice, 1 ounce orange juice, and 4 ounces rum (traditionally, Pusser's—formerly the British Royal Navy issue). Shake hard. Strain into collins glass over 4 ounces crushed ice.

GOOD OLD DAYS SOUTHERN SMUGGLER

Fill highball glass with ice, then pour in 1¼ ounces light rum, ½ ounce dark rum, 6 ounces lemonade, and 2 ounces orange juice. Stir one or two turns and garnish with slice of lemon.

PLANTER'S COCKTAIL

Shake together 1½ ounces dark rum, 1 ounce orange juice, 1 ounce sugar syrup, and 1 ounce lime juice in cocktail shaker with ice. Strain into mug containing 3 ounces crushed ice. Sprinkle a few drops of grenadine on the surface.

LAGOON PUNCH

Pour 2 ounces orange juice, 2 ounces pineapple juice, 1 ounce lemon juice, 1 ounce coconut milk, 1½ ounces grenadine, and 1½ ounces light rum over ice in cocktail shaker. Shake hard; then strain into a mug; garnish with chunk of pineapple.

THE MONTE CARLO LIVING ROOM SPECIAL

Put 3½ ounces Barbados rum, ¼ fresh papaya, ¼ fresh mango, ¼ ripe banana, 2-to-3 ounces pineapple juice, 2-to-3 ounces orange juice, 4 ounces crushed ice, and a dash of grenadine into blender. Blend until smooth. Pour into large wine glass; garnish with slice of pineapple.

PLANTER'S PUNCH I

Dissolve 1½ teaspoonfuls sugar in 2 ounces lime juice in cocktail shaker. Add ice cubes and 3 ounces Jamaica rum. Shake well, and strain into highball glass half filled with crushed ice.

Garnish, if desired, with sliver of fresh pineapple, slice of orange, and sprig of mint. Serve with straw.

PLANTER'S PUNCH II
Stir in mixing glass quarter filled with ice 1 ounce dark rum, ½ ounce grenadine, 1 dash bitters, and 1½ ounces sweet-and-sour. Strain into highball glass filled with ice; top with soda. Garnish if desired, with a cherry.

PLANTER'S PUNCH III
Pour into cocktail shaker ½ ounce sugar syrup, 1 ounce lime juice, 4 ounces rum, and 1 dash grenadine; add ice cubes and shake well. Strain into highball glass half filled with cracked ice. Garnish with lime rind and, if desired, sprinkle of nutmeg.

THE PANINI
Put 4 ounces orange juice, 2 ounces rum, 1 ripe banana, and 6 or 7 ice cubes into blender. Blend until smooth. Pour into large wine glass.

PONCE DE LEON
Frost the rim of a cocktail glass with sugar. Pour 2 ounces light rum, ½ ounce grapefruit juice, ½ ounce mango nectar into cocktail shaker. Add 1 teaspoonful lemon juice and ¼ teaspoonful superfine sugar and shake hard. Strain into cocktail glass.

GAUGUIN
Pour ½ ounce passion-fruit syrup, ½ ounce lime juice, ½ ounce lemon juice, and 2 ounces light rum into blender with 4 ounces crushed ice. Blend for 10 seconds. Pour, without straining, into rocks glass. Squeeze a strip of lime peel over drink to release the oil and toss in.

LITTLE RUM BOOGIE
Fill rocks glass with ice and pour in 1½ ounces dark rum. Top with a mixture of pineapple and coconut juices. Add a squirt of fresh lime juice.

BAHAMA MAMA
To a dash of grenadine in the bottom of large collins or hurricane glass, add ice cubes, 2 ounces sweet-and-sour, 2 ounces pineapple juice, 1½ ounces each white rum, gold rum, dark rum, and 2½ ounces orange juice. Garnish with squeeze of lime, a slice of orange, and a cherry. Sip through a straw.

THE MARTIAN TWEETIE
Stir together in a mixing glass 1½ ounces dark rum, ½ ounce light rum, ½ ounce passion-fruit syrup, ½ ounce mai tai cream mix, 2 drops honey, and 2 teaspoonfuls coconut milk. Pour mixture over ice in a rocks glass.

APPLE DELIGHT
Fill rocks glass with ice and pour in 1½ ounces Captain Morgan's Spiced Rum; top with apple cider. Garnish with a slice each of apple and orange and a cherry.

PINK VERANDAH
Pour 1 ounce gold rum, ½ ounce dark rum, ½ ounce lime juice, 1 teaspoonful superfine sugar, 1½ ounces cranberry juice, and ½ egg white over ice in cocktail shaker. Shake hard. Put ice in rocks glass and strain the mixture over it.

RUM DRINKS WITH LIQUEURS

EYE-OPENER

Pour 1½ ounces light rum, 1 teaspoonful triple sec, 1 teaspoonful white crème de cacao, 3 dashes anise-flavored liqueur, 1 teaspoonful Falernum syrup, and 1 egg yolk over ice in cocktail shaker. Shake hard. Strain into cocktail glass.

ACAPULCO COCKTAIL

Pour 1½ ounces light rum, ½ ounce triple sec, ½ ounce lime juice, 1 teaspoonful superfine sugar, and 1 egg white over ice in cocktail shaker. Shake hard, then strain into cocktail glass. Float 3 mint leaves on the surface.

SHIPPING SOUTH

Fill rocks glass with ice and pour in 1½ ounces golden rum and 1½ ounces Grand Marnier; stir.

PAGO PAGO

Pour 2 ounces light rum, ½ ounce pineapple juice, ½ ounce lime juice, ½ teaspoonful white crème de cacao, and ¼ teaspoonful green Chartreuse over 4 ounces crushed ice in cocktail shaker. Shake hard. Strain into rocks glass.

MARY PICKFORD

Pour 1½ ounces pineapple juice, 1½ ounces light rum, ¼ teaspoonful kirsch, and ¼ teaspoonful grenadine over ice in cocktail shaker. Shake hard. Strain into rocks glass.

APRICOT LADY

Pour 1½ ounces Barbados rum, ½ ounce triple sec, 1 egg white, 2½ ounces apricot nectar, and 2 ounces crushed ice into blender. Blend for 15 seconds. Pour into rocks glass half filled with crushed ice.

SUNBURN

Pour 1½ ounces light rum, ½ ounce Cointreau, 3 dashes amaretto, and ½ ounce lime juice over 4 ounces crushed ice in cocktail shaker. Shake hard. Strain into rocks glass filled with ice.

RUM DANDY

Put 2 ounces pineapple juice, 1 ounce orange juice, 1½ ounces dark rum, 1 teaspoonful banana liqueur, 1 teaspoonful lime juice, and 3 ounces crushed ice into blender. Blend at low speed for 15 seconds. Strain into rocks glass.

BERMUDA DREAM

Shake together 2 ounces orange juice, 2 ounces lime juice, 1½ ounces light rum, 1 dash peach liqueur, and 1 dash Parfait d'Amour liqueur. Pour over crushed ice in large wine glass; garnish with sprig of mint and slice of lime.

CABINET COCKTAIL

Stir together in mixing glass 1½ ounces light rum, ½ ounce Grand Marnier, ½ ounce white crème de cacao, and ½ ounce lemon juice. Pour into rocks glass filled with ice. Garnish, if desired, with jelly beans.

OLDER BUT NO WISER

Pour 2 ounces dark rum, 1 teaspoonful apricot brandy, 3 teaspoonfuls pineapple juice, and 1 teaspoonful golden rum over ice in cocktail shaker. Shake hard. Strain into cocktail glass.

FRESCO DELIGHT

Remove pulp and membrane from a grapefruit half and set shell aside. Put 4 ounces crushed ice into cocktail shaker, then pour in 1½ ounces light rum, ¾ ounce triple sec, 1½ ounces lemon juice, and 1 teaspoonful sugar. Shake hard. Strain into the grapefruit shell and stick in a short straw.

CHINESE

Pour 2 ounces golden rum, 1 teaspoonful curaçao, 3 drops grenadine, and ½ ounce passion-fruit juice, with 2 dashes Angostura bitters, over ice in cocktail shaker. Shake hard. Strain into cocktail glass.

CASA BLANCA

Pour 2 ounces golden rum, ¼ teaspoonful curaçao, ¼ teaspoonful maraschino liqueur, and ¾ teaspoonful lime juice over ice in cocktail shaker. Add dash of Angostura bitters and shake hard. Strain into cocktail glass.

HOLY MOLEY

Pour 1½ ounces light rum, 1 ounce coffee liqueur, 1 dash curaçao, and 1 ounce dark crème de cacao over ice in cocktail shaker. Shake hard. Strain into cocktail glass.

SHANGHAI

Pour 1½ ounces dark rum, ½ ounce lemon juice, 1 ounce sambuca, and 3 drops grenadine over ice in cocktail shaker. Shake hard. Strain into cocktail glass.

RIVIERA

Fill rocks glass with ice and pour in 1 ounce light rum, 1 ounce Cointreau, and ½ ounce raspberry liqueur. Top with bitter lemon soda. Squeeze a wedge of lime over drink and toss it in.

RUM RUNNER

Fill rocks glass with ice and pour in 1 ounce light rum, 1 ounce gold rum, 1 ounce dark rum, 1 ounce blackberry brandy, 1 ounce banana liqueur, and 1 ounce grenadine. Stir, then top with soda.

BANANA PEEL

Pour ¾ ounce banana liqueur, 1 ounce gold rum, and ¾ ounce Pernod over ice in cocktail shaker and shake hard. Strain into cocktail glass.

SWEET BANANA OF PARADISE

Pour 1 ounce light rum, ½ ounce Southern Comfort, 1 teaspoonful lime juice, and 1½ ounces banana liqueur over ice in cocktail shaker. Shake hard, then strain into cocktail glass.

JOLLY ROGER

Pour 1 ounce dark rum, 1 ounce banana liqueur, and 2 ounces lemon juice over ice in cocktail shaker. Shake hard. Strain over ice in large wine glass.

MANDEVILLE

Put ice cubes in cocktail shaker, then pour in 1½ ounces dark rum, 1 ounce light rum, ½ ounce lemon juice, ½ ounce cola, ¼ teaspoonful anise-flavored liqueur, and ¼ teaspoonful grenadine. Shake hard, then strain into cocktail glass.

SEMI-FREDDO COCKTAIL

Dissolve 1 teaspoonful sugar in ½ teaspoonful water and put into blender. Add 2 dashes Angostura bitters, 2 dashes curaçao, and 4 ounces light rum. Drop in 4 ice cubes and blend until ice is slushy. Spoon into large wine glass containing the juice of 1 lemon. Squeeze strip of lemon peel over drink and toss in.

HIGH IN THE BERRY PATCH

Frost rim of a cocktail glass with sugar. Pour into cocktail shaker 1½ ounces light rum, ¾ ounce raspberry liqueur, 1 teaspoonful kirsch, and ½ ounce lemon juice. Add ice and shake hard. Strain into the sugar-frosted glass.

SPIKE HEELS

Pour 1½ ounces light rum, 2 teaspoonfuls amaretto, 1 teaspoonful lime juice, ½ teaspoonful superfine sugar, 1 dash orange bitters over ice in cocktail shaker. Shake hard; strain into cocktail glass.

PLEASURE ISLAND

Pour over ice in cocktail shaker 1½ ounces light rum, ½ ounce peach liqueur, and ½ ounce dry vermouth. Shake hard. Strain into cocktail glass.

JAMAICAN BLUE MOUNTAIN

Shake together 1½ ounces dark Jamaican rum, ¾ ounce coffee liqueur, ½ ounce vodka, ½ ounce orange juice, and ice. Shake hard. Strain into rocks glass filled with ice.

BLACK AND GOLD

Into rocks glass pour 1½ ounces gold rum, 1½ ounces coffee liqueur, ½ teaspoonful powdered instant coffee, and ½ teaspoonful superfine sugar. Stir to dissolve coffee and sugar. Fill glass with crushed ice; stir one or two more turns.

CHA-CHA-CHA

Pour 2½ ounces light rum, ½ ounce pineapple liqueur, 1 ounce lime juice, ½ ounce triple sec over 4 ounces crushed ice in cocktail shaker. Shake hard. Fill rocks glass halfway with crushed ice, and strain drink into it. Garnish with slice of lime.

TROPICAL MOUTHWASH

Put 3 ounces crushed ice in cocktail shaker and pour in 1½ ounces light rum, ½ ounce peppermint schnapps, and 1 ounce mango nectar. Shake hard. Strain into large wine glass, then shake 2 drops grenadine onto surface.

TROPICAL HEAT TAMER

Pour 1½ ounces light rum, ½ teaspoonful curaçao, ½ ounce lime juice, and ½ ounce pineapple juice over ice in cocktail shaker. Shake hard; strain over ice in rocks glass.

BOARDWALK BREEZER

Combine in cocktail shaker ½ ounce crème de banane, ¼ ounce Rose's lime juice, 1½ ounces dark rum, and 4 ounces pineapple juice. Shake hard. Strain over ice in collins glass, then top with dash of grenadine. Garnish with slice of orange and maraschino cherry.

YELLOW STRAWBERRY

Pour 1 ounce light rum, ½ ounce

crème de banane, 4 ounces strawberries (either fresh or the frozen kind,
thawed out), and 1 ounce sweet-and-
sour over ice in cocktail shaker. Shake
hard. Strain into cocktail glass or large
wine glass; garnish with slice of banana.

MIAMI WHAMMY

Mix together 1½ ounces light rum, ¾
ounce Nassau Royale liqueur, 6 ounces
orange juice, and 1½ ounces grenadine. Pour into large highball or hurricane glass full of shaved ice.

BEFORE THE REVOLUTION

Pour 1½ ounces light rum, ¾ ounce
brandy, 1 teapoonful grenadine, and ½
teaspoonful lime juice over ice in cocktail shaker. Shake hard; strain into
cocktail glass.

THE SCARLET FEVER

In a large brandy snifter, combine 1
ounce rum, ½ ounce cherry brandy, ½
ounce apricot brandy, 2 ounces orange
juice, and 2 ounces cranberry juice.
Garnish with slice of orange and a
cherry.

SCORPION

Blend together 2½ ounces light rum, 2
ounces orange juice, 1 ounce brandy,
½ ounce lime juice, 2 dashes crème
de noyaux (almond), and 4 ounces
crushed ice in blender until smooth.
Strain into rocks glass; garnish with
slice of orange.

MONTEGO BAY PUNCH

Pour 1 ounce each light rum and dark
rum, ½ ounce orange tequila, ½ ounce
apricot brandy, five drops Galliano liqueur, 5 ounces pineapple juice, and a
few dashes grenadine into cocktail
shaker. Add ice and shake well. Strain
into collins glass half filled with
crushed ice. Squeeze lime wedge over
drink and drop squeezed-out wedge
into it.

ICE PALACE

In mixing glass a quarter filled with
ice, stir 1 ounce light rum, ½ ounce
Galliano liqueur, ½ ounce apricot
brandy, 2 ounces pineapple juice, and
¼ ounce lemon juice. Strain into collins glass filled with ice. Garnish with
1 orange section and a cherry.

ANKLE-BREAKER

Pour 1 ounce cherry brandy, ¾ ounce
lemon juice, 1½ ounces 151-proof dark
rum, and 2 teaspoonfuls sugar syrup
over ice in cocktail shaker. Shake
hard. Strain into rocks glass.

ADIOS, MUCHACHOS

Frost the rim of a rocks glass with sugar
and set aside. Pour ¾ ounce Mexican
brandy, ¼ ounce sweet vermouth, ¼
ounce tequila, 1 ounce light rum, and
2 teaspoonfuls lime juice over ice in
cocktail shaker. Shake hard and strain
into the prepared glass.

HAPPY APPLE

Pour 1½ ounces light rum, ¾ ounce
sweet vermouth, 1 ounce calvados, 1
dash grenadine, and 1 teaspoonful
lemon juice over ice in cocktail
shaker. Shake hard. Strain into cocktail glass.

THIRD RAIL

Pour ¾ ounce light rum, ¾ ounce

brandy, ¾ applejack, and 1 dash Pernod over ice in cocktail shaker. Shake hard. Strain into cocktail glass.

HIGH WIND OVER JAMAICA

Fill rocks glass with ice. Pour in 1½ ounces dark Jamaican rum and ½ ounce coffee liqueur; float dash of cream on surface. Stir.

BLUE HAWAII

Pour ½ ounce white crème de cacao, ½ ounce blue curaçao, 1 ounce light rum, 1½ ounces cream, and 1½ ounces pineapple juice over ice in cocktail shaker. Shake hard. Strain into cocktail glass or large wine glass.

RUM COCKTAILS WITH APERITIFS, BITTERS, AND OTHER SPIRITS

RUM MANHATTAN

Pour 3 ounces gold rum and 1 ounce sweet vermouth over ice in cocktail shaker. Add a dash of bitters and shake hard. Strain into cocktail glass.

NOSE TICKLER

Pour 2 ounces dark rum, 2 dashes orange bitters, 1 teaspoonful vodka, 1 teaspoonful Bourbon whiskey over ice in cocktail shaker. Shake hard. Strain into rocks glass and top with cola. Squeeze a strip of lime peel over drink and toss in.

RUM MARTINI

Stir 3 ounces light rum and between ¼ ounce and ½ ounce dry vermouth (depending on individual preference) in

mixing glass with ice. Strain into cocktail glass and garnish with cocktail onion.

RUM AND BITTERS

Stir 3 ounces light rum, 3 ounces water, and ½ teaspoonful superfine sugar in rocks glass. Add ice. Shake in 2 dashes Angostura bitters.

RUM CHILLER

Pour 2 teaspoonfuls lime juice, 2 ounces light rum, and ½ teaspoonful superfine sugar over ice in cocktail shaker. Shake hard. Strain into cocktail glass. Top with dry sparkling wine, then stir one or two turns.

PIRATE OF PENZANCE

Stir 1½ ounces dark rum, ½ ounce gin, ¾ ounce sweet vermouth, and 2 dashes Angostura bitters with ice in mixing glass. Strain into cocktail glass.

AFTERNOON ABANDON

Pour 1½ ounces sweet vermouth, 1½ ounces light rum, ½ ounce lemon juice, and 2 dashes Angostura bitters over ice in cocktail shaker. Shake hard. Strain into cocktail glass; garnish with maraschino cherry.

RUMBONNET

Pour 1 ounce light rum, 1 ounce Dubonnet, and 3 dashes Angostura bitters over ice in cocktail shaker. Shake hard. Strain into cocktail glass.

LAZY RHYTHM

Pour 1½ ounces dark rum, ½ ounce Dubonnet, and 3 dashes Grand Marnier over ice in cocktail shaker. Shake hard, and strain into cocktail glass.

Squeeze a strip of lemon peel above drink to release oil, then toss it in.

GOLDEN GATE
Pour two ounces light rum and 1 ounce dry sherry over ice in mixing glass. Stir. Strain into cocktail glass.

RUM DRINKS WITH CREAM, HONEY, AND EGG

MIDNIGHT STAR
Pour 2 teaspoonfuls orgeat syrup, 1 ounce dry fino sherry, 2 ounces dark rum, and ½ egg yolk into cocktail shaker. Shake hard. Strain into rocks glass, and dust top with nutmeg.

HONEY BEE
Pour ½ ounce honey, 2½ ounces dark rum, and ½ ounce lemon juice over ice in cocktail shaker. Shake hard. Strain into cocktail glass.

BEE-STUNG LIPS
Pour 2 ounces light rum, 1 teaspoonful honey, and 1 teaspoonful heavy cream over ice in cocktail shaker. Shake hard. Strain into cocktail glass.

SNOWSTORM IN JULY
Blend quickly in blender 2 dollops vanilla ice cream, 1½ ounces pineapple juice, and 1½ ounces coconut "milk." Pour into large wine glass, then stir in 1½ ounces light rum.

PRECIOUS LADY
Pour over ice in cocktail shaker 1½ ounces gold rum, ¼ ounce lime juice, 1 teaspoonful heavy cream, and ½ egg

white. Shake hard. Strain into cocktail glass.

SHORT, SPIKED AND CREAMY
Pour 2 ounces dark rum, ½ ounce dark crème de cacao, and ½ ounce heavy cream over ice in cocktail shaker. Shake hard. Strain into cocktail glass.

ALMOND CREEK
Pour 2½ ounces light rum, 1 teaspoonful cream of coconut, 1 teaspoonful lime juice over 3 ounces crushed ice in cocktail shaker. Shake hard. Strain into rocks glass; top with soda; sprinkle a big pinch of crushed almond on surface.

RUMMY CREAM POP
Put 3 ounces crushed ice in cocktail shaker. Over it pour ¾ ounce light rum, ¾ ounce triple sec, and 1 ounce heavy cream. Shake hard. Strain into cocktail glass.

HOT SPOT COCKTAIL
Pour 2 ounces gold rum, 2 teaspoonfuls coffee liqueur, and 1 teaspoonful heavy cream over ice in cocktail shaker. Shake hard. Strain into cocktail glass; garnish with a bit of shredded coconut.

RUM CACAO
Pour 1½ ounces light rum, ¾ ounce white crème de cacao, ¾ ounce white crème de menthe, ½ ounce heavy cream, and ½ ounce 151-proof rum over ice in cocktail shaker. Shake hard. Strain into rocks glass.

SEPTEMBER MORN
Pour 2½ ounces light rum, ½ ounce lime juice, 1 teaspoonful grenadine,

and 1 egg white over 4 ounces crushed ice in cocktail shaker. Shake hard, then strain into sour glass.

CROWN JEWEL
Pour 1¼ ounces lemon juice, 1½ ounces light rum, ½ ounce almond liqueur, ½ egg white, 1 ounce cream of coconut, and 4 ounces crushed ice into blender. Blend until smooth. Pour, without straining, into large wine glass. Garnish with a fresh strawberry.

CANEY
Make a cup out of a papaya as follows: Cut a thin slice off the bottom, so that it will sit flat; then cut off the top third, so that you can scoop out seeds and pulp from the bottom part of the fruit—be careful to leave the base intact. Chill. Put 4 tablespoonfuls of the papaya pulp into blender; add 2 ounces light cream, and 1 teaspoonful superfine sugar and blend for several seconds. Add 1½ ounces light rum and ¾ ounce apricot brandy and blend again. Add 8 ounces crushed ice and blend until smooth. Pour, without straining, into prepared papaya cup. Garnish, if you like, with a flower and serve with a straw.

BLACK STRIPE
Pour 3 ounces dark rum and ½ ounce molasses over 7 ounces crushed ice in cocktail shaker. Shake hard. Pour, without straining, into rocks glass.

HOT RUM DRINKS

RUM TODDY
In a mug put 1 teaspoonful sugar, 3 cloves, one-inch stick of cinnamon, and 1 thin slice of lemon. Add 1 ounce boiling water, stir, and let stand a bit. Then add 1½ ounces rum and 4 more ounces hot water. Stir again and sprinkle nutmeg on top.

HOT CIDER AND RUM
Pour 1½ ounces light rum or gold rum into mug and fill with hot apple cider. Stir. Add 2 cloves and a slice of lemon.

RUM AND COCOA
Pour 1½ ounces rum into cup of hot cocoa. Top with whipped cream and chocolate shavings.

BAJAN SNAP
Dissolve 1 teaspoonful dark brown sugar in 1½ ounces dark rum in the bottom of a mug. Add hot double-strength coffee to fill to three quarters level; stir. Top with whipped cream; garnish with sprinkling of grated lime rind.

COFFEE ALFREDO
Pour 1 teaspoonful sugar, 1 whole clove, 1 pinch cinnamon, 1½ ounces dark rum, and 1½ ounces Cognac in bottom of a mug. Bring to three-quarters full with hot espresso coffee. Put a dollop of butter on top; garnish with spiral of orange or lemon peel.

RUM HIGHBALLS

JUNTA
Pour into collins glass filled with ice 1½ ounces gold rum, 1 ounce Southern Comfort, 4 ounces tea steeped until it is dark, 2 teaspoonfuls lemon juice,

and 3 teaspoonfuls superfine sugar. Stir. Top with soda, and stir again one or two turns.

NANAN HETOS
Mix 1½ ounces rum, 4 ounces ginger ale, 1 dash bitters, and a squeeze of orange in a highball glass. Add ice and stir one or two turns.

AUBADE
Fill highball glass with ice and pour in 2½ ounces light rum, 1 ounce lime juice, and 2 teaspoonfuls grenadine. Stir, top with tonic and stir again one or two turns.

CRUISE CONTROL
Pour 1 ounce light rum, ½ ounce apricot brandy, ½ ounce Cointreau, and ½ ounce lemon juice over ice in cocktail shaker. Shake hard. Half fill highball glass with crushed ice; strain the drink in. Top with soda.

FREE MONEY
Pour ¾ ounce dark rum, 1 ounce gin, 1 teaspoonful sugar syrup, 1 teaspoonful lemon juice, and ½ ounce light cream over ice in cocktail shaker. Shake hard. Strain over ice in highball glass; top with soda.

SHARK'S TOOTH
Pour ½ ounce lime juice, 1 ounce lemon juice, ¼ ounce grenadine, ¼ ounce sugar syrup, and 1½ ounces rum over 4 ice cubes in cocktail shaker.

Shake hard. Strain into highball glass filled with ice and add 3 ounces soda.

SUNSHINE SPARKLER
Fill highball glass with ice and pour in 1½ ounces Demerara rum and 4 ounces bitter lemon. Stir one or two turns.

GINGER BREEZE
Pour 1½ ounces light rum, 4 ounces orange juice, and 1 teaspoonful cherry brandy over 4 ice cubes in cocktail shaker. Shake hard. Fill highball glass with ice, then strain drink into it and top with ginger ale. Squeeze a strip of lime peel above the drink and toss it in.

RUM AND COKE
Fill highball glass with ice and pour in 1 ounce rum. Top with Coca-Cola and stir.

JAMAICA COOLER
Dissolve 1 teaspoonful superfine sugar in 2¼ ounces dark rum in the bottom of a large wine glass. Add the juice of half a lemon, 2 dashes orange bitters, and 4 ice cubes. Top with 7-Up and stir well.

RUM ICED TEA
Pour 2¼ ounces gold rum into a highball glass. Add ½ teaspoonful sugar and 1 teaspoonful lemon juice; stir to dissolve sugar. Add ice and fill with freshly brewed—but cooled—strong tea. Garnish with slice of lemon.

Multi-Spirited Drink Recipes

See Section One for information on barware, mixing supplies, and mixing tips. For conversion to metric or other measurements, refer to tables on pages 11 and 22.

MULTI-SPIRITED COCKTAILS

PLANTATION HOUSE COCKTAIL
Shake, in cocktail shaker with ice cubes ¾ ounces each of light rum, dry vermouth, and gin. Strain into cocktail glass.

BREEZE OVER JAMAICA
Shake together with ice 1½ ounces gin, 1 ounce dark rum, ½ ounce dry red wine, and ½ ounce orange juice in cocktail shaker. Strain into rocks glass half filled with ice cubes. Garnish with wedge of lime.

K.G.B.
Shake with ice cubes in cocktail shaker 1 ounce each gin and vodka, 2 dashes each slivovitz and kirsch, and a few drops lemon juice. Strain into cocktail glass.

GREAT NOTION POTION
Combine in cocktail shaker ½ ounce each gin, dry vermouth, sweet vermouth, and vodka; add ½ ounce orange juice and ice cubes. Shake, then strain into cocktail glass.

CINQ-À-SEPT
Stir in mixing glass with ice cubes 1 ounce each crème de cassis, dry ver-mouth, and gin. Strain into cocktail glass.

AFTER DARK COCKTAIL
Put into cocktail shaker ¾ ounce each green Chartreuse and sweet vermouth; ½ ounce gin; 2 dashes orange bitters; and ice cubes. Shake. Strain into cocktail glass. Twist lemon peel over drink to release one drop of oil, drop peel in.

TRINITY COCKTAIL
Put into cocktail shaker with ice cubes, ¾ ounce each Cointreau, apricot brandy, and gin. Shake. Strain into cocktail glass.

OVAL-ROOM SPECIAL
Shake in cocktail shaker 1 ounce each dry vermouth and gin, and ½ ounce each Cointreau and apricot brandy, along with ice cubes. Shake well, and strain into rocks glass half filled with ice cubes.

BLOOD AND SAND
Pour over ice in cocktail shaker 1 ounce each scotch, cherry brandy, sweet vermouth, and orange juice. Shake. Strain into cocktail glass.

GROUND ZERO
Shake in cocktail shaker ¾ ounces each peppermint schnapps, bourbon, and vodka, and ½ ounce Kahlúa, with

ice cubes. Strain into sour glass half filled with crushed ice.

SNAKE BITE

In mixing glass with ice cubes, stir ¾ ounce each brandy, dry sherry, and light rum, and 3 dashes Angostura bitters. Strain into cocktail glass.

JUNIPER BLEND

Shake in cocktail shaker with ice cubes 1 ounce each Cherry Marnier and gin and 1 teaspoonful dry vermouth. Strain into cocktail glass.

BARBARY COAST

In cocktail shaker, shake together ¾ ounce each light rum, scotch, gin, crème de cacao, light cream, and ice cubes. Strain into cocktail glass half filled with ice cubes.

RUSH HOUR

Shake with ice in cocktail shaker 1 ounce bourbon, 1 ounce light rum, 1 ounce brandy, 2 teaspoonfuls each lemon juice and superfine sugar. Strain into cocktail glass; garnish with lemon peel.

RED TIGER

Stir in mixing glass ½ ounce each sloe gin, tequila, and green Chartreuse. Pour into brandy snifter. Top with 151-proof rum.

LOLITA

Shake with ice in cocktail shaker ½ ounce each gin, applejack, Southern Comfort, and maple syrup. Strain into cocktail glass.

TOASTER

Put with ice cubes into cocktail shaker 1 ounce each gin, calvados, and apricot brandy; add a dash of lemon juice. Shake, and strain into cocktail glass.

MULTI-SPIRITED HIGHBALLS

LONG ISLAND ICE TEA

Brew a cup of tea and refrigerate until well chilled. Stir in mixing glass with ice cubes 1 ounce each gin, vodka, tequila, white rum, and triple sec. Strain into highball glass half filled with cracked ice. Pour in chilled tea to top. Garnish with lemon wedge.

NICE TEA

Pour in mixing glass 1 ounce each light rum, gin, vodka, and tequila, add a splash of sour mix and ice cubes. Stir well. Strain into highball glass half filled with cracked ice. Top with cola. Garnish with lemon wedge.

CALIFORNIA LEMONADE

Into cocktail shaker pour ½ ounce each vodka, gin, and brandy. Add 2 ounces sweet-and-sour, 2 ounces orange juice, ¼ ounce grenadine, and ice cubes. Shake. Strain into highball glass half filled with ice cubes.

FIRST DATE

For two persons: Pour into one 20-ounce brandy snifter ½ ounce each vodka, gin, and rum; ½ ounce each triple sec and crème de menthe; 8 ounces each grapefruit juice and orange juice. Stir well. Sip through straws.

MONKEY MIX

Stir in mixing glass ½ ounce each vodka and light rum; pour mixture into highball glass filled with cracked ice. Top with orange juice. Stir well.

FOGCUTTER

Stir in mixing glass ½ ounce each brandy, rum, and gin, together with 3 ounces pineapple juice, 1 ounce sweet-and-sour, and ice cubes. Strain into collins glass filled with ice. Garnish with lemon twist.

SOMETHING BLUE

Shake in cocktail shaker 1 ounce each blue curaçao and golden rum; ½ ounce triple sec; 2 ounces orange juice and 2 ounces sweet-and-sour. Strain into highball glass half filled with ice cubes.

SECTION THREE

Americans are conducting a love affair with wine that shows signs of settling into a serious relationship. Not only do Americans drink more of it (consumption has quadrupled in the last 20 years), but they drink it on more occasions—at meals, before meals, before bed, in bed, and in bars, nightclubs, wine bars, and at home. As the quantity of wine consumed increases, so do the quality and range of wines commonly available. Gone are the days when "California wine" meant something sugar-sweet from a jug, or when the wine lists in many American restaurants featured only rosé (and bad rosé at that), or when all German wine was thought to have the same odd name of *liebfraumilch*.

But with choice comes confusion. With so many more kinds and brands and nationalities of wines available, the inexperienced imbiber may feel overwhelmed on entering the local wine store to confront the hundreds of bottles with indecipherable labels, odd shapes and colors, and prices that may range from $2.99 to $79.99. Wine, one may have been told, is a difficult subject requiring vast erudition; so, if one is not a connoisseur, one had better stick with that old reliable jug wine. Nonsense, we say.

There are only two things you have to do to become knowledgeable about wines: The first is to read a bit about them and the second is to find a good wine store and patronize it. With this section of the book under your belt, you'll know everything you need to about grapes, vines, vinification, the great wine-producing regions of the world and what wines they produce, along with what bottles you're likely to come across at a good wine store and how much you're likely to pay for them. Then you can go to that wine store, strike up an intelligent conversation with the friendly, helpful wine merchant, say which wines you'd like to sample and, later, which ones you liked, and before you can say *Chateau Lafite-Rothschild* you may be laying down cases in your own private cellar. At least you'll know which—for your dollar—are the best wines to serve with meals and to stock in your home bar. So, here we go.

Wine—to be quite basic about it—is a beverage whose character comes from the fermentation of grape sugar by yeast. Wine has been around a long time; so long, in fact, that it predates history. In early cultures, wine was considered the gift of the gods: the Egyptians thanked Osiris for it, the Greeks paid homage to Dionysus with some pretty wild parties, and the Hebrews credited Noah with its invention. The Greeks and Romans had aged wines to drink because they discovered that wine improved when the clay storage jars were made airtight by a covering of pitch; but the secret of aging wines this way was lost, and during the Middle Ages and Renaissance wines were drunk young, sometimes sweetened or flavored to mask their harshness. The modern wine bottle—glass, slender, well-rounded, and corked—was not perfected until the late 18th century, when storing wines

101

for long periods again became possible. Thus, the great red wine aged in the bottle for the requisite number of years is a relatively new phenomenon.

WINE PRODUCTION

Although the basics of wine making are quite simple, the production of a really fine wine involves a good deal of tricky cooperation between man and nature. Nature must provide the proper conditions for the vine, which, for all the world's great wines, is the same species, *Vitis vinifera:* Stony soil on a south slope is usually best; some rain, but not too much; plenty of sun, especially in late summer; and the right kinds of yeast in the air. Man must harvest the grapes at the moment when sugar and acid are in optimal balance; press them; allow them to ferment for the correct number of days under optimum conditions; then care for each variety according to its needs, especially if it is to be aged.

Skins, pulps, and seeds each contribute something to the wine, and the wine maker must decide how long to leave them in contact with the juice. The skins, in particular, are important, for these determine color and tannin, the crucial flavoring element in red wines. White wines are separated from skins as soon as they're pressed; rosé is left in contact with skins for only a short period; reds are permitted to soak up color and tannin for as long as 14 days. The astringency and harshness of the tannin decrease with time: This is why red wines need to be aged and whites don't. After fermentation all wines go into barrels, usually of oak wood, where they throw off the bulk of their sediment—gross lees—and react chemically with the oxygen that comes in through the pores in the wood. Then they are racked—that is, pumped into clean, fresh barrels —leaving the lees and sediment behind. Generally speaking, red wines are racked more often than whites, and quality reds are aged longer in the barrel than lesser reds.

Many people assume that the older a wine is the better it will taste, but this is simply not true. Quality red wines must spend several years in the bottle to mellow the tannin, to acquire bouquet and a lovely spectrum of rich, deep colors; but some reds, such as beaujolais, are best drunk young; and no red will last forever. Generally speaking, the greater the wine the longer it should be aged. Usually 15-to-20 years is enough for even the noblest of red wines; after that the wine begins to break down and die. Two-to-three years may suffice for the lesser reds of the Bordeaux and Burgundy regions of France. Dry white wines should be drunk young; but sweet whites, particularly the noble German rieslings and the great French sauternes, will develop a marvelous complexity of flavor and aroma if allowed to age for several years in the bottle. If you're unsure how long, ask your wine merchant for advice.

WINE AND FOOD

The subject of wine and food makes some people panic, some bristle, and others just throw up their hands and drink beer with meals. How do you know what goes with what? The answer is: Trust your instincts and your sense of taste. Would you eat roast beef with a scoop of vanilla ice cream on top? Of course not. Then you wouldn't serve a sweet white wine with it, either. You might, however, eat a bit of sweet chutney with a hot curry; accordingly, a spicy and lightly sweet gewürztraminer would make a very pleasant accompaniment to this dish. This is not a foolproof approach, but it will keep you from making really horrid blunders.

One good rule of thumb is that the wine should either complement or contrast with the food served. Dry wines, especially whites, go down well with seafood: Chablis and oysters is a classic combination; dry champagne, muscadet, and white burgundies are right for a seafood appetizer or main course. Dry whites are also a smart choice with many ham, veal, and chicken dishes, although red bordeaux and burgundies are often the better choice with roast chicken and turkey. Highly spiced veal or chicken dishes will require a more robust red wine, such as a rhône or a barolo. In general, the heavier the food the heavier (that is, fuller-bodied and more intensely flavorful) the wine drunk with it should be. Beef and lamb are almost always served with red wine; if you have a bottle you think might be superb, keep the meat as simple and elegant as possible. Sweet white wines are best with desserts; yet here, too, as with fine reds, the superior sweet whites will show up better when served with something simple, such as plain poundcake or nonacidic fruit.

When the occasion is an elaborate formal dinner party, it's a nice touch to serve more than one wine. If you want to do this, here are a few simple rules to keep in mind: Serve dry wines before sweet wines, white before red (except in the case of dessert wines), young before old, and lesser before greater. Many wine experts discourage serving bordeaux and burgundy at the same meal. Wines play off each other much as colors or sounds do. You may get to the point in your appreciation where you are planning meals around the wines, selecting foods to offset and enhance them.

In Europe, but especially in Germany, wine is often drunk by itself between meals, and once you become acquainted with some of the excellent German white wines you'll know why. Like champagne, many fine white wines may be sipped and savored with a simple biscuit. Rosé (or pink wine) is a good choice for picnics, light lunches, and hot summer days.

SERVING WINE

A note about serving wines: It's usually safe to assume that white wine should be served cool and red wine be allowed to breathe (that is, sit in the uncorked bottle) at room temperature for some time before it's poured. The sweeter the white wine, the colder it should be. Immerse a dry white wine in an ice bucket filled with ice cubes or shaved ice and water for 20 minutes; a sweet one needs slightly longer chilling. One can also refrigerate the bottle for two or three hours. Pink wines also taste better with a chill on. Beaujolais, a red wine that is best when young, may be cooled slightly before serving.

About breathing times: The older the wine the less time it needs to breathe. A very young and full-bodied bordeaux can be opened the day before it is to be consumed, whereas a good red wine between five years and fifteen years old might be opened two hours or so before dinner.

A very old wine, or one with noticeable sediment at the bottom, should be decanted very carefully. Red wines (with the already noted exception of beaujolais) are served at room temperature.

1

THE WINES
OF FRANCE

The greatest wines in the world come from France, center of modern civilization," says Alexis Lichine in his authoritative *Encyclopedia of Wines and Spirits* (Knopf, 1968—a new edition appeared in 1982). The part about wine, at least, is generally accepted as truth. Not only are French wines the world's greatest, but more kinds of great wines are produced in France than anywhere else. This is not to say that all French wines are great (or even good) or that only French wines are great. The bulk of the wine produced there is "vin ordinaire"—which is exactly what it sounds like.

The key to quality is the phrase *Appellation Controlée* (controlled name) on the label. This refers to a body of laws that governs what wines may be produced in which regions and in what manner. For example, the words *Appellation Margaux Controlée* on a wine label guarantee that the contents of the bottle have been made from cer-tain grape varieties (largely cabernet sauvignon) grown in the parish of Margaux (within the Médoc district of the Bordeaux region) according to the methods designated by law as proper for this wine. The more specific the words printed on the label, the better the wine: Thus, *Appellation Margaux Controlée* is better than merely *Médoc*, and *Médoc* is better than just *Bordeaux*. Best of all is *Chateau Margaux*—that's the most renowned vineyard in this parish. A French wine producer always uses the most specific controlled name that his wine qualifies for. Of the French wines imported to the United States, some 85 percent carry the words *Appellation Controlée* on their labels.

There are six major wine regions in France: Alsace, Bordeaux, Burgundy, Champagne, the Loire valley and the Rhône valley. Of these, three are preeminent: Bordeaux and Burgundy, the monarch of France's wine regions, and Champagne, without whose bubbling wine the world would be a far poorer place. (The wines of Champagne will be considered with other sparkling wines at the end of this section.)

BORDEAUX

Bordeaux, which many people consider the finest wine-producing region in the world, makes both red and white wines and they are equally distinguished. Within Bordeaux there are five major districts: **Sauternes,** known for sweet white wines; **Médoc** (with Haut-Médoc the superior section), **Pomerol** and **Saint-Émilion** for reds; **Graves** for both red and dry white wines. Each of these districts is further subdivided into communities or parishes, and some of these names are very important in recognizing fine Bordeaux wines.

In Médoc, the four parish names to know are Margaux, Pauillac, Saint-Julien, and Saint-Estèphe. In Sauternes, look for Sauternes (both a district and parish), Bommes, Fargues, Preignac, and Barsac. The last-named is so famous and enterprising a parish that it has an appellation and a style of wine all its own—sweet on the tongue, yet with a dry aftertaste. In the district around Graves, the important parishes are Pessac, Léognan, and Martillac.

Within the parishes there are individual vineyards, in French known as *chateaux.* The phrase *mis en bouteille au chateau* on a bottle of wine from Bordeaux means the wine has been bottled at the vineyard where it was grown. This is a sign—but not a guarantee—of quality.

Here is an example of a hypothetical Bordeaux label:

1978 Chateau de Rigeur
Cru Bourgeois
Appellation Graves Controlée
Mis en bouteille au chateau.

1978 is the vintage year, an indication that the wine in the bottle was made from grapes harvested in the same year. A vintage chart (available at most wine stores) gives a general idea of how good the wines from a particular year should be, but it won't specify districts or chateaus. For this one must consult the wine merchant. *"Cru Bourgeois"* tells us that Château de Rigeur, despite its classy name, is not one of the great "classified growths"—meaning, specific property or vineyard—but an average, run-of-the-mill chateau. The great ones will say *grand cru classé* or *premier cru.* "Appellation Graves" indicates that, although this wine was all grown and bottled at one chateau, it has not met the requirements to qualify for one of the Graves parish appellations. At the right price, this Château de Rigeur will make a pleasing accompaniment to a nice dinner; it will not provide one of the great drinking experiences of your lifetime.

Principal grape varieties used in making red bordeaux wines, commonly referred to as *claret,* are the cabernet sauvignon, cabernet franc, merlot, malbec, carmenère, and petit verdot. The classic white wines of Bordeaux are made from sémillon, sauvignon blanc, and muscadelle grapes.

Bordeaux wines are so various that no one word or phrase can characterize them. The médocs, often singled out as the classic clarets, are more delicate and subtle than the rich hearty clarets of Saint-Émilion; the reds of Pomerol fall somewhere between these two. Most Americans associate the Graves district with mediocre sweetish white wines; but these represent only the cheapest of the blended graves wines. This district also produces lovely dry whites and excellent, distinctive reds.

Although sweet white wines have fallen out of fashion, an exception should be made for the white wines of the Sauternes district. These are pressed from grapes that have succumbed to that state of overripeness the French term *pourriture noble* and the Germans, *edelfäule*—the noble rot. Caused by a fungus called *Botrytis cinerea*, this condition gives the wine a sublime sensual sweetness, with hints of other flavors—perhaps apricots or apples. The queen of sauternes, the legendary Château d'Yquem, may set you back as much as $50 for one bottle; but nearby vineyards, such as Château de Sudiraut and Château Filhot, produce exquisite wines that may be enjoyed for about half the price. This is true not only for sauternes but also for most really famous wines: Prices drop off much more rapidly than quality does when you move from the premier chateau to its lesser-known neighbors.

It's still a good idea to know about these premier chateaux, however, because their wines do set the standards for the world. In the Médoc district these are Château Lafite-Rothschild, Château Mouton-Rothschild, Château Margaux, and Château Latour. In Saint-Émilion, they are Château Ausone and Cheval-Blanc. In Pomerol, the leader is Château Petrus; and in Graves, it is Château Haut-Brion. Prices run anywhere from $35 to $70 for recent vintages, rising steeply as the date gets older. These wines make up the Bordeaux aristocracy: Serve them only on *very* special occasions to people who will appreciate them.

A step below are wines in the $12-to-$25 category. Chateau names to look for include Lascombes, Pichon-Lalande, Giscours, Palmer, Talbot, Lynch-Bages, and Beychevelle in Médoc; in Graves, watch for Carbonnieux and La Louvière, La Mission Haut-Brion and Pape Clement; and in Saint-Émilion and Pomerol look for Figeac, Magdelaine, Belair, Canon, and Clos Fourtet. Prices drop to the $4-to-$9 range for bordeaux wines from the so-called *petits chateaux.* Good examples include Le Tuquet (Graves), Côtes Rocheuses (Saint-Émilion), Haut-Maurac (Médoc), Larose-Trintaudon and Caufran (Haut-Medoc), and Cos d'Estournel and Gloria (Médoc). Lower still in price are the "shipper" wines: These have the Bordeaux appellation, but are blended by the shipper and labeled with a brand name. Prices run about $3.50-to-$6 a bottle. Some of the better brands are: Chevalier de Vedrines (white), Mâitre d'Estournel (red and white), Dourthe (white), Rosechâtel (white), Palais Gallien (red and white), Mouton Cadet (red and white), Verdiallac (red and white), B & G Fonset-Lacours (red), and Lacour Pavillon (red).

BURGUNDY

Burgundy, the other great region of France, has been a center of viniculture for more than two thousand years, and in that period the Burgundians have elevated wine-making into something approaching a fine art. Americans usually think of Burgundy as producing a full-bodied dark red wine, but this is not the whole story; the region also offers the light, fruity reds of the Beaujolais district and the celebrated bone-dry whites of Chablis.

The full red burgundies of the popular imagination come from the **Côte d'Or** (the Slope of Gold), a stretch of magnificent vineyards lying south of Dijon. Within this section there are two districts: The Côte de Nuits, which makes the noble reds of Chambertin, Musigny, and Romanée; and the Côte de Beaune, whose reds are a bit more delicate. Also from the Côte de Beaune come the white wines of Montrachet and Meursault, perhaps the finest white wines in the world.

Chablis and Beaujolais constitute separate sections of their own within the Burgundy region, as do Mâconnais and Chalonnais, which make lighter and lesser wines than those grown on the Côte d'Or.

Because vineyards in Burgundy tend to be small and are often worked by a number of different growers, the estate-bottling system practiced in Bordeaux does not really apply. Variations can be considerable, even among wines grown in the same vineyard. The shippers have rectified the system somewhat by blending and bottling burgundies and selling them under their own company names. These wines are usually fairly consistent in quality from year to year; so if you find a shipper's label you like, stick with it. Some of the better ones are Bouchard Père et Fils, Louis Jadot, Louis Latour, Joseph Drouhin, and Georges Duboeuf (especially for beaujolais). Estate-bottled burgundian wines will say on the label *mis au domaine, mise du domaine,* or *mis en bouteilles par le propriétaire.* These are likely to be excellent—and expensive.

The fine red wines of Burgundy are pressed from pinot noir grapes, whereas the lesser reds, such as those from the Beaujolais district, are made primarily from the highly productive gamay grape. Chardonnay and pinot blanc grapes go into the distinguished whites; aligoté into the lesser and shorter-lived whites.

Burgundy is a small, notoriously difficult region in which to grow grapes, and therefore true burgundy is rare and prices run high. As in Bordeaux, there are certain Burgundy place names to learn as guides to the finest wines. In the **Côte de Nuits** district, the most famous parishes are Fixin, Gevrey-Chambertin, Vougeot, Vosne-Romanée, and Nuits-Saint-Georges. Centuries of wine connoisseurs have rated three vineyards supreme for reds: Chambertin in Gevrey-Chambertin, Clos de Vougeot in Vougeot, and Romanée-Conti in Vosne-Romanée. Wines from the premier vineyards cost between $40 and $50 a bottle for recent vintages, perhaps half that much for parish and village appellations such as Gevrey-Chambertin, Chambolle-Musigny, Nuits-Saint-Georges, and Vosne-Romanée.

Experts rate the red wines of the **Côte de Beaune** slightly below those of the Côte de Nuits, but the whites are unparalleled. Fragrant, elegant, pale, and costly, these whites offer a drinking experience never forgotten. The three parishes for great whites are Meursault, Puligny-Montrachet, and Chassagne-Montrachet; the outstanding vineyard is Le Montrachet, and Marquis de Laguiche is a recommended domain, or estate, within the vineyard. Prices run $60 and up for Le Montrachet, but parish appellations offer much better value at between $10 and $20 for recent vintages.

Côte de Beaune reds are lighter, fruitier, and softer than those of the Côte de Nuits and need less aging. They are also a bit less expensive. Le Corton is the number-one vineyard; Pommard, the most renowned parish. Look to the parish of Santenay for good value, perhaps even under $10 a bottle.

More affordable burgundies can be had from the wine-producing regions to the south of the Côte d'Or. In Chalonnais, the two names to look for are Mercurey and Givry for medium-bodied, highly fragrant reds. Jadot, Latour, Faiveley, and Delorme are the merchant-shipper labels to look for. Prices should run under $10 a bottle.

The **Mâconnais** and Beaujolais districts occupy the southernmost area of the Burgundy region, and both produce popular, pleasant, and very drinkable wines. Mâconnais is primarily a white-wine district, its most celebrated product being pouilly-fuissé, a lovely light and very dry wine. Unfortunately, the popularity of this wine has driven prices up ($10 to $15 a bottle), and some feel quality has suffered. Domain bottling is the best guarantee of quality. Château Fuisse, by Marcel Vincent, is one of the better products. Pouilly-Loché and Pouilly-Vinzelles, from nearby properties, are quite similar, less expensive, and worth looking for. Mâcon-Villages and Saint-Veran offer good Mâcon value at about $5 to $7 a bottle.

The light, fruity red wines of **Beaujolais** seem to grow more popular and widely available each year. These are wines to be drunk with gusto, not sipped, and the younger they are, the better. Hence the hoopla each autumn when the "Beaujolais nouveau" arrives. The best Beaujolais vineyards are Moulin-à-Vent, Fleurie, Morgon, and Brouilly. Beaujolais-Villages is a controlled name signifying that the wine comes from a limited area within the Beaujolais district. Slightly lower in quality than the vineyard wines mentioned above, Beaujolais-Villages wines are the best value, with prices running between about $3.50 and $6 at the top. Georges Duboeuf, J. Mommessin, Paul Sapin, and Fessy are the shippers' names to look for.

In the north of Burgundy—and in a class by itself—is **Chablis.** Often described as "flinty," the wine from this district is among the driest and palest of all white wines. Austere, elegant, and rare, true chablis must be from a good year; otherwise it will probably taste thin and sharp rather than light and crisp. The best comes from vineyards rated *grand cru* or *premier cru*. If a label merely says *chablis*, without the name of a vineyard, it means the wine is from one of the lesser properties in the district. Prices have come down considerably the last couple of years, and a very good bottle could be had recently for less than $10; this probably represents the best value in ten years. If you find one you like, order a case!

ALSACE

The wines produced in this hilly region on the left bank of the Rhine reflect its dual French-German heritage. The grapes are for the most part German varieties, and the wines are white, delicate, and flowery, the perfect drink for a summer luncheon. Alsatian wines are bottled in tall, slender bottles known as the *Alsace flute*.

When selecting an Alsatian wine, make sure the grape variety is mentioned on the label: Unlike other French wines, this, and not the place where the grapes were grown, is the key to quality. Labels carrying grape name *and* shipper, grower, or vineyard name are likely to be the best; but place name without grape name is a sure sign of inferiority. The major grape varieties are gewürztraminer, riesling, pinot gris (known in this region as the *tokay d'Alsace*), muscat, pinot blanc, sylvaner, and chasselas. Riesling, Germany's noblest grape, is considered the best, with gewürztraminer and tokay d'Alsace placing second and third. Look for the shipper-grower firms of Trimbach,

Hugel, and Dopff & Irion. Prices run $4-$8 generally; much higher for the rare late-harvest wines.

RHÔNE

Vineyards along the Rhône river between Lyons and Avignon fall within the area known as the *Côtes du Rhône*. The wine they produce is for the most part hearty, robust, and vigorous. The three most famous Rhône valley red wines are from **Châteauneuf-du-Pape, Hermitage,** and **Côte Rotie;** each is superb in its own way. Châteauneuf-du-pape is the softest and the quickest-maturing of the three; côte rotie is a rich, fruity, heady wine with hints of violets and raspberries in its taste; hermitage is a classic, full-bodied wine that ages well, growing softer with time. There are also a white hermitage and a small amount of white châteauneuf-du-pape.

The most important grape variety in the region is the syrah, although as many as ten grape varieties go into châteauneuf-du-pape. Other noteworthy names along the Rhône include Château Grillet, Condrieu, Saint-Joseph, Cornas, Saint-Péray, Crozes-Hermitage, and Tavel—the last-named considered by many to be France's best rosé. Wines labeled simply **Côtes du Rhône** are of lesser quality and lower price, but often these are good value for money and make fine table wines for everyday consumption. A châteauneuf-du-pape from a recent year will cost $10 and more, while an average côtes du rhône could be as low as $3.

LOIRE

Delicacy, freshness, charm, and youth characterize the wines made along the Loire river, France's famed chateau country and a must on many tourist itineraries. Loire wines come in all types—red, white, rosé, sparkling, and semisparkling (or, as the French say, *pétillant*)—and they are especially good value at present. **Saumur** and **Vouvray** are the famous names in sparkling Loire wines, the former for whites made by the méthode champenoise, the latter for delightful pétillant wines. **Muscadets** are wonderfully dry and light white wines from the mouth of the Loire; Muscadet de Sèvre et Maine is the best of the lot and deserves its high reputation. Prices are in the $3-to-$7 range. **Sancerre** is another excellent dry Loire white, and there is some very fine rosé from this district, too. Similar in character to white sancerre, but more refined and delicate, is **pouilly-fumé**—not to be confused with Burgundy's pouilly-fuissé. Ladoucette is one of the most popular and best made of the pouilly-fumés; prices run about $10 to $13 a bottle. **Anjou** is a large Loire vineyard area, making red wine, sweet and dry whites, and rosé wines with prices as low as $4 a bottle. Loire wines, with the exception of some of the finest sweet whites, mature quickly; reds and dry whites alike should be drunk young.

2

THE WINES OF ITALY AND SPAIN

THE WINES OF ITALY

French wines hold the number-one spot for quality and prestige, but Italy rivals—often surpasses—France in the quantity category. In 1979, 1980, and 1981 Italy made and exported more wine than any other country; France just edged ahead in production in 1982. Italians are also the world's leading wine imbibers, putting away approximately 24 gallons per person per year. And Italian wine is now America's leading imported wine, accounting for some 60 percent of the imported wines sold here. This, however, was not always the case: It is in the last ten years that sales here of Italian wines have mounted twentyfold and the number of labels available increased by 500 percent.

What many don't yet appreciate is that with this rise in quantity came unprecedented leaps in quality. The Italian wines imported here used to have a kind of a low-brow "cheap-o" reputation—recalling jugs of poor-quality chianti served in pizza parlors with red-checked tablecloths—that they still have not entirely succeeded in shaking off. But this is only a matter of time. Wine experts now agree that Italy has—in a single generation—made far greater strides in the technology used in its wine making than any other region in the world, including California.

As with French wines, enlightened buying is largely a question of knowing a few definitions and learning a few names. First, look for the letters D.O.C. on a bottle of Italian wine: This means *Denominazione di Origine Controllata* and represents Italy's answer to France's Appellation d'Origine Contrôlée. The laws were enacted in 1963 to establish guidelines for place names, viticultural districts, grape varieties, and alcohol levels. They set in motion the upgrading that has done so much for Italian wines. A step above D.O.C. is D.O.C.G.—Denominazione di Origine Controllata e Guarantita—which shows that the statement of ori-

113

gin is not only regulated but also guaranteed. Only four wines currently qualify for this category: barolo, brunello di Montalcino, gattinara, and vino nobile di Montepulciano.

Now for the names. Italian wines usually take their names either from the town near which the grapes were grown or from the grape variety itself. Thus, a grower near Barbaresco in the Piedmont region will use this very famous name for his choice reds: but he may label the lesser reds *nebbiolo,* after the variety of grape.

Nebbiolo is Italy's most highly prized and aristocratic grape. Other varieties that commonly give their names to the wines are: **barbera,** grown for red wines in the Piedmont region; **cortese,** used for light, dry white wines in both Piedmont and Liguria; **grignolino** for light, fruity reds from Piedmont; **malvasia,** which produces a luscious, sweet dessert wine; **pinot bianco,** used for a fruity white wine made in the northeast; **pinot grigio,** which makes the dry and often quite reasonably priced whites from the north; **sangiovese,** the main grape variety of the Chianti hills, which also makes fine sturdy reds when grown in Emilia-Romagna and in Abruzzi; and **trebbiano,** the leading white wine grape of central Italy.

Italy is often described as one vast vineyard, and there's a lot of truth in this. Grapes grow everywhere and easily in Italy and have been doing so for thousands of years—which in part explains why Italians have tended to be a lot more casual about wine than, say, the French. Ubiquity does not mean uniformity, however: Generally speaking, the wine quality improves as one proceeds north. This is not to say that Sicily and Calabria don't produce some noteworthy wines; merely that Piedmont, Veneto, and Tuscany produce more of them.

PIEDMONT AND LOMBARDY

The Piedmont region, in the northwest, is particularly rich in fine wines. From here come Italy's two most celebrated reds, **barolo** and **barbaresco**—rich, full-bodied, powerful wines as complex and rewarding as the best French Burgundy or Rhône. Of the two, barolo is considered the greater: Slower to age (as long as 20 years for the most heavily tannic), deeper in color, most robust in flavor, this is an uncompromising "masculine" wine. Both barolo and barbaresco are made from the nebbiolo grape, which is known locally as *spanna,* the name for a slightly lesser but still robust and long-maturing Piedmont red wine.

Piedmont producers to look for are: Aldo Conterno, Angelo Gaja, Ceretto, Prunotto, Giacosa, and Valentino Migliorini. Prices for barolo and barbesco run high—anywhere from $7.50 to $26 for good quality. A good spanna may be had for $7, and often less. Another quality Piedmont red to look for is **gattinara,** a big, warm wine that is nonetheless elegant when it's made well. It, too, is from the nebbiolo grape: Antoniolo is the producer to look for. Prices may run between $9 and $14.

Dolcetto is the name of a grape variety that makes a good-value medium-range red wine, fruity but dry and drinkable when still young. Dolcetto d'Alba tends to be smoother than dolcetto d'Acqui and dolcetto d'Asti. Renato Ratti and Elvio Cogno are noted producers. Prices are in the $5-to-$7 range. **Carema** and **Bricco Manzoni** also offer excellent value in Piedmont reds.

A good deal of **barbera** (a productive grape variety and also a wine name) comes out of Piedmont. Much of it is cheap ($4-to-$6), strong, and harsh, though some will age well. Two of the most charming reds of Piedmont are **freisa** d'Asti and freisa di Chieri, light, fruity, and sometimes slightly sparkling wines with a wonderful raspberry bouquet.

Asti spumante, Piedmont's well-known sparkling white wine, is discussed at the end of the wine section, along with champagne.

Directly east of Piedmont is the Lombardy region. Its famous wine-producing district is Valtellina, from which come three balanced and medium-bodied reds: **sassella, grumello,** and **inferno.** Expect to pay about $4-to-$5 a bottle for these wines.

VENETO
Again moving eastward: Several excellent wines come from the Veneto region in the northeast, to which the cities of Verona and Venice belong. The best reds of Veneto are **valpolicella,** recioto amarone della Valpolicella, and bardolino. Care must be taken not to confuse the first two.

Simple valpolicella is light, smooth, rather fruity; nice, but nothing extraordinary. The special variety of it, dubbed *recioto amarone,* is a concentrated, superpotent (14-to-15 percent alcohol), extremely full-bodied red; it is made from grapes that have been dried almost to raisin condition before pressing, and then fermented up to 40 days. It needs at least ten years to age, but when it is ready, it has a texture of worn velvet and hints of violets and honeysuckle in the bouquet. At anywhere from $12 to $30 for a bottle, amarone is certainly not cheap; but it's still less than French wines of comparable quality. Quintarelli is one of the best producers. Simple valpolicella will run about $5-to-$6 a bottle.

Bardolino is a popular and rather inexpensive ($4 or so a bottle) light red, best when young. Try serving it a bit chilled.

Soave, by far the most popular of Italian whites among Americans, also comes from the Veneto region. It's light, pale, often cheap, and best when young. Many feel that success has spoiled soave, that it's been overproduced and overplayed; but Anselmi and Pieropan are still making nice wines for $3-to-$4.50.

Much **pinot grigio,** another popular white wine, also comes out of the northeast. Fuller bodied than soave, fruity and pleasantly spicy, this wine can often be had for as little as $4 a bottle. Usually the name of the region where the pinot grigio grapes were grown will be on the label.

EMILIA-ROMAGNA
Emilia-Romagna, the region around Bologna, lies between Lombardy and Veneto to the north and Tuscany to the south. It produces in bulk one of Italy's most popular wines, **lambrusco,** which is semidry, fruity, and lively.

Lambrusco is often served chilled and is at its best when it is drunk quite young.

TUSCANY

Tuscany, cradle of the Renasciamento, is also the birthplace of **chianti,** Italy's highest-profile red wine. The chianti of the popular imagination is a coarse, heady potation that flows from a squat little raffia-covered fiasco (flask) and is taken in gulps between mouthfuls of spaghetti. There is still chianti like that around. But there is also another chianti: properly aged, sold in a straight-sided bottle, and called *Chianti classico*—which means that it comes from the original Chianti district between Florence and Siena. Chianti is not one of the world's great wines; but at its best it can be superb—tangy yet elegant, sturdy without being heavy, sharp but not harsh. The word *riserva* on the label indicates that the wine is of exceptional quality and has been aged at least three years. The three largest and best-known producers of Chianti classico are Antinori, Ruffino, and Brolio, though Castello di Volpaia and Castelli del Grevepesa are also notable producers. Expect to pay around $7 for a bottle of Chianti Classico Riserva.

Also worth trying is **tignarello,** a red wine made in the Chianti region. In this wine, some cabernet sauvignon grapes—the traditional Bordeaux variety—are added to the sangiovese and canaiolo grapes standard in this part of Italy.

Other Tuscan reds include **brunello di Montalcino**—one of the four D.O.C.G. wines—made entirely from sangiovese grosso grapes. Slow to mature, potent, and expensive ($10 and more a bottle), this is the wine that many connoisseurs single out for special praise. Fattoria dei Barbi, Il Poggione, and Caparzo are among the better producers; Biondi-Santi is the most famous (and its wine the most expensive). Another splendid pure sangiovese red is known as *vino nobile di Montepulciano,* also D.O.C.G. Price may be as low as $6 for this dark, rich wine if you buy young and let it age up to 15 years. Look for the producers Avignonesi and De Farrari-Corradi. Not as well known, but worth asking for, is a Tuscan red called **carmignano riserva;** the two best vineyards are Villa di Capezzana and Villa di Trefiano.

Tuscan whites can also be first rate, particularly the dry **vernaccia di San Gimignano** (reputedly a favorite of Michaelangelo's) and the highly prized **Vin Santo,** a rich, sweet, golden dessert wine not often seen in this country. Expect to pay anywhere from $8 to $20 for Vin Santo; $4 to $5 for vernaccia.

UMBRIA AND THE MARCHES

Two other popular Italian whites are **orvieto,** from the charming region of Umbria, and **Verdicchio dei Castelli di Jesi,** a crisp dry wine from the Marches on Italy's east coast. Traditionally, orvieto was a full-bodied semisweet wine produced from the trebbiano, malvasia, and verdello grapes; but the contemporary preference for dryness has forced the produc-

116

ers to change, and now there is dry orvieto, too—it is made mostly from trebbiano grapes. Antinori's Castello della Sala Orvieto Classico is the best of this type of wine; it runs about $5 a bottle. The best known red wine of the Marches is **montepulciano di Abruzzi;** intense, dark, and full-bodied, and costing as little as $4 a bottle.

ROME'S NEIGHBORS

Latium, the region around Rome, produces primarily dry white wines, the most celebrated being **frascati.** Soft, a touch fruity, delightfully fragrant and eminently drinkable, frascati flows freely in the trattorie of the Eternal City. Est! Est!! Est!!! with its bizarre name and legend to match (it's about Bishop Fugger and the inn at Montefiascone back in 1111) is another Latium white to sample. It's pale gold, and either dry or slightly sweet. Prices for frascati range from $2.50 to $4.50; expect to pay $4 to $5 for Est! Est!! Est!!!

Taurasi is a big red wine from Italy's southern Campania region. With the proper aging, it can attain considerable complexity. Look for the riserva from Mastroberardino.

SICILY

Hot, sunny, fertile Sicily produces a variety of wines, the best known of which is **marsala,** a fortified wine of dark brown color served with dessert or used in cooking. Other nonfortified sweet dessert wines are made from the luscious muscat grape; these include golden moscato di Siracusa and densely perfumed moscato di Pantelleria

from the eponymous island. (Nice sweet moscatos are also made in Piedmont.)

The best light Sicilian table wines are **etna** and **corvo di Casteldaccia,** both of which have both red and white varieties. Etna rosso is a very full, ripe, and fruity wine, capable of aging, and often available here for less than $4. Think about Mount Etna, a still-active volcano, when you drink it. Both red and white corvo—dry and rather delicate—they are considered among the best made of southern Italy's wines. Respectable corvo will cost you about $4.50-to-$6 a bottle.

THE WINES OF SPAIN

Spain is known primarily for its fortified wines (see Section IV), but its table wines are becoming more popular in this country. The superior regions are **Rioja** and Catalonia: Their wines are distinctive and often quite inexpensive.

The best reds come from Rioja Alavesa, the lighter ones being known as *claretes* (they're similar in style to the reds, or clarets, of Bordeaux). The finest of all are labeled *reserva.* Coarser and more alcoholic red wines come out of Rioja Baja; Rioja Alta makes red, rosé, and white wines. Many people find the Spanish whites heavy and woody; but this should change, as more modern methods are being introduced. The better producers of Rioja include Age Bodegas, Berberana (look for Carta de Plata, Carta de Oro, Gran Reservas), Campo Viejo, Faustino Martinez for reds and whites in the new style, Marquès de Murrieta for reds and interesting whites, Marquès de Riscal, and Marquès de Cáceres. Prices run from $4 to $8 for top quality.

The best reds of **Catalonia** come from the regions around Tarragona and Panadés. Torres is the big producer in Catalonia: Its better whites are Viña Sol and Gran Viña Sol; Gran Coronas Reserva is an especially good dry red for about $4.50 a bottle; Sangre de Torro is a full-flavored red Torres wine. Jean Leon is experimenting with chardonnay and cabernet sauvignon grape varieties; Marquès de Monistrol makes an interesting white and a good quality red reserva. Much high-quality sparkling wine is made in Catalonia, too (see last chapter this section).

One of the supreme names in Spanish wine is Vega Sicilia: It designates a dense, complex, full-bodied red from Old Castile. A bottle of this may cost you $40 or more; but connoisseurs have been known to rave. Valbuena offers superb second quality, and, at $10-to-$15, great value.

3

THE WINES
OF GERMANY

Germany is the northern-
most of Europe's wine-
producing countries, and
the Germans have risen to the chal-
lenge of their climate with patience,
tenacity, and imagination. Despite late
springs, undependable summer sun,
and unpredictable autumns, Germany
produces some of the finest white
wines in the world from picturesque
(and painstakingly tended) vineyards.
(German reds, produced in much
smaller quantities, seldom get exported.) Many American wine lovers,
however, tend to shy away from German wines. "Too sweet," they'll say,
or, "Too hard to figure out those
labels." There is some truth in both
these notions, but only some. Many
fine German wines *are* sweet—with a
subtle, rich, nectarlike flavor that is
not at all sugary. But several German
wines—about 35 percent—are dry.
German wine labels *do* look a little
confusing; but in fact, once you know
the basic terminology you'll find they
tell you more about exactly what's inside the bottle than the labels of any
other country.

Most of the noteworthy German
wines come from the valleys of the
Rhine river and its tributaries, especially the **Mosel** (which, for labeling
purposes, the Germans lump together
with its own tributaries, the Saar and
the Ruwer). One way of telling the difference between Rhine and Mosel
wines is the bottle color: Mosel wine
comes in green bottles, Rhine in
brown. The three most important wine
regions on the Rhine itself are: the
Rheingau—Germany's single greatest
district, which makes fragrant, fruity,
firmly authoritative wine; the
Rheinhessen—for mildly sweet, mellow, and less acid wines than those
from the Rheingau; and Rheinpfalz
(also known since ancient times as the
Palatinate)—producer of the lightest of
all rhine wines, soft, lightly perfumed,
and low in alcohol. Lighter than any of
these wines are the delicate, elegant
whites of the Mosel-Saar-Ruwer water-
shed, which are sprightly when sweet

119

and delightfully fruity when dry. Some excellent, balanced, and wonderfully fragrant wines come from the region of the **Nahe** river, which deserves to be better known in this country. **Baden** and **Franken** (Franconia) are also less well known as wine-producing districts; the former has pungent, frequently dry whites similar in character to those of Alsace across the river; Franconia's wines are stronger and earthier than Rhine wines and come in a distinctive flagon-like bottle known as the *bocksbeutel.*

In Germany, one grape variety lords it over all the rest, and this is the **riesling.** Some lovely soft wines come from the **sylvaner;** uniquely spicy wines are made from the **gewürztraminer** grape in Baden and Rheinpfalz; and the **Müller-Thurgau,** a crossing of the riesling and sylvaner grapes, produces larger and larger quantities of pleasant wine throughout the country. But the riesling unquestionably produces the finest German wines. All the great wine from the Mosel and Rheingau comes from this grape, and so the word is often left off the labels of these wines. But make sure you see "riesling" somewhere on the label of a wine from Rheinpfalz or Rheinhessen—it's your assurance of a certain level of quality.

In addition to the name of the grape variety, German wine labels usually include the following helpful information: quality category; region of origin; subregion (*Bereich,* in German), collective site (*Grosslage*) or town name, followed by name of individual vineyard; vintage date; name of producer or bot-

tler, and certification number. The essential thing to look for on a bottle of quality wine is the village name (usually with *-er* appended to it) and the vineyard name. Bernkasteler Doctor, to take one very famous example of quality wine from the Mosel-Saar-Ruwer, means the wine comes from the Doctor vineyard in the town of Bernkastel. As with French wines, the more specific the designation of place, the better the wine. For example, if a wine is labeled simply *Bereich Nierstein,* you'll know it is a blend of wines from the different properties in the district to which the town of Nierstein has given its name. This bottle is likely to be inferior to one labeled *Niersteiner Brudersberg,* which indicates the wine comes only from the individual vineyard of Brudersberg. *Erzeugerabfüllung* means the wine was estate-bottled, another sign of quality.

Aside from vineyard, town, and subregion names, many German wines carry the terms *moselblümchen* and *liebfraumilch.* The first means that the wine falls in the lowest quality category—tafelwein, or table wine—that it is a blend of various Mosel region wines, and that if it's not cheap, it's not worth it. **Liebfraumilch** wines, however, offer consistency and a good general level of quality, usually at quite reasonable prices ($3 to $6 a bottle). They must be made from certain authorized grape varieties grown only in the Rheinhessen and Rheingau regions, but they are sold under such various brand names as Blue Nun, Hanns Christof, and Madonna.

There are two major categories in

the quality wines of Germany: **Qualitätswein bestimmter Anbaugebiete (QbA)** and *Qualitätswein mit Prädikat* (QmP). These refer not only to classes of quality but also to degrees of natural sweetness—much prized in Germany, where the sun seldom shines long enough to bring the grapes to full ripeness.

QbA is the driest of the quality categories; the wines may even have sugar added before fermentation to keep them from being too harsh. These are decent, well-made wines, suitable for everyday drinking (liebfraumilch falls in this category).

The QmP category is a big step up. These are wines of special distinction, made only in years when the grapes achieve their full natural ripeness and no sugar is added. Wines in this superior class are rated according to five levels of ascending natural sweetness and quality. First comes **kabinett,** wine from fully matured grapes, the driest in the prädikat category. Next is **spätlese**—"late harvest"—from grapes picked late in the season to produce a fuller and rounder taste. While kabinett and spätlese wines are usually sweet, they can be vinified bone-dry. **Auslese,** the next category up, comes from specially selected late-harvest grapes and will always be sweet. Better still is **beerenauslese,** meaning that the grapes have turned to berries, have been attacked by that wondrous mold *Botrytis cinerea* (which the Germans call *Edelfäule),* and have been picked off the cluster individually. And, at the very summit, **trockenbeerenauslese**—made from grapes that have shriveled nearly to raisins and are covered with edelfäule. These luscious wines achieve an exquisite depth, complexity, concentration of nectar-like sweetness, and balance.

Prices, as one might expect, rise with each level: The most revered "trocks" may go for hundreds of dollars, though $55-to-$60 is not unheard of for some still superb bottles, whereas the finest beerenauslese can be had for between $30 and $60.

Dry German wines will be labeled either *trocken*—which means dry to the taste and is not to be confused with trockenbeerenauslese, which means that the grapes themselves have dried—or *halbtrocken* (semi-dry).

In a class by itself is **eiswein,** a rare and splendid beverage made from grapes that are harvested so late they are actually frozen. Only wines in the beerenauslese and trockenbeerenauslese classes may qualify; prices run from $30 to $100.

There is some debate among connoisseurs about how best to savor the consummate pleasure afforded by beerenauslese and "trocks." The purists will tell you to drink—no, sip—them alone, as dessert or before dinner, so that nothing interferes with this most cerebral of drinking experiences. Epicureans given to elegant counterpoints allege that these wines show their full quality when drunk with foie gras at the start of the meal. Devotees of contrastive tastes say there is nothing like the juxtaposition of a superbly sweet trock and a sharp blue cheese. So, take your pick.

Even lesser German wines may

benefit from similar treatment. The Germans themselves frequently drink their wines between meals, at parties, in the evenings—customs we have adopted for dry Italian and French white wines and might well try for some of the fine sweet German wines. For those who wish to drink German wine with dinner: Try serving the less sweet varieties with seafood or fried foods, for instance soft-shelled crabs or chicken.

MOSEL AND TRIBUTARIES

Village names to look for in the Mosel-Saar-Ruwer region include Bernkastel (site of the renowned Doctor vineyard, of which the part owned by the Thanisch family makes the best wine), Zell-Merl, Piesport, Brauneberg, Erden, Graach, Wiltingen (look for the vineyard of Scharzhofberg, which will appear without the town name; best producer is Egon Müller), Ayl and Wehlen (J.J. Prüm is the name to look for here). Raciness, freshness, and delicacy are words that come to mind in association with these mosels.

All German wines are rather low in alcohol (9 to 10 percent) and hence low in calories; but mosels are the lowest of all. They tend to be acidic and to have a fragrance of flowers and pine trees.

A Zeller Schwarze Katz, Piesporter Michelsberg, or Bereich Bernkastel (three very popular labels showing Mosel river region bereich and grosslage) will run about $3.50 to $5; while wines of fine vineyards, such as Wehlener Sonnenuhr or Bernkasteler Doktor from Thanisch, will be in the $11-to-$15 range for auslese.

THE RHEINGAU

The **Rheingau** holds the greatest wine estates in Germany—Schloss Johannisberg, Schloss Vollrads, Steinberg—with names so great and famous they will stand alone (without village name) on the label. Village names to look for are Rüdesheim, Geisenheim, Winkel, Hattenheim, Hochheim, Erbach (site of the famous Marcobrunn vineyard, a favorite of Thomas Jefferson's), Hallgarten, and Kiedrich. At their best, Rheingau wines exhibit all the great characteristics of German wine: delicacy of bouquet, a full-bodied elegance, and just the right balance of fruitiness and austerity. They should be aged longer than other German wines, needing a minimum of three to four years—longer, as the quality class ascends. Beerenauslesen and trocks should be kept in the bottle between 10 years and 20 years to achieve their full potential. Prices for the premium Rheingau vineyards are likely to start in the $10-to-$15 range and climb steeply. You'll get better value from neighboring vineyards: for example, Hallgartener Schönhell, adjacent to Schloss Vollrads; and Bereich Johannisberg is a popular, medium-priced label.

PALATINATE

Fuller (and lesser) wines come from the **Rheinpfalz**—the Rhineland Palatinate—south of the Hesse district. Here there are three producer names to know: Dr. Bürklin-Wolf, Dr. von Bassermann-Jordan, and von Buhl (known in the region as the three B's). Less than 20 percent of Pfalz wines are made from riesling grapes; about half are made from Müler-Thurgau. Dr. Bürklin-Wolf produces a lovely dry gewürztraminer from his Wachenheimer Königswingert property.

HESSE

The **Rheinhessen** produces a great deal of wine, much of which goes into various brands of liebfraumilch. These softer and less distinctive wines come from a large number of different grape types. Nierstein, Oppenheim, and Worms are the towns from which the better wines come. Franz Karl Schmitt is a producer with a good reputation. A bereich Nierstein should cost between $3 and $6.

OTHER DISTRICTS

The **Nahe** river valley, less well known that the Mosel or Rhine, has vineyards that produce lovely, delicate, and often good-value wines. Some say these wines combine the sprightliness of those from the Mosel with the firmness of fine Rhine wines. Although they rarely achieve the heights of their better-known neighbors, wines made here from riesling grapes can be superb. Bad Kreuznach and Schloss Böckelheim are the names to look for. You might have to pay $11-to-$13 for an estate-bottled wine from Bad Kreuznach; the regional (bereich) wines are priced in the middle range.

For those who remain unconvinced, and find all these wines too sweet, there are the whites of the **Baden** region, which tend to be dry, fresh, simple, and vigorous. Expect to pay $4-to-$6.

4

THE WINES OF
THE UNITED STATES

CALIFORNIA

Even the most chauvinistic French oenophile will now admit (albeit grudgingly) that some of the great wine in the world comes out of California. How could it be otherwise after the Great Paris Tasting of 1976? At that now-legendary blind tasting of white wines made from the chardonnay grape (the principal grape of Burgundy's great whites) and reds made from the cabernet sauvignon (Bordeaux's most presitigious grape variety), nine eminently qualified French judges awarded first and second prices to—two California wines! This kind of honor seems nothing short of miraculous when one considers how short a time high-quality wines have been made in the state. Prohibition practically wiped out the domestic wine industry, and from Repeal until the early 1960s reconstruction was fitful. In the last 20 years or so, though, wine production in California has really taken off, not just in terms of quantity but

also in quality and variety: Superb wines are being made. The state's wine industry is currently in a period of upheaval, with new wineries setting up and shutting down all the time, new methods being experimented with in established wineries, new wines being developed and discarded, and prices fluctuating. Things may not settle down for some time; meanwhile, the consumer reaps the benefits. There is more good California wine around than ever before, and prices, which skyrocketed through the 1970s, seem to be coming down at last.

Like all great wine-growing areas, California is divided into regions with their own characteristics. More important than regional divisions is the distinction between generic and varietal labeling.

Generics are for the most part "jug" wines, made from blends of various grapes and named after the style of European wine they supposedly resemble. The most common generic names are *chablis* for white, *burgundy* and *moun-*

125

tain *claret* for red (or often simply *california white* or *red table wine*) and *vin rosé* for rosé.

Varietals are the class California wines. *Vitis vinifera*, the European grape vine, grows in astonishing numbers of varieties; and an astonishing number of these thrive in the various climates and regions of California. Chardonnay and cabernet sauvignon are the acknowledged kings of white and red California wines, respectively, but superior whites also come from the chenin blanc, sauvignon blanc (also known as fumé blanc), gewürztraminer, johannisberg riesling, sémillon, sylvaner, pinot blanc, and French colombard. The other excellent grape varieties for reds are barbera, gamay and gamay beaujolais, petite syrah, pinot noir, ruby cabernet, and zinfandel. This last has been dubbed California's "mystery" grape because no one was really sure where it originated. It used to be that a wine with a varietal label had to be made of 51 percent of that variety; now the figure has risen to 75 percent.

Although the styles of the wines change—depending on where the grapes are grown—it holds as a general rule that chenin blanc, johannisberg riesling, gewürztraminer, and sylvaner grapes make off-dry or slightly sweet whites, while chardonnay, sauvignon blanc, sémillon and pinot blanc yield drier and crisper white wines. The classic reds come from **cabernet sauvignon** grapes, while **pinot noir** and its clone, gamay beaujolais, generally produce lighter, less assertive red wines. **Gamay beaujolais** and gamay (also called *napa gamay*) are actually different grapes. In

fact the gamay beaujolais is misnamed—it is actually a strain of the pinot noir, whereas the napa gamay is the French beaujolais grape. In California, the latter makes a full and rather intense wine unless it is subjected to a special fermentation technique known as *carbonic maceration*, when it will yield a sprightly, frothy beverage resembling France's beloved nouveau beaujolais.

Zinfandel grapes produce wines in a range of styles—everything from light and fruity to rich, heavy, and astringent. The demand for zinfandel has tapered off in recent years, and prices are low as a result. **Petite syrah** and **barbera** grapes both yield reds on the tart and tannic side, full-bodied and deep-colored, even though the two varieties thrive in different parts of the state. **Ruby cabernet** is a hybrid grape planted in large quantities in the Central Valley, where it produces some very nice reds, similar in character to cabernet sauvignon but less refined.

California has two important wine regions—close to the coast in the north and central areas, and the great Central Valley; in addition, a good deal of sweet and not very distinguished wine comes out of Southern California. There are subdivisions within each region. The bulk of the state's wine flows from the Central Valley (this is E. & J. Gallo territory), but the best California wine is made in the cooler north and central coastal valleys.

THE NAPA VALLEY

Just as Bordeaux has its Médoc and Burgundy its Côte d'Or, so California has its **Napa Valley,** the small, beautiful wine district north of San Francisco that every wine expert places at the head of the class. Napa has been home to wine grapes since the middle of the 19th century, and such wineries as Beaulieu Vineyards, Beringer/Los Hermanos, Christian Brothers, Inglenook Vineyards, and Charles Krug have been around for decades. But Napa, perhaps more than any other wine district in the state, reflects the upheaval of the last few years. In 1960 Napa had about 25 wineries; now there are some 135, many of which opened up in the giddy years of the late 1970s when California wine became all the rage. The small ones are known as *boutiques:* They produce limited quantities of fine (and expensive) wine, some of which never leaves the state. It sometimes seems, of late, as if the lifespan of a new boutique winery is shorter than that of the excellent wine it produces. Outfits like the ones mentioned above are likely to weather the storm, however, along with important names like Louis M. Martini, Robert Mondavi Winery (one of the more innovative in Napa), Carneros Creek Winery, Clos du Val Wine Company, Heitz Cellars, Joseph Phelps Vineyards, Mayacamas Vineyards, Stag's Leap Wine Cellars, and Stony Hill Vineyard.

Premium Napa red wines include Beaulieu Vineyard Georges de Latour Private Reserve, Mondavi Reserve, Joe Heitz's Martha's Vineyard Cabernet Sauvignon, Stag's Leap California Cabernet Sauvignon, Clos du Val Zinfandel and Cabernet Sauvignon. Prices run anywhere from $12 to $20 per bottle, although Mondavi Reserve can be as high as $40 for a recent vintage and much more for an older one.

In 1983, with the California wine market depressed, many of the better Napa vineyards were bottling excellent generic reds—often using mostly fine varietal grapes—and pricing them at $5 or less a bottle. You may still be able to find relative bargains in Carneros Creek Red Table Wine (from 100 percent zinfandel grapes), Clos du Val Red Table Wine, Beaulieu Vineyards Burgundy, or Joseph Phelps California Vin Rouge. B.V. Beau Tour Cabernet Sauvignon and Charles Krug Cabernet Sauvignon were also offering attractively low prices.

Lovely white **chardonnays** are coming out of the Joseph Phelps, Mayacamas, Carneros Creek, Heitz, and Stony Hill vineyards (you may have to look hard for the last-named label). Prices start at $12 for the best ones. Less prestigious (and expensive) than chardonnay is the increasingly popular napa sauvignon blanc (also know as *fumé blanc*). Producers doing well with this grape variety are Robert Mondavi (Fumé Blanc Reserve), Joseph Phelps, and Charles Krug. Grgich Hills Cellar is often singled out as one of the best wineries in Napa for white wines, particularly chardonnay, **riesling,** and fumé blanc. An excellent introduction to the pleasures of sweet white dessert wine can be had with the Joseph Phelps Late Harvest Riesling, although you may have to pay as much as $25 for a half-bottle. At the time of the recent drop in prices, some splendid whites (both varietals and generics) could be had for $5 or less. Look for Carneros Creek White Table Wine,

Joseph Phelps Vineyards Vin Blanc, Heitz Cellars Chablis, and Robert Mondavi White.

SONOMA AND MENDOCINO

Stretching from the Napa Valley north and to the Pacific Ocean is **Sonoma County,** rated by many just one notch below Napa as a wine-producing region. The Russian River valley to the north is dotted with wineries, the most important being Simi Winery, for mild zinfandels and lively gewürztraminers; Joseph Swan Vineyards, for distinctive zinfandels; Sonoma Vineyards, for riesling and chardonnay grapes; J. Pedroncelli, for quality zinfandel wines at prices as low as $5 a bottle; and the relatively new Dry Creek Vineyard, excellent for such whites as chardonnay, chenin blanc, and fumé blanc. Chateau St. Jean is another Sonoma name to look for in good-quality chardonnay, johannisberg riesling, and gewürztraminer varietal wines. Most prices are in the $6-to-$10 range.

In the southern part of Sonoma County lies the **Valley of the Moon,** dear to the heart of Jack London, the writer. Here the notable wineries are the historic Buena Vista (B.V.), for fine riesling and fumé blanc; Clos du Bois, for chardonnay, cabernet sauvignon, and riesling; and the large Sebastiani Vineyards, known for its excellent robust Reserve Barberas. You probably won't pay more than $9 a bottle for any of these wines.

Parducci Wine Cellars and Fetzer Vineyards, two wineries in **Mendocino County** (north of Sonoma), are making very lovely zinfandels and cabernet sauvignons, often at excellent value.

Even better value are the generics— Fetzer Vineyards Premium Red and Parducci Mendocino Chablis are each less than $5 a bottle.

CENTRAL COAST

South of San Francisco, in a region defined loosely as the **Central Coast,** a number of big and very big firms have been making wine for a hundred or more years. Almadén, Paul Masson, Concannon, and Wente Brothers dominate this region. Massive production hasn't brought down the quality of Almadén and Paul Masson wines: Both make reliable, consistent, middle-range products, often very good value. Look to Almadén for gewürztraminer, cabernet sauvignon, merlot, and gamay rosé, and a wine named Eye of the Partridge, at prices ranging from $4 to $7. A wine called Charles le Franc is their top-of-the-line vintage product. Paul Masson's chardonnay and zinfandel make excellent everyday wines, as does its Emerald Dry (made from Emerald riesling grapes). Concannon Vineyard has good value in sauvignon blanc, petite syrah, and zinfandel rosé; while nearby Wente Brothers offer well-made chardonnay, sauvignon blanc, and blanc-de-blancs, also at attractive prices ($4-to-$6 is the range). Ridge Vineyards is making a name for itself among connoisseurs with its superb late-harvest zinfandel.

Monterey County is becoming a more and more important name in California wines as such wineries as The Monterey Vineyard, Monterey Peninsula, and Mirassou Vineyard (an old, established firm that has expanded into Monterey from Santa Clara) turn out quality whites in the riesling, chenin blanc, and sauvignon blanc varieties. The cool damp, foggy climate encourages growth of *botrytis cinerea*—the "noble rot" described in the chapters on German and French wines. Look for its effects in sauvignon blanc from The Monterey Vineyard. You probably won't be paying more than $6 for most of these wines. The tiny Chalone Vineyard is making a big reputation for its excellent chardonnay and pinot noir. Prices for the chardonnay start at $20.

SAN JOAQUIN VALLEY

The **San Joaquin Valley,** the northern part of the great Central Valley, produces enormous quantities of wine, most of it ordinary generic table wine and most made by four big companies: E. & J. Gallo, Guild Wineries and Distilleries, Franzia Brothers, and I.S.C. Wines of California. Compared to the everyday table wines of Europe, these are superior, carefully made, and consistent wines. Gallo Hearty Burgundy and Gallo Chablis Blanc have pleasurably washed down many a meal; and such Gallo varietals as sauvignon blanc, gewürztraminer, riesling, and chardonnay are not at all bad for the price ($2.50 to $5). The big brand of Guild Wineries has been Vino da Tavola, a semi-sweet red; their Winemasters zinfandel gets high marks. Franzia Brothers also has an interesting zinfandel and a reliable burgundy worth sampling.

For sparkling California wines, see the following chapter.

NEW YORK STATE

In the past, most New York State wines were made from grapes native to the American northeast, unlike California wines, which came primarily from the European species *Vitis vinifera.* Concord, catawba, and delaware are the prominent American varieties. These native grapes impart a "foxy" taste to the wine, a kind of pungent grapiness (take a swallow of Taylor's Pink Catawba and you'll know what that means). More recently, New York growers have been experimenting with French-American hybrid grapes, such as baco noir, de chaunac, and seyval blanc—which may be the best of the lot. The result is less foxiness and more classic European style. Benmarl, Bully Hill, Clinton Vineyards, and Glenora are all experimenting successfully with the hybrids. Prices should be about $5 a bottle. Taylor is the state's largest winery and uses mostly traditional native grapes.

Hargrave Vineyards literally broke new ground a few years back by planting vines out on Long Island's North Fork. They seem to have started a trend: Now there are many others, including the Bridgehampton Winery on the South Fork and Lenz Vineyards on the North. Whites seem to do better here than reds, particularly chardonnay and riesling grapes.

129

5

SPARKLING WINES

The time is the late 17th century. The place is France; the hero, a blind Benedictine monk named Dom Pérignon. The legend goes that, when he took his first sip of the bubbling wine he had just perfected, he murmured ecstatically, "I am drinking stars!"

Fanciful, perhaps, but anyone who has ever tasted Champagne knows exactly what he meant. Champagne differs from still wine as diamonds do from quartz. Nothing so rapidly and delightfully buoys people up. It adds brilliance to any occasion, be it a wedding, a cocktail party, or an evening for two. Champagne—like money —is always in good taste. Wine lovers looking forward to a long evening of different wines will take a glass before sitting down to the dinner table; true devotees will drink it all the meal; in its sweeter incarnation, it can be excellent with (or as) dessert.

FRENCH CHAMPAGNE

Many different kinds of wine have the word *champagne* printed on their labels. But there is only one true Champagne, and this is the sparkling white wine made in the traditional way—called *méthode champenoise*—in the Champagne region of France. At the heart of this method is the tricky business of capturing bubbles (preferably tiny ones) in each individual bottle. This involves a second fermentation inside the bottle and a delicate operation of removing sediment without letting the bubbles escape. Nearly all Champagnes have a bit of sugar added (the "dosage"), the amount determining the style of the resulting sparkling wine. The driest is brut; the next, extra-sec ("sec" is the French word for "dry"), then sec, demi-sec, and doux (the French for "sweet"). The last three categories taste rather sweet and are best as dessert wines. The three principal Champagne grape varieties are chardonnay, pinot noir, and pinot meunier. A blanc-de-blancs Champagne is made entirely from white grapes (usually the chardonnay) and is generally brut.

The other method for making champagne is called the *bulk* or *Charmat* process: The second fermentation occurs in large tanks rather than in individual bottles, and the wine is bottled under pressure. No true Champagne from France uses this process, nor do any of the finer Spanish, American, or German sparkling wines.

Unlike other French wines, Champagne is generally sold under a brand (not vineyard) name; it does not carry the words *Appellation Controlée* on the label (the name *Champagne* is guarantee enough); and more often than not it has no indication of vintage year. Most Champagnes are blends of wines from different grapes and different years. Taste and style remain fairly constant, so that when you buy a bottle of Dom Pérignon, you don't have to worry—about *anything*.

Only in exceptionally good years will Champagne producers declare a vintage. Then the year of the crop will appear on the bottle, and you'll know that only wines from that harvest have been used. **Vintage Champagnes** are richer, fuller, more complex, and more expensive (about 20 percent more) than nonvintage; they will also age better. An even higher distinction than vintage is indicated by the term *cuvée spéciale*, the very top of the line in this luxury product. Dom Pérignon is in this class, as are Perrier-Jouët

Fleur de Champagne, Taittinger Comtes de Champagne, Roederer Cristal, Mumm's René Lalou, Veuve Clicquot Grande Dame, Piper Heidsieck Florens Louis, and Krug Grand Cuvée. Prices run between $30 and $50 for a bottle.

The best Champagne firms are clustered about the towns of Rheims and Épernay. In addition to the producers of cuvée spéciale mentioned above, look for these names: Charles Heidsieck, Heidsieck Monopole, Pommery & Greno, Ruinart Père et Fils, Taittinger, Moët et Chandon, Mercier et Cie., Pol Roger (especially their nonvintage White Foil brand). Bollinger is the leading Champagne house near the town of Ay. Figure between $15 and $25 for typical nonvintage brut.

A note about serving Champagne: It's best chilled, not iced. The ideal way is to place the bottle in an ice-filled bucket for 30 minutes. Twist the cork off gently into your hand: Popping it out across the room may be dramatic—but it wastes the wine and the precious bubbles. Champagne tastes best in an elegant flute- or tulip-shaped glass; the shallow, saucer-shaped variety lets the fizz dissipate too quickly, and the fizz is, after all, the whole point. The magnum (1.5 liter bottle) allows the wine to achieve its second fermentation under optimal conditions. A split is 187 ml (just over half a pint); a Jeroboam is 3 liters; a Methuselah is 6 liters and a Salmanazar, 9 liters—open one only when you're having some friends!

CALIFORNIA SPARKLING WINES

French Champagne is the supreme, but by no means the only, sparkling wine. Perched one notch down, the California sparkling wines made by the méthode champenoise offer a superb alternative. The French themselves recognized California's potential and arrived on the scene: The firms of Moët-Hennessy (maker of Moët et Chandon and Dom Pérignon) and Piper-Heidsieck have both set up sparkling-wine operations in the Golden State. They use the classic French grapes, technology, equipment, and expertise to produce delicate, classy sparkling wine that no one need apologize for. Moët-Hennessy's winery is Domaine Chandon and it produces two kinds: Chandon Napa Valley Brut and the more full-bodied Blanc de Noirs, a luscious coral-hued bubbly from red wine grapes. Piper-Heidsieck's winery is Piper-Sonoma and the wines it produces, unlike those of Domaine Chandon, are vintage-dated. Lighter and drier than the California Chandon wines, Piper-Sonoma's Brut, Blanc de Noirs, and Tete de Cuvée are superelegant champagnes that virtually bubble right out of the glass.

F. Korbel and Brothers, one of the older growers of fine California champagne, produces a crisp, reliable, and very popular brut; a blanc-de-blancs from chardonnay grapes only; Korbel Natural, which is even drier than brut; and a blanc-de-noirs or a lovely pale salmon color. Prices for the Korbel bubblies go from $10 to $16. At $18 to $20 a bottle, Schramsberg's blanc-de-noirs pushes the upper limit for California prices, but it's considered among the best. Other excellent California sparkling wines include an Almadén blanc-de-blancs with a fruity aroma, soft, faintly sweet finish, and reasonable price ($10 or less); and Hans Kornell Extra Dry—fresh, clean, and appealing. Beaulieu Vineyards and Mirassou also make well-regarded sparkling wines.

SPANISH AND ITALIAN SPARKLING WINES

Spanish sparkling wines offer the best value for money, with prices for well-made wines running as low as $4 a bottle. Two firms—Cordorníu and Freixenet—dominate the U.S. market. Cordorníu, one of the world's largest producers of sparkling wines, has two labels available here; Blanc de Blancs, which is slightly fruity but crisp, and Brut Clasico, nice and dry and less than $5. The firm is gearing up for a massive American marketing effort, and has even bought vineyard land in California. Freixenet wines, in their distinctive black bottles, outsell Cordorníu, however. Look for Freixenet's Cordon Negro Brut, Carta Nevada Brut, and Brut Nature labels. Both these companies use the French méthode champenoise.

Asti spumante heads the roster of Italian sparkling wines. Made from the fragrant muscat grape, it is sweet, light, flowery—though some dry is now being made—and usually low in alcohol.

This is a lighthearted, jovial wine, easy to consume in quantity. Prices run from $7 to $12. Cheaper than the sparkling wine from the Asti region, and thus increasingly popular, is moscato spumante. Ferrari makes the best dry sparkling wine in Italy. Contratto is a producer to look for in Asti.

GERMAN SEKT

German sparkling wine, known as *sekt*, is produced throught the country's wine regions, particularly Rheinhessen (Hesse) and Rheinpfalz (the Palatinate). The best of the Sekt wines will have the name of the village or vineyard on the label—such as Bernkastel, Schloss Johannisberg, Scharzberg—but most German sparkling wines are blends from different districts (and even different countries: a good deal of Italian and French white wine may be mixed in) and most are sold under producer brand names.

Henkell and Deinhard have managed to wrap up most of the American market. Look for Deinhard's Lila Imperial for about $8.50 a bottle. Fürst von Metternich is a recommended premium brand that contains a good deal of riesling wine from the Rheingau. Dry sekt will be labeled *trocken*. Sekt made by the méthode champenoise will specify this on the label.

Wine Recipes

See Section One for information on barware, mixing supplies, and mixing tips. For conversion to metric or other measurements, refer to tables on pages 11 and 22.

FIVE WINE STANDARDS

WHITE WINE SPRITZER
Half fill highball glass with ice, then pour in 5 ounces chilled dry white wine. Top with soda; stir one or two turns. Garnish with a strip of lemon peel or sprig of mint.

CHAMPAGNE COCKTAIL
In the bottom of champagne glass, put 1 cube sugar, 1 dash bitters, and a twist of lemon. Fill to the top with chilled champagne.

MIMOSA
Fill a champagne glass with equal parts chilled champagne and chilled orange juice, preferably freshly squeezed.

KIR
Add 1 or 2 teaspoonfuls crème de cassis to 6 ounces chilled dry white wine in a wine glass. Garnish with twist of lemon.

KIR ROYAL
Add 1 or 2 teaspoonfuls crème de cassis to 6 ounces chilled nonvintage sparkling wine in a champagne glass. Stir one or two turns.

WHITE WINE DRINKS

SAUTERNE COCKTAIL
Fill rocks glass with ice and pour in 2 ounces California or New York State sauterne, 1 teaspoonful lemon juice, and 3 ounces lemon-flavored soda. Stir. Squeeze strip of lemon peel over drink to release drop of oil, then toss in.

CRANBERRY SPRITZER
Put 3 ice cubes in highball glass, then pour in 3 ounces cranberry juice, $4\frac{1}{2}$ ounces California or New York State sauterne, $1\frac{1}{2}$ ounces Grand Marnier. Top with soda.

MEDICATO
Add 1 or 2 teaspoonfuls Campari to 6 ounces dry white wine in a wine glass. Stir one or two turns. Garnish with twist of orange peel.

LE MARQUIS
Add 1 or 2 teaspoonfuls of framboise liqueur to 6 ounces dry white wine in a wine glass. Stir gently.

POUSSE RAPIER
Half fill a highball glass with ice. Pour in $1\frac{1}{2}$ ounces orange juice, $1\frac{1}{2}$ ounces brandy, and 2 ounces dry white wine; stir. Top with soda; garnish with slice of orange.

DRAWBRIDGE

Pour 5 ounces dry white wine over ice in wine glass. Top with soda and add a splash of blue curaçao. Garnish with lemon twist.

FROZEN ON THE VINE

Pour 3 ounces dry white wine, 2 teaspoonfuls curaçao, 1 teaspoonful lemon juice, and ½ teaspoonful orgeat syrup over 4 ounces crushed ice in blender. Blend at low speed for 10 seconds. Strain over ice in large wine glass. Add 2 dashes Grand Marnier to the surface.

CHABLIS COOLER

Frost the rim of a highball glass with sugar. Pour in 1 ounce vodka, 2 teaspoonfuls grenadine, 2 teaspoonfuls lemon juice, and 1 dash vanilla extract and stir well. Fill glass with ice, then pour in 4 ounces chilled California chablis.

L.A. COOLER

Pour over 5 ounces crushed ice in blender ½ ounce bourbon, ½ ounce banana liqueur, 2 teaspoonfuls Cointreau, 1 teaspoonful lemon juice, and 2 ounces pineapple juice. Blend at low speed for 15 seconds. Half fill collins glass with crushed ice, and strain blender mixture over it. Add 3 ounces chilled California chablis.

COLD AND COMFORTABLE

Pour 2 ounces dry white wine, 3 ounces orange sherbet, and 2 dashes Southern Comfort into blender. Blend at low speed until smooth. Pour into sour glass and garnish with cherry.

RED AND ROSÉ WINE DRINKS

LOADED COOLER

Pour 1½ ounces brandy, 1 ounce triple sec, and 3 ounces soda into a highball glass and stir. Add wedge of orange and wedge of lemon. Top with red burgundy.

7-UP COOLER

Put 4 ounces crushed ice in highball glass and pour in 4 ounces red burgundy. Top with 7-Up, stir one or two turns; garnish with cherry.

RED WINE COBBLER

Dissolve 1 teaspoonful superfine sugar in 1 teaspoonful lemon juice and 1 dash maraschino liqueur in the bottom of a highball glass. Fill with ice. Pour in 8 ounces dry red wine; stir. Garnish, if desired, with a spear of pineapple.

CLARET ORANGEADE

Dissolve 1 teaspoonful superfine sugar in the juice of one orange in highball glass. Fill glass with ice and top with dry red wine. Stir.

ROSÉ DAIQUIRI

Pour 3 ounces rosé, ¾ ounce lime juice, and 1 teaspoonful superfine sugar over ice in cocktail shaker. Shake hard. Strain into cocktail glass. Garnish with slice of lime.

FRENCH FLAG

Shake 1½ ounces apricot liqueur and 3 dashes blue curaçao with ice in cocktail shaker. Then pour 1 teaspoonful white crème de violette into a large wine glass. Carefully strain the shaker mixture into glass so that it floats on, but does not mix with, the crème de violette. Now carefully float 4 ounces dry red wine on top.

RED FROST
Fill large wine glass most of the way up with crushed ice and pour in 4 ounces dry red wine. Add 1 teaspoonful crème de cassis. Squeeze strip of lemon peel over drink to release drop of oil, then toss it in.

DOUBLE DERBY
Pour into highball glass 1 ounce Kentucky Bourbon, 2 ounces strong tea (chilled), 3 ounces dry red wine, 2 teaspoonfuls lemon juice, and ½ ounce crème de cassis; stir thoroughly. Add 3 ice cubes, and garnish with slice of orange.

RUSSIAN BLUSH
Stir 3 ounces dry red wine, ½ ounce vodka, and a teaspoonful Grand Marnier with ice in mixing glass. Strain into wine glass.

TURKISH BLOOD
Pour 2 ounces chilled red burgundy into wine glass and add 2 ounces chilled champagne. Stir one or two turns.

RED HOUSE LEMONADE
Put juice of half a lemon, 4 ounces red wine, and a dash of grenadine into collins glass. Stir in 1 teaspoonful sugar until sugar dissolves, then taste—adjust sweetness if necessary. Add cracked ice and fill to top with club soda. Garnish with thin slice of lemon.

WINE COLLINS
Pour 4 ounces red wine and ½ ounce lime juice into collins glass half filled with cracked ice. Fill to top with lemon-lime soda. Garnish with maraschino cherry.

RED WINE FLIP
Put 3 ounces dry red wine, 1 egg, 1 teaspoonful superfine sugar, and ice in cocktail shaker and shake hard. Strain over ice in large wine glass. Sprinkle surface of drink with nutmeg.

CHAMPAGNE AND OTHER SPARKLING WINE DRINKS

FRENCH 75
Fill collins glass with ice. Pour in 1 ounce gin and 2 ounces sweet-and-sour; stir well. Top with champagne and stir one or two turns more.

FRENCH 125
Fill collins glass with ice. Pour in 1 ounce brandy and 2 ounces sweet-and-sour; stir well. Top with champagne; stir again one or two turns. Garnish with twist of lemon.

STRAWBERRY SAVIOR
Slice 3 strawberries and put them in champagne glass. Gently add and stir in 1½ ounces black raspberry or red currant syrup. Top with chilled brut champagne.

RASPBERRY ROYALE
Add ½ teaspoonful raspberry liqueur to glass of chilled champagne. Stir gently. Garnish with lemon peel that has been marinated in Grand Marnier.

CHARLIE'S GEORGETOWN SPECIAL

Add ¼ ounce strawberry liqueur to glass of chilled champagne. Garnish with a fresh strawberry. Stir gently.

JEALOUSY

Put 4 or 5 seedless grapes in freezer for about an hour; then try one—they should be chewy. Pour 1 teaspoonful green Chartreuse into champagne glass and add 3 or 4 of the grapes. Fill glass with champagne and stir one or two turns.

ROYAL SCREW

Pour into champagne glass 2 ounces chilled orange juice and 1 ounce cognac; then fill up with chilled champagne. Stir gently.

PUCCINI

Pour 2 ounces fresh tangerine juice over cracked ice in champagne glass. Add 6 ounces dry sparkling wine; stir.

CALIFORNIA ROSY DAWN

Stir 1 dash crème de cassis and 2 ounces orange juice with ice in mixing glass. Strain into wine glass. Top with chilled sparkling pink wine.

BELLINI

Purée a fresh peach—this can be done in a food processor or a blender. Pour it into highball or champagne glass, and top with chilled champagne.

AS THE PEACH TURNS

Remove fuzz from 1 small peach, but do not peel; pierce it all over with a fork. Put it into large wine glass or goblet. Fill glass with dry sparkling wine. Set the peach spinning before serving.

PEACH TREAT

Shake together 1 ounce peach brandy and 2 ounces orange juice with ice in cocktail shaker. Strain into collins glass filled with ice. Add 4 ounces chilled champagne; garnish with slice of peach.

CHAMPAGNE FRAMBOISE

Run enough fresh raspberries through a sieve to make 2 ounces of purée. Pour into large wine glass. Add 6 ounces chilled champagne.

TINTORETTO

Pour ½ ounce pear purée into champagne glass. Top with champagne; add a dash of pear brandy.

SPARKLING FRUIT CUP

Marinate, in enough white wine to cover, several thin slices apple and lemon with pinch of sugar and dash of cognac. Wait a few hours, then pour fruit and marinade into champagne glass and top with chilled champagne.

TIZIANO

Stir together 6 ounces white grape juice and 2 ounces sparkling wine (preferably from Asti) in champagne glass.

FRENCH LIFT

Half fill champagne glass with dry chilled sparkling wine; pour in ½ ounce grenadine; top with chilled Perrier water or soda. Garnish with 3 blueberries.

STRAWBERRY BLONDE

Blend together with shaved ice 7 hulled strawberries, 1 pinch sugar, 2 dashes lemon juice, 2 dashes cognac, and 2 dashes strawberry liqueur in blender for 10 seconds or until smooth. Pour into champagne glass, and top with chilled champagne.

REMBRANDT

In blender or food processor, purée 1 cup fresh strawberries. Pour into highball or champagne glass and top with champagne.

ITALIAN HOLIDAY

Fill large wine glass with ice and pour in 1 ounce lemon juice, 1 teaspoonful melon liqueur, and 4 ounces dry Italian sparkling wine; stir gently. Garnish with sprig of mint.

AMBROSIA COCKTAIL

Pour 1½ ounces brandy, 1½ ounces apple brandy, and 1 dash raspberry liqueur over ice in cocktail shaker. Shake hard. Strain into sour glass, and top with dry sparkling wine; stir one or two turns.

RAZZMATAZZ

Pour 1½ ounces Chambord Royale black raspberry liqueur into champagne glass; add 4 ounces chilled champagne.

ON YOUR TOES

Fill champagne glass with ice, add 1 teaspoonful cognac; pour in chilled champagne to top. Garnish with orange peel.

THE CONCORDE

Stir together 2 ounces cognac and 2 ounces chilled pineapple juice in mixing glass. Strain into champagne glass over cracked ice, then fill glass with chilled champagne.

MOSCOW MIMOSA

Pour 3 ounces chilled champagne, 3 ounces chilled orange juice, and ½ ounce vodka into wine glass. Stir gently.

DEATH IN THE AFTERNOON

Pour 1½ ounces chilled Pernod into champagne glass; fill to top with chilled champagne.

ROYAL HIGHNESS

Pour ½ ounce apricot brandy into large wine glass or brandy snifter. Top off with as much chilled champagne as you like.

CHICAGO

Frost rim of a rocks glass with sugar. Pour 1½ ounces brandy, 4 drops triple sec, and 2 dashes Angostura bitters over ice in cocktail shaker. Shake hard. Strain into prepared glass and top with chilled dry sparkling wine.

EVE

In a small glass, dissolve 2 teaspoonfuls superfine sugar in 2 teaspoonfuls curaçao. Coat inside of a large wine glass with ½ teaspoonful Pernod, then pour in ½ ounce cognac. Now add sugar mixture to large glass and stir. Put in 3 or 4 ice cubes; top with chilled pink sparkling wine.

EARLY ENGAGEMENT
Coat inside of a champagne glass with 1 teaspoonful Grand Marnier. Fill with chilled dry sparkling wine and float 1 tea rose bud on top.

POINSETTIA
Half fill large wine glass with ice, then pour in ½ ounce triple sec, 3 ounces cranberry juice, and stir. Add 4 ounces dry sparkling wine.

CHAMPAGNE CUP
Half fill large wine glass with ice. Pour in ¼ ounce Bénédictine and ¼ ounce brandy; add 4 ounces chilled champagne and stir. Garnish with strawberry, slice of orange, and sprig of fresh mint.

SPARKLING WINE POLONAISE
Moisten rim of champagne glass with blackberry liqueur and frost with sugar. Pour in 1 teaspoonful blackberry brandy, ½ teaspoonful cognac, and 3 ounces chilled dry sparkling wine. Stir gently.

PATRIARCA
Stir in mixing glass with ice ½ ounce lime juice and ½ ounce crème de framboise. Strain into champagne glass. Top with chilled Italian dry sparkling wine.

COUNT DOWN
Pour 4 drops green Chartreuse and 4 drops cognac into champagne glass. Top with chilled dry sparkling wine. Squeeze strip of lemon peel over drink to release drop of oil, then drop peel into glass.

GREENE STREET COCKTAIL
Pour chilled champagne into champagne glass and add a floater of melon liqueur.

THE GAINSBOROUGH
Pour chilled champagne over 1 teaspoonful blueberry liqueur in a champagne glass. Garnish with fresh blueberries.

CREOLE COCKTAIL
Mash several slices of orange, lemon, and lime in bottom of a highball glass. Add 2 ounces dry vermouth, 1 cube of sugar, 1 dash of crème de cassis. Fill with chilled champagne. Garnish with mint.

LE COQ HARDI
Over a cube of sugar in bottom of a champagne glass, pour 1 drop Fernet Branca bitters, 1 drop Grand Marnier, 1 drop Cognac, 1 dash Angostura bitters. Top with chilled sparkling wine; garnish with slice of orange.

GREEN POOL
Put 2 small scoops lemon sherbet in bottom of rocks glass; add ½ ounce green crème de menthe. Top with chilled Italian sparkling dry wine—preferably Asti—and stir. Garnish with spring of mint.

ALTO PARLARE
Blend 1 ounce orange sherbet with ½ ounce Cointreau in bottom of large wineglass. Top with chilled dry Italian sparkling wine, and stir well. Add dash of grenadine to surface of drink.

SOYER AU CHAMPAGNE
Blend 1 ounce vanilla ice cream, 4 drops brandy, 4 drops maraschino liqueur, and 4 drops cognac in a large wine glass. Top with chilled dry sparkling wine; stir one or two turns. Garnish with slice of orange.

FANCY FOUNTAIN
Pour ½ ounce brandy, ½ ounce kirsch, 1½ teaspoonfuls sugar syrup, and 3 dashes Angostura bitters into highball glass; stir until mixed. Fill glass halfway with chilled dry sparkling wine. Drop in 1 scoop lemon or orange sherbet and fill with more sparkling wine.

29 FIZZ
Half fill highball glass with chilled champagne. Add 1 dash framboise and top with vodka. Squeeze a quarter of lime over drink.

NUMERO UNO
Pour juice of one lime, 2 ounces vodka, 1 teaspoonful sugar, and some crushed fresh mint into cocktail shaker. Shake hard. Strain into champagne glass; top with chilled champagne.

FROBISHER
Pour 2 ounces gin and 4 dashes Angostura bitters into highball glass and stir. Fill glass with ice, then top with dry sparkling wine. Squeeze strip of lemon peel over drink and toss in.

STARS IN A TROPICAL SKY
Pour ½ ounce light rum, 1 ounce lime juice, 1 ounce pineapple juice, and ½ teaspoonful banana liqueur over ice in cocktail shaker. Shake hard. Strain mixture over ice in collins glass; top with chilled sparkling wine.

AMERICANA
Stir 1 teaspoonful bourbon, 1 dash orange bitters, and ½ teaspoonful superfine sugar in mixing glass. Pour into champagne glass. Top with chilled dry sparkling wine *but do not stir*. Toss in 1 slice brandied peach.

FORTIFIED WINES AND APERITIFS

1

FORTIFIED WINES

To fortify a wine means to add alcohol to it, a practice that began as a means of stabilizing wines so that they would make it unspoiled through long trips in ships' holds. The two leaders in the field are sherry and port, offspring of Spain and Portugal, respectively, but adopted children of England, the country that developed their styles, corrupted their names, and still controls their trade. Other types include madeira and marsala (both now used more for cooking than drinking), and the less common málaga and montilla. Alcoholic content of fortified wines ranges from 14 percent to 24 percent, as compared with 8-to-16 percent for table wines. For the most part, the alcohol used as the fortifying ingredient is wine distilled into grape brandy.

SHERRY

When Falstaff roars for "a cup of sack" in Shakespeare's Henry IV plays, what he craves is sherry. This delightful fortified wine arrived in 16th-century England in casks marked *Vino de Jerez, Saca*—meaning: Wine from the town of Jerez for export. The Brits of the day loved the drink and, ever unwilling to bother with foreign words, dubbed it *sherris sack*, which was shortened to *sack*, and later "Jerez" became *sherry*. True Sherry still comes from the district around the town of Jerez, in the torrid Andalusian region of southern Spain. There the palomino grape variety bakes in the sun to a state of superripeness; all the considerable sugar in its juice is fermented into a strong dry wine. It's not until after fermentation that the grape brandy is added, and at this point the wines are classed either *fino* or *oloroso*: the first will become a lighter and drier style of sherry; the second, a sweeter, stronger, and more intensely fragrant sherry. Finos develop a thick yeast film on top—known as *flor* (flower)—which gives them their distinctive tang. No flor grows on the olorosos; they are fortified at once to 18 percent alcohol.

All sherries are aged and blended in wooden casks in a complex process known as the *solera system.* Casks are placed in tiers according to age, each tier a year apart. The wine must run through as many as 12 tiers before it is drawn off and bottled; but in any given year no more than one third of the wine in the bottom tier is ever drawn off for bottling. The solera system ensures consistency of style and quality from year to year. Because the casks are never emptied, sherry is always a blend. There is no such thing as vintage sherry.

Within the two broad classes of **fino** and oloroso, there are further subdivisions. Finos may be classed as simply *fino,* or as **manzanilla** or **amontillado.** Fino and Manzanilla are similar in character, both being very dry and pale. The difference arises from the places they are produced: Manzanilla, made near the Atlantic Ocean, has a discernible salty bite that inland finos lack. Both should be served chilled. Amontillados are fuller in body, not as dry or as pale as the other finos, and have a rich nutty flavor and a higher alcohol content. Serve either at room temperature, chilled, or on the rocks.

Sherry labeled simply *oloroso* is a golden, full-bodied, and strong wine, sometimes dry but much more often sweet. **Cream sherry,** the most popular type, is a rich, sweet and smooth oloroso that has acquired considerable mellowness from long aging. Serve cream sherries and the richer olorosos at room temperature; the drier olorosos may also be served on the rocks.

Finos, and particularly the light, dry manzanillas, make excellent aperitifs. The sweet olorosos and cream sherries are splendid at the end of the meal with fruit, pastry, or coffee and nuts, although they, too, are popular as aperitifs.

PORT

Even more than sherry, port is the fortified wine one associates with the English at their most eccentrically English. It is port that is passed around the table (strictly in a clockwise direction, if you please, sir!) at the end of dinner once the ladies have left; port that is poured from those elaborate cut-crystal decanters; port that used to be laid down (by the pipe, a traditional measure equivalent to 115 imperial gallons) for one's godson at his birth. Curiously, the world's largest importer of port is now France, where it is downed without much ado as an aperitif.

Port must be made from grapes grown in a strictly delimited region of the Douro River valley, upstream from the town of Oporto (the origin of its name) in the north of Portugal. The juice from as many as 15 different grape varieties goes into port wine. Like sherry, port is fortified with grape brandy; but there is a crucial difference: In port, the brandy is added *before* fermentation is complete, and it halts the process. Unfermented grape sugar therefore remains in the wine, making it necessarily sweet. Once it is fortified, port is strong (20 percent or more alcohol), deep in color, and heavily tannic.

The port trade has always been dominated by British shippers, among them Cockburn, Croft, Graham, Sandeman, Warre, Calem, and Mackenzie. These firms have wine lodges at the mouth of the Douro, and there they determine the style of the port through careful blending. They also decide which port is worthy of the distinction of being declared a vintage, something that happens only about three times a decade. **Vintage port** is the royalty of fortified wines: It is a blend of the best port wines from a single superior harvest, bottled after two years in wood and then aged for decades. Fifteen-to-twenty years is about the right length of time to wait before opening a bottle of vintage port, although it will maintain its character for fifty. When ready to drink, its color is the deepest ruby red, its body thick, and its bouquet intensely fruity. Vintage port throws a sediment during its long stay in the bottle and must be decanted carefully before serving.

One step down is the category known as *late-bottled vintage* (L.B.V.) —port wine from a single good harvest that has been set aside to age unblended in wood for ten years or more. Unlike true vintage ports, these wines require no additional aging in the bottle, nor do they need to be decanted. They are also cheaper than vintage ports. Yet another category is called *vintage-character* port; similar in taste to L.B.V., it has been aged for only about half of the time in wood. These wines are bottled when ready to drink but will improve in the bottle, with time.

Wood ports constitute a separate (and lower) class and come in three basic types: ruby, tawny, and white.

The wood ports get all the aging they need in the cask and are ready to drink when bottled. **Ruby** is the youngster of the port family, aged for about 3-to-8 years, very fruity and sweet and bright ruby red in color. Being the youngest, it is also the least expensive. **Tawny** port is a blend of more mature wooded ports, ten years in wood being the average. The longer aging period mellows both color and body; and tawny port is usually drier than ruby. **White** port is made in the same way as ruby, the difference being that only white grapes are used. The French drink it chilled as an aperitif.

MADEIRA

After sherry and port, the next most important fortified wines are madeira and marsala. Nowadays, both are more likely to be seen in the kitchen than on the bar, though madeira enjoyed a particular vogue in America during Colonial times. Madeira hails from a tiny Portuguese island of the same name out in the Atlantic. Among its several peculiarities are the post-fermentation heat treatment it is subjected to (the wine matures in an estufa, or hothouse, at temperatures ranging from 95 degrees to 120 degrees F), the facts that it benefits from motion and that it lives so extraordinarily long, continuing to improve even after 100 years. Madeiras run the gamut from very dry to very sweet, with **sercial** being the palest and driest, **malmsey** the sweetest, and **verdelho** in between. (The names derive from the dominant grape types.) Sercials and verdelhos are excellent chilled as aperitifs, or at room temperature between or after meals. Malmsey's intense sweetness best suits the after-dinner hour. Madeira is the indispensable ingredient in Sauce Madère, a classic of French cuisine.

MARSALA

Marsala, named for a town on the west coast of Sicily, comes in a variety of styles. They range from dry to very sweet, but all share richness of flavor and the bite of high acidity. Most marsalas that make it out of Sicily are suitable only for cooking. For drinking, look for the amber-colored, delightfully aromatic Marsala Vergine (known also as Marsala Soleras).

MONTILLA AND MÁLAGA

Montilla and málaga are Spanish fortified wines that have never achieved quite the prestige of sherry. Montilla—rather light and dry, as fortified wines go—comes from Pedro Ximenez grapes grown in the chalky soil of the Montilla mountains, due west of the Jerez region. It is used mostly as an aperitif. Málaga's taste spectrum veers decidedly toward the sweet; its alcohol content may be as high as 23 percent; its color is usually dark. The rich, fragrant muscat and the Pedro Ximenez grapes are the dominant varieties. Málaga, popular before the Second World War, is a rarity today. It's simply too sweet to suit most contemporary palates.

Fortified Wine Recipes

See Section One for information on barware, mixing supplies, and mixing tips. For conversion to metric or other measurements, refer to tables on pages 11 and 22.

THE DEVIL HIMSELF
Shake together 1 ounce port, 1 ounce dry vermouth, and 1 teaspoonful lemon juice in cocktail shaker with ice. Strain into cocktail glass.

ANY PORT IN A STORM
Blend 3 ounces ruby port, 1 ounce brandy, ½ ounce maraschino liqueur, and cracked ice in blender for 10 seconds at medium speed. Strain into collins glass half filled with cracked ice. Top with soda.

PORTE ALEGRE COOLER
Blend 3 ounces tawny port, 1½ ounces bourbon, ½ ounce sweet vermouth, 3 dashes orange bitters, and cracked ice in blender for 10–15 seconds at medium speed. Pour into collins glass. Top with soda. Taste, and add sugar syrup if desired.

FREEPORT FIZZ
Shake in cocktail shaker with ice 1½ ounces port, 1½ ounces dark rum, 1 ounce lemon juice, 1 egg white, and a pinch of sugar. Strain into highball glass over ice cubes. Top with club soda.

JEREZ COCKTAIL
Shake 2 ounces dry sherry, 1 dash orange bitters, and 1 dash peach bitters with ice in cocktail shaker. Strain into cocktail glass. Alternatively, this can also be made by pouring sherry over 2 or 3 ice cubes in a large wine glass, adding the bitters, and stirring.

ADONIS
Pour 1 ounce dry sherry, ½ ounce sweet vermouth, and 1 dash orange bitters over 2 or 3 ice cubes in large wine glass. Stir. Garnish with strip of orange peel.

BRAZIL
Pour 1 ounce dry sherry, 1 ounce dry vermouth, 1 dash Pernod, and 1 dash Angostura bitters over 2 or 3 ice cubes in large wine glass. Stir. Squeeze a strip of lemon peel over drink to release drop of oil, then toss it in, too.

NUTCRACKER SUITE
Pour into wine glass 2 ounces each cream sherry and Nocello liqueur. Stir gently.

SHERRY COBBLER
Put shaved ice in a cocktail glass and pour over it 2 ounces sweet sherry and ¾ ounce sugar syrup. Garnish with slice of orange and sprig of mint.

CUPID
Pour 3 ounces dry sherry, 1 egg, 1 teaspoonful superfine sugar, and 1 dash cayenne pepper over ice in cocktail shaker. Shake hard. Strain into cocktail glass.

SPANISH DAIRY QUEEN

Pour 1 ounce cream sherry, 1 ounce orange juice, 1 teaspoonful brandy, and 2 teaspoonfuls heavy cream over 3 ounces crushed ice in cocktail shaker. Shake hard, then strain into cocktail glass.

SPANISH KISS

Blend briefly 3 ounces sherry, 1 ounce light rum, and 3 ounces orange juice with crushed ice in blender. Strain into wine glass.

MOSS ROSE

Shake in cocktail shaker with ice cubes 3 ounces of fino sherry, 4 ounces grapefruit juice, and 1 ounce sloe gin. Strain into wine glass over 3 ice cubes.

PACT

Pour 2 ounces dry sherry and 1 ounce gin over ice in mixing glass; stir until mixed and cold. Strain into cocktail glass. Twist a strip of lemon peel over drink and toss in.

GREEN HORNET

Pour 1 ounce sherry, 1 ounce melon liqueur, 1 teaspoonful lemon juice, and ½ teaspoonful Falernum over ice in cocktail shaker and shake hard. Strain into cocktail glass.

HIGH AND FINE

Half fill highball glass with ice, then pour in 1 ounce fino sherry, 1 ounce brandy, and ½ ounce Cointreau; stir. Top with tonic.

MADEIRA COOLER

Blend briefly 1½ ounces madeira, 1½ ounces cognac, juice of a lime, 1 ounce each pineapple juice and passion-fruit juice, and a dash of orange bitters with cracked ice in blender. Pour into collins glass; garnish with orange slice and pineapple spear.

MADEIRA M'DEAR?

Blend briefly 1½ ounces each madeira and bourbon, the juice of half a lemon, ½ ounce curaçao, and orgeat or sugar syrup to taste. Blend with cracked ice 10 to 15 seconds. Pour into cocktail glass.

PLAYA DEL REY

Shake 2 ounces madeira, 1 ounce brandy, and ½ ounce curaçao in cocktail shaker with cracked ice. Strain into cocktail glass; garnish with lemon peel.

REGENT'S PUNCH

Heat—but don't boil—4 ounces sauterne, 2 ounces madeira, and 1 ounce dark rum in saucepan. Warm a mug; spoon a little honey into it, and pour in mixture from saucepan. Stir to dissolve honey. Top mug with hot tea. Add dash or 2 of curaçao on top.

2

APERITIFS

An aperitif is anything one drinks before a meal, be it white wine, champagne, or whiskey. In Europe, and particularly in France, most people who drink aperitifs choose vermouth or one of the other aromatic wines. And as more and more Americans discover what perfect aperitifs these drinks make, our notion of the word is coming to be the same as the European one. With their relatively low levels of alcohol and their mouth-tingling astringency, aromatized wines leave the palate undulled, the taste buds primed, and the appetite heightened. In short, they create the ideal prelude to an evening of eating good food and drinking the wine one wishes to appreciate fully.

Aromatized wines go fortified wines one better: Not only are they strengthened by the addition of alcohol (to about 16-to-20 percent), they are also flavored with infusions from a range of herbs, flowers, roots, barks, and other ingredients known as *botanicals*. Vermouth heads this rather small family; other members include Dubonnet, Lillet, Punt e Mes, Byrrh, and St. Raphaël. Closely related is a beverage known as *mistelle*, a mixture of unfermented grape juice and brandy; in fact, this is what many aromatized wines consist of before they are made aromatic by the addition of botanicals.

Also popular as aperitifs are the bitters—such as Campari—and the anise-flavored spirits—such as Pernod. Technically, these are not classed with the aromatized wines because their base alcohol is different: distilled spirits.

VERMOUTH

It used to be that Americans knew vermouths only for what they could mix with them: dry vermouth for martinis, sweet vermouth for manhattans. It also used to be that sweet vermouth meant Italian and dry meant French. These days, however, Americans have discovered the joys of vermouth straight

151

up (always cold) as well as on the rocks or with soda. And now both French and Italians are making vermouths that are sweet, dry, extradry; red, white, and rosé. Who says there's no such thing as progress?

Vermouth's commercial history stretches back to 1786, when Antonio Benedetto Carpano first sold it out of Turin, Italy. In France, Joseph Noilly began bottling a drier version in 1800. But the drink had been around in some form during the Dark Ages, and probably back in ancient Rome, as well. The name itself comes to us through the German word *Vermutwein*—wormwood wine. Wormwood is still one of the botanicals flavoring vermouths, along with nutmeg, cloves, coriander seeds, marjoram, angelica root, camomile, linden, gentian, elder flowers, and many more. Each maker naturally keeps its formula secret.

The French make vermouth this way: Once the flavoring ingredients have been selected and combined, a mixture of fortified wine and mistelle is poured over them and the brew is allowed to steep for a few weeks; then the wine is drawn off and the process repeated until all the flavor has been extracted from the botanicals. A number of these flavored wines (known as *infusion*) are blended together for consistency and then mixed in a proportion of 1-to-5 with unflavored wines. Next, brandy is added to raise the alcohol level; then the vermouth is chilled nearly to freezing to force out any sediment.

In Italy, the process is a bit less involved: Various white wines are blended together first, and then the flavoring agents are infused. When all the flavor has been incorporated into the wine, it is drawn off, fortified with brandy, filtered, and tinted brown with caramel. Often, Italian vermouths (and various other aromatized wines, as well) have a small amount of quinine added. This is a holdover from the age of imperialism, when European settlers and soldiers in tropical colonies were given quinine regularly to guard against, as well as to treat, malaria. The stuff was too bitter to take by itself; so they mixed it with sweetened wine. Once established, the taste for this "medicine" proved to be enduring.

The best-known makers of vermouth also make the best. In Italy, these are Martini & Rossi, Cinzano, Riccadonna, Stock, and Carpano—the last-named for its bittersweet brown Punt e Mes. Martini & Rossi and Cinzano both produce rosso (sweet), bianco (dry), and the more recently introduced rosé, which is delightfully light and fruity. The class French vermouth is Noilly Prat, followed by Vernat. Both make it sweet, dry, and extradry; Vernat also has a product flavored with wild strawberries.

There are all sorts of ways to serve vermouth, but one constant is *always to have it chilled*, either straight up from a refrigerated bottle or on the rocks. Try it with a slice of peel of lemon. Splash in soda, too, if you like; but take care not to overdilute, particularly the dry and rosé vermouths. Some folks have taken to mixing half-and-half sweet and dry.

OTHER APERITIFS

Once you've acquired a taste for vermouth, you'll want to move on to some of the other aromatic wines. France offers bracing, astringent **Dubonnet** (both red and white); the drier and more subtle **Lillet** (also red and white—and best served with orange slice or peel); **Byrrh** (biting, red, and quinined); and **St. Raphaël** (available here only in red, and rather full-bodied and sweet). Italian competitors to vermouth include **Cynar,** whose strong, unique flavor comes from artichokes, and Blackberry Julep.

Campari, perhaps the best known of all Italian aperitifs, is classified as a bitters because it's based on spirits—classic with soda and orange. Fernet, another Italian bitters, of which **Fernet Branca** is the best-known variety, has an even stronger bitter tang.

The Cognac region of France produces a very charming mistelle known as **Pineau des Charentes,** a mix of unfermented sweet grape juice and—what else?—cognac. Look for the Reynac label; drink on the rocks or with soda. Mistelle made in France's Champagne region is known as *ratafia*. Now there is a splendid California ratafia named **Panache;** it's made by Domaine Chandon, the Franco-Californian sparkling wine concern.

ANISE-FLAVORED SPIRITS

For those whose taste buds are truly adventurous, there are the anise-flavored spiritous aperitifs with their odd properties, licorice bite, and dangerous reputations. **Pernod** from France, a kind of toned-down younger brother of the notorious (and now illegal) absinthe, is the best-known example. Pernod—the name of the maker has become synonymous with the drink—flows from the bottle a yellow-green color and 90 proof; mix it with an equivalent amount of water and it swirls with milky clouds; mix in even more water and it clears. The usual mixture is 5-to-1, water-to-Pernod. Each Mediterranean country has its own anise-flavored speciality, to note: ojen from Spain; pastis from France—flavored with licorice, not anise, and sold mostly by Ricard; anesone from Italy; **ouzo** and mastikha from Greece; raki from Turkey; and arak from Israel.

Aperitif Recipes

See Section One for information on barware, mixing supplies, and mixing tips. For conversion to metric or other measurements, refer to tables on pages 11 and 22.

FOUR APERITIF STANDARDS

CAMPARI AND SODA
Fill highball glass with ice. Pour in 2 ounces Campari and 4 ounces soda. Twist a strip of orange peel over the drink to release drop of oil and toss in.

AMERICANO
Fill rocks glass with ice and pour in 1 ounce Campari and 1 ounce sweet vermouth. Add splash of soda, twist of lemon peel over drink and toss in.

NEGRONI
Fill rocks glass with ice and pour in 1 ounce Campari, 1 ounce sweet vermouth, and 1 ounce gin. Stir. Twist a strip of lemon peel above drink, then toss in.

VERMOUTH CASSIS
Mix 1 ounce crème de cassis with 3 ounces chilled dry vermouth in highball glass. Add 3 ounces soda; stir one turn.

VERMOUTH COCKTAILS

PERFECT COCKTAIL
Stir 1 ounce sweet vermouth, 1 ounce dry vermouth, and 1 ounce gin with ice in mixing glass. Strain into cocktail glass. Twist strip of lemon peel above surface, then toss it in to drink.

HIGH AND DRY
Pour 1½ ounces dry vermouth, ½ ounce light rum, 1 teaspoonful lime juice, and ½ ounce curaçao over ice in cocktail shaker. Shake hard. Strain into cocktail glass.

TIGHT DENIM JEANS
Pour ½ ounce dry vermouth, ½ ounce Bourbon whiskey, 2 dashes Angostura bitters, and 1 dash blue curaçao over ice in cocktail shaker. Shake hard. Strain over 2 ice cubes in an old-fashioned or rocks glass. Twist strip of lemon peel over drink, and toss it in.

BITTERSWEET
Stir 2 ounces sweet vermouth, 1 ounce Fernet Branca bitters, 1 teaspoonful sugar syrup, and 1 dash Angostura bitters with ice in mixing glass. Strain into cocktail glass.

VERMOUTH COCKTAIL
Stir 3 ounces dry vermouth, 3 dashes orange bitters, and 3 dashes Angostura bitters with ice in mixing glass. Strain into cocktail glass. Twist strip of orange peel over drink and toss in.

JUST MOONING AROUND
Pour 1½ ounces sweet vermouth, 1

154

ounce pineapple juice, 2 teaspoonfuls gin, 2 dashes curaçao over ice in cocktail shaker. Shake hard. Strain into cocktail glass.

ROOM FOR ONE MORE

Stir 1 ounce brandy, 2 ounces dry vermouth, and 2 dashes orange curaçao over ice in mixing glass. Strain into cocktail glass.

KNOCK-OUT

Pour ½ ounce gin, ½ ounce dry vermouth, ½ ounce Pernod, and 1 teaspoonful crème de menthe over ice in cocktail shaker. Shake hard. Strain into cocktail glass.

FOURTH DEGREE

Stir ½ ounce gin, ½ ounce dry vermouth, ½ ounce sweet vermouth, and 2 dashes Pernod in mixing glass with ice. Strain into cocktail glass.

ADDINGTON

Pour 1 ounce dry vermouth, 1 ounce sweet vermouth, and 1 teaspoonful lemon juice over ice in cocktail shaker. Shake hard. Strain into rocks glass; add 3 ounces soda; twist strip of lemon peel over drink and toss in.

HIGH HEELS WITH ORANGE SHOELACES

Stir 1 ounce sweet vermouth, 1 ounce dry vermouth, 1 ounce orange juice, 2 drops triple sec, and 1 teaspoonful gin with ice in mixing glass. Strain into rocks glass half filled with crushed ice. Garnish with slice of orange.

APPLE KICKER

Stir in mixing glass with ice 1 ounce each sweet vermouth, dry vermouth, and calvados. Strain into cocktail glass.

MARTINEZ

Put into blender cracked ice, 1 ounce each gin and dry vermouth, and 3 dashes each curaçao and orange bitters. Blend at medium speed for 10 seconds. Strain into cocktail glass, and garnish with cherry.

LIPSTICK ON THE COLLAR

Pour ¾ ounce sweet vermouth, ¾ ounce dry vermouth, 1 ounce gin, and 1 teaspoonful strawberry liqueur over ice in cocktail shaker. Shake hard. Strain into cocktail glass filled with crushed ice. Garnish with strawberry.

KINGDOM COME

Shake ¾ ounce gin, 1½ ounces dry vermouth, 1 teaspoonful white crème de menthe, and ½ ounce grapefruit juice with ice in cocktail shaker. Strain into rocks glass filled with crushed ice. Garnish with strip of grapefruit peel.

PUNTEGRONI

Stir 1 ounce Punt e Mes, 1 ounce dry vermouth, and 1 ounce gin with ice in mixing glass. Strain into cocktail glass. Twist strip of orange peel over drink, and toss it in.

WHIP

Pour 1 ounce brandy, 1½ ounces dry vermouth, 1 dash curaçao, and 2 drops Pernod over ice in cocktail shaker. Shake hard. Strain into cocktail glass.

MORNING BECOMES ELECTRIC
Stir 2 ounces dry vermouth, 1 ounce brandy, 2 teaspoonfuls port wine, and 1 dash curaçao with ice in mixing glass. Strain over ice in rocks glass.

GREEN ROOM
Pour 1½ ounces dry vermouth, ½ ounce brandy, and 1 teaspoonful green crème de menthe over ice in cocktail shaker. Shake hard. Strain into cocktail glass.

STRIKE ONE
Stir 1½ ounces dry vermouth and ¾ ounce curaçao with ice in mixing glass. Strain into cocktail glass; top with soda. Sprinkle surface with a bit of cinnamon, if desired.

HARPER'S FERRY
Pour 1½ ounces dry vermouth, ½ ounce Southern Comfort, ½ ounce light rum, and ½ ounce curaçao over ice in cocktail shaker. Shake hard. Strain into cocktail glass.

CAT'S EYE
Pour 2 ounces dry vermouth, ½ ounce yellow Chartreuse, and 2 dashes orange bitters over ice in cocktail shaker. Shake hard. Strain into cocktail glass.

AMERICAN BEAUTY ROSE
Pour ¾ ounce dry vermouth, ¾ ounce orange juice, ½ ounce peppermint schnapps, and 1 dash strawberry liqueur into cocktail shaker. Shake hard, then strain into cocktail glass. Float ¾ ounce port wine on surface of drink.

CAMPARI COCKTAILS

BITTER BIKINI
Pour 1½ ounces Campari, 1 ounce dry vermouth, and ½ ounce triple sec over ice in cocktail shaker. Shake hard. Strain into rocks glass filled with crushed ice.

VIA VENETO
Fill rocks glass with ice and pour in 1 ounce lemon liqueur and 2 ounces Campari. Squeeze in the juice from a lemon wedge; fill to top with grapefruit juice; stir. Garnish with the squeezed-out lemon wedge.

IN THE PINK
Fill highball glass with ice and pour in 1 ounce Campari and ½ ounce peach brandy; stir. Top with bitter lemon, and stir again one or two turns.

CAPRI COCKTAIL
Pour 2 ounces Campari, 1 ounce vodka, 2 dashes Angostura bitters, and 1 teaspoonful sugar over ice in cocktail shaker. Shake hard. Strain into cocktail glass; twist strip of lemon peel above surface, then toss in.

DUBONNET DRINKS

DUBONNET COCKTAIL
Stir 1 ounce red Dubonnet, 1 ounce gin, and 1 dash Pernod with ice in mixing glass. Strain into cocktail glass, twist a strip of lemon over drink and then toss in.

MOONSHINE COCKTAIL
Shake ½ ounce white Dubonnet, 1 dash Pernod, ½ ounce brandy, and ½ ounce peach brandy with ice in cocktail shaker. Strain into cocktail glass.

BENTLEY
Stir 1 ounce red Dubonnet and 1 ounce calvados with ice in mixing glass. Strain into cocktail glass.

MIXED MARRIAGE
Stir 1½ ounces each red and white Dubonnet with ice in mixing glass. Strain into cocktail glass. Twist orange peel over drink to release a drop of oil, then toss it in.

FRENCH WENCH
Pour 3 ounces Dubonnet into highball glass. Drop in a few ice cubes, and fill to top with ginger ale. Stir gently. Garnish with lemon or lime wedge.

DUBONNET NEGRONI
Stir with ice in mixing glass 1½ ounces Dubonnet, 1½ ounces gin, and 1½ ounces Campari. Strain into wine glass. Twist lemon peel over drink; drop it in.

DUBONNET FIZZ
Into highball glass filled with ice cubes, pour 1½ ounces each Dubonnet and gin. Add ½ ounce curaçao and stir well. Top with club soda; stir again gently. Garnish with lemon peel.

LILLET COCKTAILS

HOOPLA
Pour ½ ounce Cointreau, 1 ounce Lillet, ½ ounce lemon juice, and ½ ounce brandy over ice in cocktail shaker and shake hard. Strain into cocktail glass.

RED MAPLE FLAMER
Pour 2 ounces red Lillet, 1 ounce brandy, 1 ounce fresh orange juice, and 2 dashes grenadine over ice in cocktail shaker. Shake hard; strain into brandy snifter. Twist a large section of orange rind until oil exudes, hold a match to it and ignite, plunge flaming rind into drink. Swirl snifter, holding it by its foot.

BLUE STAR
Pour 1 ounce Lillet, 1 ounce orange juice, ½ ounce gin, and ½ ounce blue curaçao over ice in cocktail shaker; shake hard. Strain into cocktail glass.

MOUNT RAINIER
Fill rocks glass with ice and pour in ½ ounce gin, 1½ ounces Lillet, and 2 dashes crème de noyaux. Twist strip of lemon peel over drink and toss in.

DEPTH-CHARGE
Pour 1 ounce gin, 1 ounce Lillet, and 2 dashes Pernod over ice in cocktail shaker. Shake hard. Strain into cocktail glass.

BARONIAL
Pour 1 ounce Lillet, ½ ounce gin, 2 dashes Angostura bitters, and 2 dashes

Cointreau over ice in mixing glass. Stir. Strain into cocktail glass.

BYRRH COCKTAILS

BYRRH CASSIS

Stir together in wine goblet 1½ ounces Byrrh and 1 ounce crème de cassis. Add a few ice cubes; top with club soda. Stir gently. Garnish with orange peel.

LE WAGON BYRRH

Fill rocks glass with ice and pour in 3 ounces Byrrh and 2 ounces dry sherry. Stir, then twist lemon peel over drink and drop it in.

GYPSY'S TOKEN

Stir 1½ ounces dry vermouth, 1½ ounces Byrrh, and 1½ ounces rye whiskey in mixing glass with ice. Strain into cocktail glass.

BYRRH COCKTAIL

Stir 1 ounce Byrrh and 1 ounce gin with ice in mixing glass. Strain into cocktail glass.

PERNOD COCKTAILS

GLAD EYE

Stir 1 ounce Pernod with ½ ounce crème de menthe with ice in mixing glass. Strain into cocktail glass.

PERNOD AND WATER

To ¾ ounce Pernod in rocks glass, add 4 ounces ice water. Stir.

SUISSESSE

Shake 1 ounce Pernod, 1 ounce lemon juice, and 1 egg white with ice in cocktail shaker. Strain into rocks glass. Top with splash of soda.

KISS-ME-QUICK

Fill rocks glass with ice and pour in 2 ounces Pernod and 1 teaspoonful Cointreau. Add 2 dashes Angostura bitters. Top with soda.

OTHER APERITIF COCKTAILS

BLACK TIE

Pour 4 ounces Pineau des Charentes and 2 ounces dry sparkling wine into large wine glass. Garnish with black grape.

FALL SUNSET

Pour 3 ounces Pineau des Charentes and 1 ounce fraise eau-de-vie over 3 ice cubes in large wine glass. Stir one or two turns. Garnish with slice of melon.

ST. GENNARO'S FANFARE

Fill rocks glass with ice and pour in 1½ ounces Cynar, 1½ ounces vodka, and 1 dash sweet vermouth. Stir thoroughly and garnish with slice of orange.

BONFIRE COCKTAIL

Stir 1 ounce Punt e Mes, 2 ounces Cognac, and 1 ounce Calvados with ice in mixing glass. Strain into cocktail glass. Twist strip of lemon peel over drink and toss in.

AFTER-DINNER DRINKS

The brandies, cordials and liqueurs of the after-dinner hours are mood drinks. One doesn't take them to quench the thirst, nor to complement food, nor to tie one on; rather, they are spirits for the mind. A mere sniff of fine cognac or armagnac clears away the day's accumulated cobwebs. A sip of clear eau de vie chases out old vapors and brings clarity to the mind. The sweeter and softer liqueurs induce contemplation, more finely tuned appraisals, and romance. Each type of after-dinner drink has its moment, a time of the evening best suited to its properties; and each has a way of heightening that moment.

1

BRANDIES

We begin with brandy because it is preeminent: There is nothing more elegant or elevating than a snifter of fine brandy as the evening winds down. Brandy has its roots in the Dutch word *brandewijn*, meaning "burned wine"—a reference to the heating of wine for distillation. Today the term *brandy* applies to any spirit distilled from fruit, even though when we use it without qualifier we're speaking of a wine or grape distillate.

Although brandies are made all over the world—fine ones come from Italy, Spain, Portugal, Peru, and California—it is France that holds the highest honors. The reasons are simple: Cognac and Armagnac. These are brandy at its most superb; Cognac superb for sublety and sophistication, Armagnac superb for its full-flavored pungency tempered by smoothness. Dispute as to superiority is pointless, especially as it's much more enjoyable to keep both on hand.

COGNAC AND ARMAGNAC

The town of Cognac in the center of the Charentes region of southwestern France is the hub of Cognac production. There is something about the chalky limestone soil here that makes the white wine grapes especially suited to distillation (oddly, the district's table wine is merely average). The Armagnac region lies 150 miles to the south in the wild, hot, sandy hills of Gascony (birthplace of D'Artagnan of *Three Musketeers* fame). If more prestige attaches to Cognac, more romance surrounds Armagnac, the production of which remains in the hands of small, fiercely independent growers. Cognac is distilled twice, Armagnac only once—which means that greater flavor comes through to the latter spirit. Alcoholic strength of both is 40-to-43 percent; both are aged in oak barrels (though the types of oak and the forests they come from are different); both are carefully blended by expert cellar masters who rely almost entirely on their noses to discriminate subleties of flavor.

The labels of Cognac and Armagnac display an identical grading system involving mysterious groupings of stars, letters, and high-flown names. The mystery, however, is easily unraveled: Three stars indicate a maker's least expensive blend, aged at least 2½ years; 3-to-5 years is a more common aging period. V.S.O.P. stands for *Very Special Old Pale* and means the brandy has spent at least 4½ years in wood (7-to-10 years being the norm). Terms such as *Extra, Napoléon,* and *Vieille Réserve* may only be used by brandies 6½ years old or older: These will be the highest achievements of the Cognac house. Some connoisseurs believe the best brandies are those aged about 20 years. After 70 years, the spirit decays in the cask. Unlike wine, no Cognac or Armagnac ages or improves at all in the bottle. Cognac labeled *Fine Champagne* has nothing to do with the bubbling wine from the similarly named region far to the northeast. It is made from grapes grown in two coincidentally named districts of the Cognac region—Grande Champagne and Petite Champagne. At least half must be from Grande Champagne, considered the better district.

OTHER BRANDIES

Calvados, the third of the world's great brandies, is made from apples and comes from Normandy. Calvados is double distilled and aged for at least a year, and generally more, in oak casks that give it a rich, dark color. It can be tart and rough when young, but with proper aging it smooths out and develops a pungent, distinctive bouquet. Our American applejack is a poor (and distant) relation.

In the Burgundy region a woody-tasting, strong brandy known as **marc** is produced from the pulpy mass left in the wine press after the juice of the grapes has been extracted. Italians know it as **grappa,** and more and more people are developing a taste for this sharp, bracing spirit.

California produces some light and mellow brandies from grapes grown primarily in the San Joaquin Valley. Although most go through a continuous still and come out quite clean, more and more producers are using the traditional pot still and the old methods developed for cognac. United States law requires a minimum two years in oak barrels; the better ones will get four or even eight.

Spanish brandy is sweeter and heavier than the cognac and armagnac types. Some is distilled from sherry, but more is from wines grown in other regions but processed and marketed by the sherry shippers.

The best South American brandy is **Peruvian pisco,** distilled from muscat grape wines and matured (briefly) in jars of porous clay.

All these brandies should be served in balloon-shaped snifters, warmed in a cupped hand to release the spirit's flavor. Sophisticated drinkers eschew oversized snifters and flamed heating devices.

EAU-DE-VIE

The true fruit brandies, known as *eaux-de-vie* or *alcools blancs*, are not to be confused with the syrupy, pastel-colored brandies that are merely flavored with fruit. The eaux-de-vie are unsweetened and usually crystal clear. The sugar has disappeared after the fruits have been mashed (usually in considerable quantities—which accounts for the high prices demanded for these drinks) and fermented. They're colorless because aging takes place after distillation in wax-lined casks, earthenware, or glass. (The exception is **slivovitz,** which gets a deep gold color from wooden casks.) While cognac doesn't age in the bottle, most eau-de-vie does.

Fruits that produce the most distinctive types are cherry (for **kirsch** or kirschwasser), plum (for slivovitz, mirabelle, and quetsch), pear (for poire and poire william—some types come with a whole pear that has actually been grown in the bottle), raspberry **(framboise),** and strawberry **(fraise).** Unlike Cognac and Armagnac, alcools blancs are best when served chilled (or even straight from the freezer). Late in the evening, after coffee, is the best time.

All brandies are meant to be sipped and savored, rolled over the tongue, then swallowed. They flood the mouth with flavor and the brain with wonders.

2

CORDIALS AND LIQUEURS

Simply said, a liqueur or cordial is an alcoholic beverage prepared by combining a spirit, usually brandy, with flavorings and then adding sugar syrup in excess of 2.5 percent of the total weight—although many contain as much as 35 percent. The line dividing a liqueur from a cordial is a fuzzy one; indeed, it has all but vanished. Some maintain that the name *cordial* applies to the ancient herbal drinks created as medicines or aphrodisiacs, while *liqueur* describes those essences of fruits and flowers distilled for the pleasure, rather than health, of the drinker.

In no other beverage does man play such an important role in determining style, color, flavor, and aroma. As a result, liqueurs often have an element of the fanciful, not to say bizarre, in their composition and taste. The Chinese reputedly distill one from the ground-up bones of tigers. Some contain the essences of as many as 130 aromatic herbs. Various liqueurs are served with flakes of gold leaf suspended in them, or with coffee beans or flower petals floating on top. The crowning achievement in the serving of liqueurs is the pousse-café, a liquid layering of colorful liqueurs kept tenuously in place by minute differences in specific gravities.

Production techniques vary widely, but there are three basic processes for making liqueurs: by distillation; by adding essential oils to brandy or grain alcohol; by steeping various aromatic roots, herbs, and seeds in grain spirit. Recently, something called *cream liqueur* has been developed. This involves the blending of fresh cream with spirits and stabilizing agents. Bailey's, the original Irish cream liqueur, was first on the market; the spirit, naturally, is Irish whiskey. Many other cream liqueurs have followed. In fact, the whole liqueur field is expanding rapidly, with new brands and styles and uses appearing all the time. France and Holland are the major liqueur-producing nations, but almost every country has its specialties.

By tradition, liqueurs have been served after dinner in tiny glasses; but today, with so many new types on the market, people are using them as aperitifs, pouring them over ice, mixing them in cocktails, and adding them to dessert recipes. Every seasoned drinker has his favorites. Ours are described below.

TRADITIONAL LIQUEURS

These classic liqueurs have been around in some cases for centuries, during which time their various makers have perfected the formulas. They are not likely ever to go out of fashion or be considered outré.

Bénédictine: The granddaddy of them all and still one of the best. Its formula has been a secret since 1510, when Dom Bernardo Vincelli invented it at the monastery in Fécamp in Normandy. The spirit base is Cognac. Also available mixed with brandy—ask for **B & B.** The initials D.O.M. on the label are for *Deo Optimo Maximo* (to God, most good, most great).

Chartreuse: The other great monastic liqueur—credit goes to the Carthusian Fathers of Grenoble. Also has a secret formula, with about 130 herbs in it. Green Chartreuse is a bit stronger than yellow, which is a touch more sweet.

Cointreau: Made from the skins of curaçao oranges, this is the classiest proprietary brand of triple sec. It used to be called Triple Sec White Curaçao, until other makers began using the name. (Curaçao is the generic term

for all liqueurs made from the curaçao orange—see next part.)

Drambuie: Highland malt whiskey and heather honey are the base ingredients in this smooth and wonderfully warming drink from Scotland. The story goes that Bonnie Prince Charlie gave the Mackinnon family the secret recipe when they saved his life back in 1745. The family still makes it today.

Fior d'Alpe Isolabella: An unusual spicy Italian liqueur flavored with herbs found in the Alps, from a recipe hundreds of years old.

Liquore Galliano: A spicy golden liqueur made from herbs and flowers. It is named after a 19th-century major in the Italian army, Guiseppe Galliano.

Grand Marnier: One of the best, and best-known, of the curaçao-type liqueurs. It is made on a base of fine-quality cognac.

Irish Mist: Irish whiskey and heather honey combine to give this one a pleasantly spicy taste.

Kahlúa: Mexico's coffee-flavored liqueur, made on a sugarcane-spirit base. Perfect with or in coffee.

Nassau Royale: Vanilla and citrus, with hints of coffee, based on sugarcane spirit. A favorite in the Bahamas.

Peter Heering: Used to be called *Cherry Heering.* By whatever name, one of the best cherry liqueurs. From Denmark.

Sambuca: A well-known Italian liqueur with licorice flavor. Often served *con mosche* (with flies), the "flies" being three coffee beans floating on top.

Southern Comfort: An American classic blending of Bourbon whiskey, peach liqueur, and fresh peaches. Potent and delicious.

Tía Maria: A popular coffee-flavored liqueur from Jamaica.

Vieille Cure: A blend of Cognac, Armagnac, and aromatic herbs made in Bordeaux. Both green and yellow.

THE GENERICS

The term *generic* means that a liqueur may be made by a number of different producers. While the basic style remains the same, quality does vary from brand to brand. Sip around until you find your favorite.

Advocaat: A Dutch classic, made from sweetened egg yolks and brandy. Try it in eggnogg.

Amaretto: An Italian offering now in vogue. The distinctive almond flavor comes, surprisingly enough, from apricot kernels. Hiram Walker now has a liqueur on the market called **Amaretto & Cognac.**

Anisette: Sharp aniseed flavor, like liquid licorice. Marie Brizard's is generally considered the best.

Crème de cacao: Has a rich chocolate flavor and comes either in brown or white. Look for *Chouao* on the label: This is Venezuela's premier cacao-growing region.

Crème de cassis: Black currants supply the flavor. Mixed with white wine, it gains the name *kir*. Add a dash of (nonvintage) champagne and you have the delightful Kir Royal.

Crème de noyaux: Flavoring from fruit pits gives a bitter-almond taste.

Crème de menthe: Mint with a touch of menthol is the flavor; the colors are green or white. Get's (pronounced jetz) Peppermint crème de menthe is our preference.

Curaçao: The rich-tasting liqueur from the peel of the curaçao orange. This liqueur can be orange, blue, or white in color. When it's redistilled clear, it's called **triple sec.**

Framboise: The heady essence of raspberries; very tasty on fresh fruit or ice cream.

Kümmel: Caraway seeds, cumin, and aniseed contribute the flavor, which may not be to everyone's taste. However, it's highly prized as a remedy for dyspepsia. **Goldwasser** is a German version flecked with gold.

Mandarine: A citrus liqueur that uses the dried peels of tangerines. For those who have tired of Grand Marnier and Cointreau, try the excellent Mandarine Napoleon.

Maraschino: The flavoring is from the Dalmation marasca cherry.

Peppermint schnapps: Light and minty and good for mixing.

Sloe gin: A fruity drink made from the sloe berry, steeped in gin. The sine qua non of the sloe gin fizz.

Strega: A spicy, citrusy liqueur, from Italy.

Swedish Punsch: An aromatic, warming liqueur based on the pungent Batavia arak, a rum from Indonesia.

FRUITS AND NUTS

Here is a sampling of some of the newer liqueurs based on fruit and nut flavors.

Aki Plum: Dark rose in color, it

smells of cherries and almonds, tastes distinctively of plum.

CocoRibe: The flavor of wild coconuts in a rum base.

Boggs Cranberry Liqueur: The taste and smell of real cranberries. A Thanksgiving and Christmas favorite.

Frangelico: A lovely taste of hazelnuts, from Italy. Softer and drier than amaretto. Try it over ice cream.

Midori Melon: This one is pale green, with the deep, cleansing fragrance of fresh melon.

Praline: A 40-proof liqueur from New Orleans, with the pecan-and-brown-sugar smell of praline candy.

Nocello: An Italian liqueur with a walnut flavor.

CREAM LIQUEURS

Not to be confused with *crème* liqueurs—such as crème de menthe or crème de cacao—the *cream* liqueurs have real cream mixed in with the alcohol and flavorings. They tend to be smooth, sweet, rich, and easy to drink. A fast-growing category.

Bailey's Original Irish Cream: The pioneer on the cream scene. In addition to cream and Irish whiskey, it has coffee, chocolate, and coconut in it. Recently joined by **O'Darby Irish Cream Liqueur** and **Waterford Cream**—but Bailey's outsells them all.

Demi-Tasse: The flavor is coffee, the cream comes from Ireland, and the spirit is French Cognac.

Trénais Nouvelle Liqueur: The new twist is yogurt instead of cream. Spiked with cognac.

Venetian Cream: Italy enters the cream competition with a mixture of Italian brandy, chocolate, hazelnuts, vanilla—and more. Slightly higher proof than the others.

Brandy and Liqueur Recipes

See Section One for information on barware, mixing supplies, and mixing tips. For conversion to metric or other measurements, refer to tables on pages 11 and 22.

FIVE BRANDY AND LIQUEUR STANDARDS

GRASSHOPPER
Shake ½ ounce green crème de menthe, ½ ounce white crème de cacao, 2 ounces cream, and 3 ounces crushed ice in cocktail shaker. Strain into cocktail glass.

THE SIDECAR
Pour 1 ounce Grand Marnier, 2 ounces cognac, and ½ ounce lemon juice in cocktail shaker with ice cubes. Shake well. Strain into cocktail glass.

BRANDY ALEXANDER
Shake ½ ounce each white crème de cacao, brandy, and heavy cream with ice cubes in cocktail shaker. Strain into cocktail glass.

THE STINGER
Shake 1½ ounces brandy and 1 ounce white crème de menthe with cracked ice in cocktail shaker. Strain into cocktail glass.

SLOE GIN FIZZ
Shake 3 ounces sloe gin, ½ ounce lemon juice, and 1 teaspoonful superfine sugar in cocktail shaker with ice cubes. Strain into wine glass over one inch of cracked ice; top with club soda. Stir gently.

STINGER AND GRASSHOPPER VARIATIONS

ITALIAN STINGER
Stir in mixing glass 1½ ounces brandy and ½ ounce Galliano. Strain into rocks glass filled with ice cubes.

INTERNATIONAL STINGER
Stir in mixing glass 2 ounces Metaxa Greek brandy and ½ ounce Galliano. Strain into rocks glass filled with ice cubes.

GREEN HORNET
Pour into mixing glass 1½ ounces brandy and ½ ounce green crème de menthe. Stir. Strain into rocks glass filled with ice cubes.

NUTTY STINGER
Shake 1½ ounces nut-flavored liqueur (amaretto—or try walnut or hazelnut liqueur) and 1 ounce white crème de menthe with ice cubes in cocktail shaker. Strain into cocktail glass.

PEPPERMINT STINGER
Blend 1½ ounces brandy, 1 ounce peppermint schnapps, and ½ cup cracked ice in blender until smooth. Pour into rocks glass.

ROMAN STINGER
Shake ½ ounce sambuca, ½ ounce

white crème de menthe, and 1 ounce brandy with ice cubes in cocktail shaker. Strain into cocktail glass.

ICEHOPPER
Shake ½ ounce green crème de menthe, ½ ounce peppermint schnapps, 2 ounces cream, and 3 ounces cracked ice in cocktail shaker. Strain into cocktail glass.

SLOEHOPPER
Shake ½ ounce green crème de menthe, 1 ounce sloe gin, 2 ounces cream, and a dash of lemon juice in cocktail shaker with 3 ounces crushed ice. Strain into cocktail glass.

THE POUSSE-CAFÉ AND VARIATIONS

SEVEN-LAYER POUSSE-CAFÉ
If executed with care, the instructions that follow should yield a layered, multi-colored drink. The liqueurs are poured according to their density, each liqueur being lighter than the one below it. Use a 2-ounce pony glass.
  (1) Begin with white anisette. Pour in ¼ ounce, taking care not to splash the sides of the glass.
  (2) Pour ¼ ounce dark crème de cacao over the rounded back of a spoon. This is most easily accomplished by placing the tip of the spoon, hollow side down, against the inside of the glass just above the anisette layer. Again, don't splash the sides of the glass.

  (3) In the same fashion, pour in this order ¼ ounce each: white crème de menthe, apricot liqueur, triple sec, green Chartreuse, and Cognac.
You can use a larger or smaller glass, and you can increase or decrease the amount of liqueur in each layer, but always keep the layers equal.

NEON TETRA
Follow technique for Seven-Layer Pousse-Café. Use a 1½-ounce shot glass and add—in order listed—¼ ounce each of the following: grenadine, anisette, blue curaçao, and 151-proof rum. Chug this one.

TORTUGA VERDE
Follow technique for Seven-Layer Pousse-Café, but pour into 2-ounce pony glass—in order listed—layers of: melon liqueur, yellow Chartreuse, Peter Heering, dark crème de cacao, and peppermint schnapps.

FIRE AND ICE
Pour ½ ounce cranberry liqueur into shot glass or pousse-café glass. Pour 1 ounce peppermint schnapps over back of a spoon so that it floats on top.

TRAFFIC LIGHT
Pour ⅓ ounce green crème de menthe into brandy snifter. Float as second layer ⅓ ounce crème de banane, and, on top, ⅓ ounce sloe gin.

'57 CHEVY WITH A WHITE LICENSE PLATE
In rocks glass filled with ice cubes, stir 1 ounce white crème de cacao and 1 ounce vodka.

AUNT JEMIMA

Pour 1 ounce brandy into snifter. Float as second layer 1 ounce dark crème de cacao and, on top, 1 ounce Bénédictine.

SIMPLE BRANDY AND LIQUEUR DRINKS

SAMBUCA CON MOSCA

Pour 1 ounce sambuca into liqueur glass. Float 3 roasted coffee beans on top. At your own risk: Light with a match before drinking.

PEARL

Pour Cointreau to almost fill rocks glass filled with ice cubes. Squeeze in juice of quarter of a lime.

BRANDY OLD-FASHIONED

Put 1 sugar cube in rocks glass with 1 teaspoonful water and 1 dash Angostura bitters. Muddle to dissolve sugar. Pour in 3 ounces brandy, twist lemon peel above glass to release drop of oil, and stir. Add ice cubes and garnish with the lemon peel.

BRANDY GUMP

Shake well with ice cubes ½ ounce brandy and ½ ounce lemon juice. Strain into cocktail glass. Dribble a couple of drops of grenadine on top.

BRANDY AND LIQUEUR DRINKS WITH APERITIFS AND OTHER SPIRITS

GODFATHER

Stir gently 2 ounces amaretto with 2 ounces Scotch whiskey. Pour over ice cubes in rocks glass.

GREEN LIZARD

Stir gently ½ ounce 151-proof rum and ½ ounce green Chartreuse in brandy snifter.

BETSY ROSS

Stir 1½ ounces brandy, 1½ ounces port, 2 dashes Angostura bitters and 2 drops blue curaçao with ice cubes in mixing glass. Strain into brandy snifter.

BETSY ROSSO

Stir with ice in mixing glass 1½ ounces each brandy and Rosso Antico aperitif, 3 dashes Angostura bitters, and 2 drops blue curaçao. Strain into brandy snifter.

WEEP NO MORE

Shake 1 ounce brandy, 1 ounce Dubonnet, and 1 ounce lime juice with ice cubes in cocktail shaker. Strain into cocktail glass.

THE FRENCH QUARTER

In rocks glass filled with ice cubes, stir 2 ounces Praline liqueur and 1 ounce bourbon.

HARVARD

Shake 1½ ounces sweet vermouth, 1½ ounces brandy, 1 teaspoonful lemon juice, 1 teaspoonful sugar syrup, and ice cubes in cocktail shaker. Pour into rocks glass half filled with ice cubes.

SUNBEAM

Pour into rocks glass filled with ice 1½

ounces Galliano and ½ ounce sweet vermouth. Stir.

ANTONIO
Shake 1 ounce brandy, 1 ounce gin, ½ ounce maraschino liqueur, and ½ ounce crème de cacao with ice cubes in cocktail shaker. Strain into cocktail glass.

BRANDY MANHATTAN
Shake 1½ ounces brandy, ¼ ounce sweet vermouth, and ice cubes in cocktail shaker. Strain into rocks glass filled with ice. Garnish with cherry.

DRY BRANDY MANHATTAN
Shake 1½ ounces brandy, ¼ ounce dry vermouth, and ice cubes in cocktail shaker. Strain into rocks glass filled with ice. Garnish with olive.

MOULIN ROUGE
Shake well 1½ ounces sloe gin, ½ ounce sweet vermouth, 2 dashes Angostura bitters, and ice cubes in cocktail shaker. Strain into rocks glass half filled with ice cubes.

AMERICAN BEAUTY
Pour into cocktail shaker ½ ounce brandy, ½ ounce dry vermouth, ½ ounce orange juice, 1½ ounces port; add 1 dash crème de menthe, 1 dash grenadine, and ice cubes. Shake, then strain into cocktail glass.

RUSSIAN MIST
Stir in mixing glass 1½ ounces Irish Mist and 1½ ounces vodka. Strain into cocktail glass; garnish with lime slice.

DEBUTANTE
Pour into mixing glass 2 ounces Praline liqueur and 1 ounce vodka. Add ice cubes; stir; strain into cocktail glass. Garnish with cherry.

ATOM BOMB
Shake 1½ ounces brandy with 1½ ounces Pernod in cocktail shaker with ice cubes. Strain into cocktail glass.

MIXED BRANDY AND LIQUEUR DRINKS

PAVAROTTI
Shake together with ice cubes 1½ ounces amaretto, ½ ounce brandy, and ½ ounce white crème de cacao in cocktail shaker. Place ice cubes in rocks glass and pour mixture over them.

FRIAR TUCK
Shake 2 ounces Frangelico, 2 ounces lemon juice, and 1 teaspoonful grenadine in cocktail shaker with ice cubes. Strain into rocks glass half filled with ice cubes. Garnish with orange slice.

SOUTHERN BELLE
Shake with ice cubes 1½ ounces brandy, ½ ounce Southern Comfort, and 2 dashes orange bitters. Strain into cocktail glass over a little crushed ice.

SARATOGA
Shake 2 ounces brandy, ½ ounce pineapple juice, 1 teaspoonful lemon juice, 2 dashes Angostura bitters, and 2 dashes maraschino liqueur in cocktail glass with ice cubes. Strain into sour glass half filled with cracked ice. You can substitute for the pineapple

juice 1 tablespoonful crushed pineapple or 1 teaspoonful pineapple liqueur.

LA JOLLA
Shake with ice cubes 1½ ounces brandy, ½ ounce crème de banane, 1 teaspoonful orange juice, and 2 teaspoonfuls lemon juice in cocktail shaker. Strain into cocktail glass.

THE INTREPID
Stir ½ ounce amaretto, ½ ounce Kahlúa, and ½ ounce Grand Marnier in mixing glass. Strain into cocktail glass filled with ice cubes.

B & B
Pour into brandy snifter ½ ounce each brandy and Bénédictine. Swirl gently.

FRENCH WALNUT
Pour 1 ounce each Nocello and Cognac into brandy snifter and swirl.

CHICAGO CRUSTA
Moisten rim of cocktail glass with brandy and sugar-frost it. Shake 1 ounce brandy, 1 ounce Cointreau, and 1 dash Angostura bitters in cocktail shaker with ice. Strain into prepared glass.

BRANDY CRUSTA
Moisten rim of cocktail glass with lemon juice and sugar-frost it. Cut rind off a lemon in one long spiral and place in glass. In cocktail shaker with ice, shake ¾ ounce triple sec, 1½ ounces brandy, 1 dash Angostura bitters, and 1 teaspoonful each maraschino liqueur and lemon juice. Strain into prepared glass.

HELL
Shake 1 ounce brandy and 1 ounce crème de menthe in cocktail shaker with ice cubes. Strain into cocktail glass, and sprinkle with cayenne pepper.

DIRTY MOTHER
Stir 1½ ounces brandy and ½ ounce Kahlúa in mixing glass. Strain into rocks glass filled with ice.

DIRTY WHITE MOTHER
Stir 1½ ounces brandy and ½ ounce Kahlúa with ice in mixing glass. Strain into rocks glass. Float cream on top.

SLOE BRANDY COCKTAIL
Shake ½ ounces brandy, ½ ounce sloe gin, the juice of a lemon wedge, and ice cubes in cocktail shaker. Strain into cocktail glass.

SEPTEMBER BRIDE
Stir in mixing glass with ice 1 ounce anisette and 1 ounce blackberry brandy. Strain into brandy snifter.

SPECTATOR
Shake with ice cubes ½ ounce cranberry liqueur, 1½ ounces brandy, 1 teaspoonful kümmel and 1 teaspoonful lemon juice. Strain into rocks glass half filled with ice cubes. Garnish with lemon peel.

THE ROYAL COUPLE
Shake 1 ounce brandy, 1 teaspoonful orange curaçao, 2 teaspoonfuls pineapple juice, 1 dash Angostura bitters, and ice cubes in cocktail shaker. Strain into cocktail glass. Garnish with twist of lemon.

MR. DICO'S COCKTAIL

Shake with ice cubes in cocktail shaker 1 ounce brandy and 1 ounce sambuca. Strain into cocktail glass. Twist lemon peel over drink to release a drop of oil; toss peel in.

HONEYMOON

Put 1 ounce each Bénédictine, calvados, and lemon juice in cocktail shaker with 3 dashes orange curaçao and ice cubes. Shake. Strain into cocktail glass.

GILBERT COCKTAIL

Shake with ice cubes 1½ ounces brandy, ½ ounce Cointreau, and ½ tablespoonful sambuca. Strain into cocktail glass.

GOOD AND PLENTY

In liqueur glass, stir ½ ounce ouzo with ½ ounce anisette.

TÍATINI

Pour ⅓ ounce Tía Maria, ⅓ ounce Grand Marnier, and ⅓ ounce gold tequila into shot glass. Stir gently.

PEPPERMINT ROMANA

Shake 1 ounce peppermint schnapps, 1 ounce vodka, and 1 teaspoonful sambuca in cocktail shaker with ice cubes. Put about an inch of crushed ice in cocktail glass; strain drink into glass.

APRÈS SKI

Shake 1 ounce peppermint schnapps, 1 ounce Kahlúa, and 1 ounce white crème de cacao with ice cubes in cocktail shaker. Pack about an inch of crushed ice in cocktail glass; strain drink into glass.

PEPPERMINT ANNETTE

Pour into cocktail shaker 1 ounce peppermint schnapps, ½ ounce sambuca, 1 ounce white crème de cacao, and ice cubes. Shake. Strain into cocktail glass containing 1½ ounces crushed ice. Twist lemon peel above glass to release drop of oil, then toss it in.

OFF-RAMP SHOOTER

Shake in cocktail shaker with ice cubes 1½ ounces Southern Comfort and ½ ounce peppermint schnapps. Add a floater of 151-proof rum.

ORANGE MINT COCKTAIL

Shake 1½ ounces Cointreau, 1 ounce peppermint schnapps, 1 teaspoonful brandy, and ice cubes in cocktail shaker. Strain into cocktail glass.

PEPPERMINT MOOSE

Shake well 1 ounce peppermint schnapps, ½ ounce crème de cacao, 2 ounces orange juice, ½ egg white, and crushed ice in cocktail shaker. Strain into wine glass.

THE SAUNA

Shake 1 ounce vodka, 1 ounce peppermint schnapps, ½ ounce cranberry juice, and 1 dash orange bitters in cocktail shaker with ice cubes. Pack about an inch of crushed ice into cocktail glass, then strain drink over it.

MINTINI

Stir in mixing glass 1 ounce peppermint schnapps and 1½ ounces gin with ice. Strain into cocktail glass; then squeeze in drop of oil from a lemon peel and drop it in.

VODKA MINTINI
In mixing glass, stir 1 ounce vodka, 1 ounce peppermint schnapps, and ice cubes. Strain into cocktail glass. Twist orange peel over drink to release a drop of oil, and toss it in as garnish.

POLAR BEAR
Shake 1 ounce banana liqueur, 1 ounce peppermint schnapps, 1 ounce light cream, and crushed ice in cocktail shaker. Strain into sour glass.

PEPPERMINT FRAPPÉ
Stir in mixing glass 2 ounces peppermint schnapps and 1 teaspoonful brandy. Shape crushed ice into mound in cocktail glass. Pour drink over mound.

FIRST FROST
Put an inch of crushed ice into cocktail glass. Shake 1½ ounces peppermint schnapps, ½ ounce golden rum, ½ ounce Cointreau, and ice cubes in cocktail shaker. Strain into prepared glass.

THE OTHER WOMAN
Shake vigorously with ice cubes 2 ounces Kahlúa and ½ ounce peppermint schnapps. Strain into cocktail glass half filled with ice cubes.

ALFONSO COCKTAIL
Pour 1½ ounces Cointreau, ½ ounce gin, 1 teaspoonful dry vermouth, 1 teaspoonful sweet vermouth, and 2 dashes Angostura bitters into cocktail shaker. Add ice cubes, shake well, and strain into cocktail glass.

CLASSIC
Moisten rim of cocktail glass with brandy and sugar-frost it. Shake 1½ ounces brandy, ½ ounce each lemon juice, orange curaçao, and maraschino liqueur in cocktail shaker with ice cubes. Strain into prepared glass.

APPLES AND ORANGES
Shake ½ ounce Calvados apple brandy, 1 ounce orange juice, 1½ ounces Cointreau, and ice cubes in cocktail shaker. Strain into cocktail glass.

CITY SLICKER
Shake 2 ounces cognac and 1 ounce triple sec in cocktail shaker with ice cubes. Strain into cocktail glass.

BETWEEN THE SHEETS
Shake 1 ounce Cointreau, 1 ounce brandy, 1 ounce golden rum, and the juice of a lemon wedge with ice cubes in cocktail shaker. Strain into cocktail glass. Garnish with the squeezed out lemon wedge, if desired.

BARBARELLA
Shake 2 ounces Cointreau and 1 ounce sambuca with ice cubes in cocktail shaker. Strain into rocks glass half filled with cracked ice.

COSTA DEL SOL
Shake in cocktail shaker 1 ounce apricot brandy, 2 ounces gin, 1 ounce

Grand Marnier, and ice cubes. Strain into rocks glass half filled with ice cubes.

ONE-AND-A-HALF COCKTAIL
Shake 1½ ounces each Cointreau, kirsch, and Punt e Mes in cocktail shaker with ice cubes. Strain into cocktail glass.

MIXED EMOTIONS
Shake with ice cubes 1½ ounces Grand Marnier, ½ ounce dry vermouth, 1½ ounces gin, and 2 dashes lemon juice. Strain into wine glass; garnish with lemon peel.

BLACK-EYED SUSAN
Shake 2 ounces Grand Marnier, ½ ounce white crème de menthe, and ½ ounce brandy with ice cubes in cocktail shaker. Strain into cocktail glass.

CHIQUITA COCKTAIL
Shake ½ ounce banana liqueur, 1 ounce Cointreau, ½ ounce light cream, and ice cubes in cocktail shaker. Fill sour glass to halfway mark with crushed ice. Strain mixture into glass.

CHIQUITA COCKTAIL II
Stir 1 ounce banana liqueur and 1 ounce brandy in mixing glass with ice cubes. Strain into cocktail glass.

BANANA FRAPPÉ
Shake 1 ounce banana liqueur, 1 ounce Kahlúa, and ice cubes in cocktail shaker. Strain into cocktail glass half filled with crushed ice, and top with club soda.

TOKYO DAWN
Shake 1½ ounces melon liqueur, ¾ ounce Cointreau, 2 ounces orange juice, and 2 teaspoonfuls lime juice in cocktail shaker with ice. Strain into rocks glass filled with ice cubes.

OFF-OFF BROADWAY
Shake in cocktail shaker 1½ ounces brandy, ½ ounce melon liqueur, 1 teaspoonful crème de noyaux, and ice cubes in cocktail shaker. Strain into cocktail glass one-quarter full of crushed ice.

MELON MADNESS
Shake 1 ounce melon liqueur, ½ ounce vodka, and 2 ounces light cream with ice cubes in cocktail shaker. Strain into cocktail glass.

APRICOT SOUR
Pour into cocktail shaker 1 ounce lemon juice and ½ teaspoonful superfine sugar. Stir to dissolve sugar. Add 2 ounces apricot brandy and ice cubes; shake. Strain into cocktail glass. Garnish with lemon peel.

INFERNO
Shake ½ ounce apricot liqueur, 1½ ounces brandy, and ½ ounce lemon juice in cocktail shaker with ice cubes. Strain into cocktail glass. Light match over drink, and drop lemon peel in next to flame.

FLAMINGO SOUR
Pour into blender with cracked ice 3 ounces apricot liqueur, 1 ounce gin, 1 ounce rum, and 1 ounce sweet-and-sour. Blend for 10 seconds, then pour into collins glass.

STONE SOUR
Shake 1 ounce apricot brandy, 1 ounce orange juice, and 1 ounce sweet-and-sour in cocktail shaker with ice cubes. Strain into wine glass.

PEACH VELVET
Pour 1½ ounces peach brandy, ½ ounce white crème de cacao, ½ ounce heavy cream, and cracked ice in blender. Blend at medium speed until smooth. Pour into rocks glass and garnish with one thin slice of fresh peach.

SCARLETT O'HARA
Peel and quarter one fresh peach; soak the quarters in 1 tablespoonful Cointreau at least 15 minutes. Toss peach, 1½ ounces Southern Comfort, and 1 ounce lemon juice into blender with crushed ice; blend at medium speed until almost smooth. Pour into rocks glass.

FUNNY VALENTINE
Moisten rim of cocktail glass with cherry liqueur and sugar-frost it. Then shake together 1½ ounces cognac, 1 ounce cherry liqueur, 3 dashes grenadine, and 1 tablespoonful lemon juice in cocktail shaker with ice cubes. Strain into cocktail glass; garnish with maraschino cherry, if desired.

SWEDISH LULLABY
Shake 1½ ounces Swedish Punsch liqueur with 1 ounce cherry liqueur and ½ ounce lemon juice. Strain into cocktail glass.

YULETIDE SOUR
In cocktail shaker, combine 1½ ounces cherry liqueur and 1 tablespoonful lemon juice, with ice cubes. Shake; strain into cocktail glass. Garnish with slice of lemon or lime—or both.

MY FAVORITE MARASCHINO
Shake 1½ ounces maraschino liqueur, 1½ ounces calvados, 2 dashes crème de noyaux, and ice cubes in cocktail shaker. Strain into cocktail glass. Garnish with maraschino cherry.

LIBERTY COCKTAIL
Shake 1½ ounces calvados, 1 ounce golden rum, ½ teaspoonful sugar syrup, and ice cubes in cocktail shaker. Strain into cocktail glass a quarter full of cracked ice.

STAR DAISY
Shake 1 ounce calvados, 1 ounce gin, ½ ounce grapefruit juice, 1 teaspoonful grenadine, and 3 dashes lemon juice in cocktail shaker with ice cubes. Strain into cocktail glass.

SPECIAL ROUGH
Shake 1½ ounces brandy, ½ ounce Calvados apple brandy, and 2 dashes Pernod in cocktail shaker with ice cubes. Strain into sour glass half filled with cracked ice.

STONE FENCE
Shake 2½ ounces applejack, 3 ounces apple cider, and 2 dashes Angostura bitters in cocktail shaker with ice cubes. Strain into rocks glass half filled with ice cubes.

DIKI-DIKI
Shake 1 ounce calvados, ½ ounce Swedish Punsch liqueur, and ½ ounce

grapefruit juice in cocktail shaker with ice cubes. Strain over a packed inch of crushed ice in cocktail glass.

DEAUVILLE
Shake with cracked ice ½ ounce each Calvados, Cointreau, brandy, and lemon juice. Strain into cocktail glass.

APPLE JACQUES
Shake well 1½ ounces Lillet, 1½ ounces Calvados apple brandy, and ice cubes in cocktail shaker. Strain into cocktail glass. Twist lemon peel over glass to release drop of oil, and toss it in as garnish.

APPLE SOUR
Combine 2 ounces calvados, 1 teaspoonful superfine sugar, and the juice from a lemon wedge in cocktail shaker. Add ice cubes; shake. Strain into cocktail glass, and garnish with the squeezed-out lemon wedge.

APPLEJACK RABBIT
Pour into cocktail shaker 1½ ounces calvados, ½ ounce orange juice, ½ ounce maple syrup, ½ ounce lemon juice, and ice cubes. Shake. Strain into rocks glass half filled with ice cubes.

APPLEJACK RABBIT II
Pour into cocktail shaker 1½ ounces calvados, 1 ounce Cointreau, and 1 teaspoonful lemon juice. Add ice cubes, shake. Strain into rocks glass filled with ice cubes.

JACK ROSE
Shake 1½ ounces applejack, 1 teaspoonful grenadine, and the juice from half a lime in cocktail shaker with ice cubes and strain into cocktail glass.

THE BLUEBERRY
Blend 1½ ounces blueberry liqueur, 1½ ounces heavy cream, and cracked ice in blender. Blend at medium speed until smooth. Pour into wine glass.

THE BLUEBERRY II
Stir in rocks glass 1½ ounces blueberry liqueur, 1½ ounces heavy cream, and ½ ounce amaretto. Add ice cubes.

PEAR SOUR
Cut one slice of fresh pear and sprinkle with lemon juice; set it aside. Pour into cocktail shaker 1½ ounces lemon juice, 2½ ounces pear liqueur, 1 tablespoonful superfine sugar, and ice cubes. Shake, then strain mixture into sour glass and garnish with the pear slice.

DARLING DOLL
Shake 2 ounces Southern Comfort, 1 ounce strawberry liqueur, 1 ounce vodka, 1 ounce orange juice, and 2 ounces sweet-and-sour in cocktail shaker with ice. Strain into wine glass half filled with cracked ice. Drizzle grenadine on top.

METAXA SUNRISE
Put into cocktail shaker 1 ounce Metaxa brandy, 1 ounce golden rum, ½ ounce strawberry liqueur, ½ ounce lemon juice, 1 teaspoonful sugar syrup, and ice cubes. Shake; strain into rocks glass half filled with cracked ice.

UNDER THE MISTLETOE
Put an inch of cracked ice into cocktail

glass; pour in 1 ounce each raspberry liqueur and white rum; stir. Drop in one green maraschino cherry.

BERRY BUBBLY

Stir in mixing glass 1½ ounces cognac, ½ ounce raspberry liqueur, and ice cubes. Strain into champagne glass, and top with champagne.

BRANDY AND LIQUEUR DRINKS WITH FRUIT JUICES

SOURBALL

Stir in mixing glass with ice cubes 1½ ounces apricot brandy, 2 ounces orange juice, and 1 ounce lemon juice. Strain into rocks glass. Add ice cubes to fill, and stir.

LUCY'S JUICE

Shake ½ ounce Grand Marnier, ½ ounce gin, 1 ounce brandy, and 2 ounces orange juice with ice cubes in cocktail shaker. Strain into cocktail glass.

ALABAMA K.O.

Pour into collins glass filled with cracked ice ½ ounce sloe gin, ½ ounce crème de banane, and orange juice almost to top. Stir well. Top off with Southern Comfort.

WALRUS

Into highball glass filled with ice cubes, pour 1 ounce Yukon Jack Canadian Liqueur and ½ ounce tequila. Top with orange juice, and stir. Garnish with wedge of orange.

BAL HARBOUR

Stir into highball glass filled with ice cubes 1 ounce Kahlúa and enough orange juice to fill glass.

OXBEND

In highball glass filled with ice cubes, stir 1 ounce Southern Comfort, ½ ounce tequila, 6 ounces orange juice, and a dash of grenadine.

NEGRIL LIGHTHOUSE

Shake 1½ ounces coconut liqueur, 1½ ounces pineapple juice, 1½ ounces golden rum, 1 teaspoonful light cream, and a dash of sweet-and-sour in cocktail shaker with ice cubes. Strain into highball glass half filled with crushed ice. Garnish with pineapple slice.

YUKON GRAPE

Pour into rocks glass half filled with ice cubes 1½ ounces Yukon Jack Canadian liqueur and 1 ounce grapefruit juice; stir.

BREAKFAST IN BED

Shake 1½ ounces brandy, 1½ ounces vodka, 3 ounces grapefruit juice, and ice cubes in cocktail shaker. Strain into wine glass.

SOUTHSIDE SOUR

Shake 1 ounce crème de cassis, ½ ounce Campari, 4 ounces grapefruit juice, and ice cubes in cocktail shaker. Strain into rocks glass half filled with ice cubes. Garnish with orange slice.

JACK'S CAPE CODDER

Shake 1½ ounces Yukon Jack Canadian Liqueur, 1½ ounces cranberry juice, juice from one lime wedge, and ice cubes in cocktail shaker. Strain into rocks glass half filled with ice cubes, and toss in the squeezed-out lime wedge. If preferred, 1 ounce cranberry liqueur can be substituted for the cranberry juice.

CLOISTER COOLER

Blend 1½ ounces Frangelico, 2 ounces pineapple juice, 2 dashes Angostura bitters, and 3 ounces crushed ice in blender at medium speed until smooth. Pour into rocks glass. Garnish with pineapple spear.

ON THE BEACH

Shake 1 ounce rum, 1 ounce crème de almond, 2 ounces orange juice, and 2 ounces pineapple juice. Pour into rocks glass half-filled with ice cubes. Garnish with orange slice.

BLACKBERRY PUNCH

Shake 1 ounce blackberry brandy, ½ ounce vodka, and 2 ounces pineapple juice in cocktail shaker with ice cubes. Strain into rocks glass half filled with ice cubes.

CHELSEA COOLER

Pour into brandy snifter 1½ ounces Grand Marnier, 2 ounces pineapple juice, 2 ounces 7-Up, and 2 ounces sweet-and-sour mix. Stir; garnish with lemon wedge.

HAWAIIAN SUNRISE

Shake ½ ounce rum, ½ ounce apricot liqueur, 1 ounce pineapple juice, 1 ounce cream, 1 ounce crushed pineapple (fresh or canned), and ice in cocktail shaker. Strain into wine glass.

BLOODY MUCHACHO

Shake with ice cubes 2 ounces Kahlúa and 6 ounces tomato juice. Strain into highball glass half filled with ice cubes. Garnish with celery stalk, if desired.

BOCCI BALL

Into highball glass half filled with crushed ice, pour 1½ ounces amaretto and orange juice almost to the top. Stir, then splash soda on top.

MALIBU SCREWDRIVER

Shake 2 ounces Malibu Coconut Rum Liqueur, ¾ ounce vodka, and 2 ounces orange juice with ice cubes in cocktail shaker. Strain into rocks glass half filled with ice cubes.

MELONADE

Shake with ice cubes ¾ ounce melon liqueur, ½ ounce each vodka and rum, and 4 ounces orange juice. Strain into rocks glass half filled with ice cubes.

DANISH ORANGEADE

In highball glass, stir 1½ ounces gin, ½ ounce Peter Heering, and 4 ounces orange juice. Add crushed ice to almost fill glass. Top with club soda.

STRAWBERRY PONYTAIL

Blend 1½ ounces crème de almond, 1 ounce grenadine, and 3 ounces fresh strawberries with ice until mixture is slushy. Pour into wine glass; top with a dollop of whipped cream.

WATERMELON ICE

With ½ cup chopped-up watermelon and ice, blend the following: 1½ ounces melon liqueur, 1 teaspoonful each lemon juice and lime juice, a pinch of sugar, and a dash of sweet-and sour. Pour into rocks glass.

BRANDY AND LIQUEUR DRINKS WITH CREAM AND EGG

GOLDEN VELVET
Shake 1½ ounces brandy, ½ ounce Cointreau, 1 egg yolk, and 1 teaspoonful grenadine into cocktail shaker with ice cubes. Strain into cocktail glass.

WHITE VELVET
Blend 1½ ounces sambuca, 1 egg white, and 1 teaspoonful lemon juice with cracked ice in blender at medium speed 15 seconds. Strain into cocktail glass.

MIXED BLESSINGS ON THE ROCKS
Shake 1½ ounces brandy, 1½ ounces orange curaçao, 1½ ounces white crème de cacao, and 1 egg white with ice cubes in cocktail shaker. Strain into rocks glass half filled with cracked ice.

WIDOW'S DREAM
In cocktail shaker, shake 2 ounces Bénédictine, 1 ounce heavy cream, and 1 egg along with cracked ice. Strain into cocktail glass.

RUSSIAN QUAALUDE
Shake ½ ounce Frangelico, 1 ounce vodka, and ¾ ounce cream in cocktail shaker with ice cubes. Strain into cocktail glass.

PEPPERMINT PATTY
Pour into rocks glass filled with ice ½ ounce peppermint schnapps, ½ ounce dark crème de cacao, and 1 ounce cream. Stir.

SAMBUCA CAFFÈ
Shake vigorously 1 ounce sambuca and 1 ounce heavy cream in cocktail shaker. Pour over ice cubes in cocktail glass. Dust top of drink with pinch of finely ground (or instant) espresso.

CUERNAVACA NIGHTCAP
Pour 3 ounces Kahlúa, 1½ ounces golden rum, and 2 ounces heavy cream into cocktail shaker; add ice cubes, and shake. Strain into rocks glass. Give drink one stir with stick of cinnamon, then use stick as garnish.

REINDEER MILK
Pour into blender 1½ ounces peppermint schnapps, 1 ounce bourbon whiskey, 8 ounces milk, 1 teaspoonful superfine sugar, and crushed ice. Blend at medium speed for 15 seconds, or until smooth. Pour into highball glass and garnish with sprig of mint.

'50S CADILLAC
Stir in rocks glass 1½ ounces Frangelico, 1½ ounces brandy, and about an ounce of light cream. Stir and taste; add more cream as needed to reach preferred consistency. Garnish with a lime wedge.

BERRYETTO
Combine in blender 2 ounces strawberries, 1 ounce amaretto, 2 ounces half-and-half cream, and crushed ice. Blend 15 seconds. Pour into wine glass.

PACIFIER
Shake well 1 ounce Bailey's Irish Cream, ½ ounce Irish whiskey, and 4 ounces cold coffee in cocktail shaker with ice cubes. Strain into brandy snifter.

SEPARATOR
Fill highball glass with ice. Pour in 1½ ounces brandy and ½ ounce Kahlúa. Top with cream, and stir well.

CREAM DREAM
Pour into cocktail shaker 1 ounce triple sec, 1 ounce vodka, 1 ounce orange juice, and 1½ ounces cream. Shake well with ice cubes, then strain into rocks glass filled with ice cubes.

SOMBRERO
Into rocks glass filled with ice, pour 1½ ounces Kahlúa and ½ ounce cream. Stir.

GOLDEN CADILLAC
Blend until smooth 1 ounce Galliano, 1 ounce crème de cacao, 1 ounce sweet cream, and 2 ounces crushed ice. Strain into wine glass.

GOLDEN DREAM
Shake 4 ounces orange juice, 1 ounce white crème de cacao, 1 ounce Galliano, and ½ ounce heavy cream with cracked ice in cocktail shaker. Strain into rocks glass.

GOLDEN LADY
Pour into cocktail shaker 1½ ounces triple sec, 1½ ounces brandy, ½ ounce crème de cacao, ½ ounce Galliano, 2 ounces light cream, and 2 ounces orange juice. Shake, then strain into highball glass half filled with cracked ice.

LADY LUCK
Pour into cocktail glass ½ ounce each blackberry brandy, amaretto, and sambuca; add 2 ounces light cream. Stir gently.

DUTCH VELVET
Shake ½ ounce chocolate mint liqueur, ½ ounce banana liqueur, 2 ounces cream, and cracked ice in cocktail shaker. Strain into wine glass. Shave sweet chocolate, preferably into curls, over top of drink.

BLUE CARNATION
Pour into cocktail shaker ½ ounce white crème de cacao, ½ ounce blue curaçao, 2 ounces cream, and cracked ice. Shake, then strain into wine glass.

PRETTY BABY
Pour into cocktail shaker ½ ounce amaretto, ½ ounce vodka, ½ ounce cream, and a drop of grenadine. Shake with ice. Strain into champagne glass.

BUTCHIE'S SPECIAL
Shake ½ ounce each vodka, Kahlúa, dark crème de cacao, white crème de cacao, and amaretto in cocktail shaker with a dash of heavy cream. Strain into rocks glass filled with ice. Garnish with cherry.

BRANDY MILK PUNCH
In highball glass, stir 2 ounces brandy, generous pinch of sugar, and 4 or 5 ounces cold milk. Add a few ice cubes, and dust top of drink with nutmeg.

RASPBERRY NOG

Shake 1½ ounces prepared eggnog, 1½ ounces raspberry liqueur, and ice cubes in cocktail shaker. Strain into wine glass half filled with crushed ice. Stir once or twice.

MOVER AND SHAKER

Shake well with ice cubes 1½ ounces melon liqueur, ¼ ounce blue curaçao, ¾ ounce pineapple juice, and ¾ ounce light cream. Strain into champagne glass.

MALIBU COLADA

Blend well with cracked ice 3 ounces Malibu Coconut Rum liqueur, 2 ounces pineapple juice, and 1 ounce milk. Pour into highball glass; garnish with slice of pineapple.

BAILEY'S B-52

Pour in cocktail shaker 1 ounce Bailey's Irish Cream, 1 ounce Kahlúa, and 1 ounce Grand Marnier. Shake well, and strain into rocks glass filled with ice.

VENETIAN BLIND

Stir in mixing glass 1 ounce Venetian Cream liqueur and 1 ounce rum. Pour into rocks glass filled with ice cubes.

FRANK AND TARA

Shake 1½ ounces Frangelica, 1½ ounces Bailey's Irish Cream, and ½ ounce brandy in cocktail shaker with ice cubes. Pour into rocks glass.

ORGASM

Shake in cocktail shaker ½ ounce white crème de cacao, ½ ounce amaretto, ½ ounce triple sec, ½ ounce cream, ½ ounce vodka. Add ice cubes. Strain into rocks glass.

FOXY

Shake ½ ounce amaretto, ½ ounce dark crème de cacao, 2 ounces cream, and ice cubes in cocktail shaker. Strain over ice cubes in rocks glass.

LA MACHINE

Shake 1 ounce Bénédictine, 1 ounce triple sec, and ½ ounce light cream in cocktail shaker with ice cubes. Strain over ice cubes in rocks glass.

VELVET HAMMER

Shake ½ ounce crème de cacao, ½ ounce triple sec, and 2 ounces cream with ice cubes in cocktail shaker. Strain into cocktail glass.

ZOOM

Pour 1 tablespoonful boiling water into cocktail shaker and stir in 1 teaspoonful honey; stir until honey is dissolved. Add ½ ounce light cream, 2½ ounces brandy, and ice cubes. Shake lightly, and strain into cocktail glass.

PINK SQUIRREL

Shake 1 ounce crème de noyaux, ½ ounce white crème de cacao, and 2 ounces cream with ice cubes in cocktail shaker. Strain into cocktail glass.

WHITE LADY

Shake ½ ounce vodka, ½ ounce white crème de cacao, and 2 ounces cream in cocktail shaker with ice cubes. Strain into cocktail glass.

WHITE HEART

Stir in mixing glass ½ ounce sambuca,

½ ounce white crème de cacao, and 2 ounces cream. Strain into cocktail glass.

BLACK LADY

Shake 2 ounces Grand Marnier, ½ ounce Kahlúa, and 1 tablespoonful brandy with ice cubes in cocktail shaker. Strain into cocktail glass.

BRANDY AND LIQUEUR DRINKS WITH ICE CREAM

HUMMER

Blend 1 ounce Kahlúa, 1 ounce golden rum, and 2 scoops vanilla ice cream in blender, briefly, at medium speed. Pour into large wine glass. Garnish with shaved bittersweet or sweet chocolate, as desired.

CHAMBORD HUMMER

Blend briefly at medium speed 1½ ounces brandy, 1 dash of Chambord Royale, and 2 scoops vanilla ice cream. Pour into large champagne or wine glass; top with raspberries.

CHOCOLATE BLACK RUSSIAN

Blend well 1 ounce Kahlúa, ½ ounce vodka, and 3 scoops chocolate ice cream. Pour into wine glass.

CHOCOLATE SNOWBALL

Place 1 large scoop chocolate ice cream in wine glass. In mixing glass stir together 1 ounce amaretto, 1 ounce crème de cacao, and ¼ ounce chocolate syrup. Pour over ice cream, and serve with a spoon.

GUILT TRIP

Blend until smooth 1½ ounces Bailey's Irish Cream, 1 ounce orange juice, ½ ounce Frangelico liqueur, and 2 scoops vanilla ice cream. Pour into brandy snifter.

MOCHA ALMOND FREEZE

Blend 1 ounce dark crème de cacao, 1 ounce amaretto, a scoop of vanilla ice cream, and cracked ice for about 15 seconds. Pour into rocks glass, and sprinkle nutmeg on top.

SWEET TOOTH NIGHTCAP

Blend until smooth 1 ounce Grand Marnier, ½ ounce Swiss chocolate liqueur, 1 ounce orange juice, and 2 scoops chocolate ice cream. Pour into highball glass; garnish with orange slice.

MELON HUMMER

Blend until smooth 1½ scoops vanilla ice cream, 1½ ounces milk, 1 ounce melon liqueur, and ½ ounce crème de noyaux. Pour into wine glass. Garnish with melon slice.

HARRY SLYBANGER

Blend until smooth 1 ounce vodka, 1 ounce Galliano, 6 ounces orange juice, and 2 scoops vanilla ice cream. Pour into highball glass.

DANISH SNOWBALL

Put 1 large scoop cherry-vanilla ice cream into wine glass. Stir in mixing glass 1½ ounces Peter Heering liqueur, ½ ounce peppermint schnapps, and 3 dark, sweet cherries. Pour mixture over ice cream in glass. Serve with a spoon.

EMERALD ISLE COOLER

Blend until smooth 3 scoops vanilla ice cream, 1 ounce green crème de menthe, and 1 ounce Irish whiskey. Pour into highball glass, top with club soda, and stir again—gently—to mix.

CARAMEL NUT

Blend until smooth 1 ounce crème de cacao, 1 ounce caramel liqueur, and two scoops vanilla ice cream. Pour into wine glass. Garnish with chopped nuts.

CHOCOLATIER

Blend well 1 ounce golden rum, 1 ounce crème de cacao, and 3 scoops chocolate ice cream. Pour into wine glass and shave sweet chocolate over top.

THE MACAROON

Blend until smooth 1 ounce golden rum, 1 ounce CocoRibe liqueur, a small scoop of vanilla ice cream, and 1 teaspoonful heavy cream. Pour into wine glass and sprinkle toasted shredded coconut on top.

STRAWBERRY SHORTCAKE

Blend 2 scoops vanilla ice cream, 1 ounce amaretto, ½ ounce crème de cacao, and 6 fresh strawberries until very smooth. Pour into wine glass. Garnish with one more sliced strawberry.

SILVER LINING

Blend well 1 ounce amaretto, ½ ounce dark crème de cacao, 1 ounce chocolate syrup, and a small scoop vanilla ice cream. Pour into wine glass.

THE BIRTHDAY PARTY

Blend at medium speed 1½ ounces banana liqueur, half a fresh banana, and 3 scoops vanilla ice cream. Pour into large wine glass or brandy snifter, and top with sliced banana.

LADIES' AUXILIARY SUNDAE

Blend 2 scoops vanilla ice cream, 1½ ounces amaretto, and 1 ounce Kahlúa at medium speed for 15 seconds. Pour into wine glass.

FROZEN TUMBLEWEED

Put into blender a scoop of vanilla ice cream, 1 ounce dark crème de cacao, ½ ounce Kahlúa, and a little cracked ice. Blend at medium speed for 15 seconds. Pour into highball glass, and top with whipped cream and chocolate shavings.

BIT-O-HONEY

Blend 1½ ounces Bailey's Irish Cream, ½ ounce white crème de cacao, and 2 scoops vanilla ice cream in blender at medium speed until smooth. Pour into wine glass.

PIÑA COLADA FREEZE

Blend until smooth 1½ ounces rum, 1 ounce Coco Lopez Piña Colada, 2 scoops vanilla ice cream, and a dash of grenadine. Pour into brandy snifter; garnish with a pineapple spear.

KENNEBUNKPORT SNOWBALL

Place 2 scoops vanilla ice cream in brandy snifter. In mixing glass, stir 1½ ounces blueberry liqueur, 1 ounce brandy, and a few blueberries. Pour over ice cream, and serve with a spoon.

BRANDY ICE

Blend until smooth 1½ ounces brandy, ½ ounce crème de cacao, 2 scoops French vanilla ice cream, and a little shaved ice. Pour into large brandy snifter and garnish with shaved sweet chocolate.

CHAMBOOGIE MARIA

Blend 1 ounce Tía Maria and 1 ounce Chambord Royale liqueur with 1½ scoops vanilla ice cream at medium speed for 15 seconds. Pour into rocks glass, and drizzle a bit more Chambord on top.

HOT BRANDY AND LIQUEUR DRINKS

MEXICAN COFFEE

Pour into a coffee cup ½ ounce tequila and ½ ounce Galliano, then fill up with coffee. Stir with a cinnamon stick and top with whipped cream. Sprinkle with powdered cinnamon, if desired.

APPLE GROG

Heat in saucepan 1½ ounces applejack, ½ ounce 151-proof rum, 1 tablespoonful brown sugar, and 4 ounces water. Stir in 2 whole allspice. Pour into mug. Twist 1 lemon peel above drink to release a drop of oil, then drop it in. Float rum on top.

COGNAC TODDY

Pour hot coffee until mug is just less than full. Stir in 1 ounce cognac and 3 whole cloves. Garnish with a thin, flat slice of lemon and a cinnamon stick.

KOKI COFFEE

Pour into coffee cup 1½ ounces each brandy, Kahlúa, and dark crème de cacao. Fill cup with coffee. Stir.

CAFÉ AMARETTO

Put into coffee cup a pinch of brown sugar and 1½ ounces Chocolate Amaretto liqueur. Pour in hot espresso until cup is three-quarters full; stir. Top with whipped cream, shaved sweet chocolate, and a dusting of crushed toasted almonds.

CAFÉ COINTREAU

Put into coffee cup a teaspoonful each of grated lemon peel and honey. Fill cup to three quarters with hot espresso. Pour in 1½ ounces Cointreau. Stir with—and leave in as garnish—a cinnamon stick. Top with whipped cream.

CAFÉ ZURICH

Pour into coffee cup 1½ ounces each cognac and anisette; add ½ ounce amaretto and fill with hot coffee to three-quarter mark. Float teaspoonful of honey on top. Stir with licorice stick. Top with whipped cream.

STEAMY PEPPERMINT PATTY

Pour into coffee cup 1½ ounces peppermint schnapps, ½ ounce crème de cacao, and 1 teaspoonful crème de menthe. Fill cup with hot chocolate.

CAFE MARNIER

Put 1 teaspoonful sugar and 1 ounce Crème de Grand Marnier into coffee cup. Add strong coffee or espresso until cup is three-quarters full. Stir. Top with whipped cream.

CAPPUCCINO SETTOBELLO

Pour into coffee cup 1 teaspoonful chocolate powder and ⅓ ounce each Galliano, anisette, and brandy. Stir, and set cup aside. Heat ½ cup milk until steamy, and pour into cocktail shaker. Shake vigorously, then pour the frothy milk into the cup. (This drink can be made with a cappuccino machine, too.)

SAMBUCA COFFEE

Add 1½ ounces sambuca to hot espresso. Stir with licorice stick.

CAPPUCCINO MOCHA

Half fill cup with hot espresso. Add 1½ ounces each coffee liqueur and crème de cacao. Stir. Top with whipped cream.

MONK'S COFFEE

Half fill coffee cup with hot espresso. Add 1½ ounces Frangelico. Top with whipped cream, and stir with cinnamon stick.

NAPOLEON'S BREAKFAST

Pour 1½ ounces Mandarine Napoleon to 1 cup English Breakfast tea. Toss in orange twist.

CAFÉ COGNAC

Pour ½ ounce cognac into a cup of espresso and set aside. Then tip 1 teaspoonful sugar into a tablespoon or dessert spoon and fill it up with cognac. Hold filled spoon carefully over a candle flame to heat mixture, then, using a long kitchen match, ignite it and float the blazing mixture on top of the coffee. Stir until the flame subsides.

SNOWBERRY

Heat in saucepan, but *do not allow to boil,* 1 ounce each vodka and strawberry liqueur, ½ ounce sugar syrup, 1 ounce lemon juice, and 5 ounces water. Pour heated mixture into large, warm mug. Drop in strawberry.

DEMITASSE FRAMBOISE

Pour into saucepan 1 ounce raspberry liqueur, ½ ounce brandy, ½ ounce water, a tablespoonful raspberry preserves, and a few dashes lemon juice. Heat, but *don't boil;* stir until jelly dissolves. Pour into demitasse cup. Float lemon peel on top.

BLUEBERRY DEMITASSE

Follow recipe for Demitasse Framboise, but substitute blueberry liqueur for the raspberry liqueur and blueberry preserves for the raspberry preserves.

CARUMBA

Frost rim of brandy glass with sugar. Pour in ½ ounce brandy and ignite. When sugar is caramelized, add ½ ounce Kahlúa and ¾ ounce each light and dark rum. Fill glass with hot coffee; add a dash of Bailey's Irish Cream. Top with whipped cream.

CAFÉ THÉÂTRE

Pour into coffee cup ½ ounce each Bailey's Irish Cream and white crème de cacao. Add enough hot coffee to almost fill glass, then add a dash each of amaretto and dark crème de cacao. Top with whipped cream. Serve with a cinnamon stick.

HIGHLAND COFFEE

Pour 1½ ounces Drambuie into coffee

cup, then fill with hot espresso. Float a little honey on top to sweeten to taste.

POLISH HOLIDAY TEA

Pour into saucepan 1 ounce plum brandy, 1 ounce white crème de menthe, 5 ounces hot dark tea, 1 teaspoonful sugar, and ½ ounce heavy cream. Heat until steamy, but *do not allow to boil.* Pour into large tea cup or coffee cup. Stir and garnish with cinnamon stick; sprinkle coriander on top.

BRANDY AND LIQUEUR HIGHBALLS

SLEEPYHEAD

Pour 3 ounces brandy into rocks glass half filled with ice cubes. Twist orange peel above drink to release drop of oil. Top with ginger ale.

APRICOT COOLER

Shake with ice cubes in cocktail shaker 1½ ounces apricot brandy, ½ ounce lemon juice, and 2 dashes grenadine. Strain into highball glass half filled with cracked ice. Top with club soda.

PETER'S CHERRY COLA

Fill highball glass with ice cubes. Pour in 1 ounce Peter Heering liqueur and 3 or 4 ounces cola. Stir gently. Garnish with lime wedge.

STIRRUP CUP

Shake 1½ ounces Southern Comfort, 1 ounce cranberry liqueur, and 3 ounces grapefruit juice in cocktail shaker with ice. Strain into highball glass containing 2 or 3 ice cubes. Top with club soda, and stir gently.

TALL ONE
WITH ORANGE

Fill highball glass with cracked ice and pour in 1½ ounces curaçao. Stir well. Top with tonic water; garnish with thin orange slice.

TALL ONE
WITH LIME

Fill highball glass with cracked ice and pour in 1½ ounces melon liqueur. Stir well. Top with club soda; garnish with lime wedge.

SPANISH SODA

Stir in highball glass half filled with ice cubes 1½ ounces brandy, 1 ounce dry Sherry, and 3 dashes curaçao. Fill with tonic water.

COCONUT COLA

Pour 1½ ounces Malibu Rum Liqueur into highball glass filled with cracked ice. Top glass with cola; garnish with lime wedge.

PIMM'S CUP AND SODA

Shake 2 ounces Pimm's Cup No. 1 with 4 ounces club soda in cocktail shaker with ice cubes. Strain into highball glass half filled with ice cubes. Garnish with cucumber slice or lime wedge.

AMARETTO SODA

Shake 1 ounce amaretto and 1 ounce gin with ice cubes in cocktail shaker. Strain into highball glass half filled with ice cubes. Top with club soda. Garnish with lemon wedge.

CHAMBORD ROYALE SPRITZER
Pour 1½ ounces Chambord Royale liqueur into wine glass. Add splash of champagne, and top with club soda. Twist lemon peel over drink to release drop of oil; toss peel in.

SANTA CLARA COOLER
Pour into highball glass filled with cracked ice 1½ ounces Santa Clara liqueur. Top with cola and stir gently.

NUTTY SPRITZER
Pour 1½ ounces Nocello liqueur over ice cubes in highball glass. Fill to top with club soda and stir gently.

WHITE CLOUD
Pour 1½ ounces sambuca over ice cubes in highball glass. Fill to top with club soda. Stir gently with a stick of licorice, if desired, or a spoon.

BREWS, WATERS AND MIXERS

1

BEER AND ALE

So far as history can tell us, as long as man has been drinking, he's been drinking beer. Not only does the origin of beer date back to the dawn of time but also the beverage has been produced and enjoyed in some form in nearly every major culture in the world. Six thousand years before Christ, Babylonian priests were brewing a special beer for their kings. There was beer in ancient Africa, China, and pre-Columbian America. The Jews took the art of beer-making with them to Israel when they freed themselves from bondage in Egypt. The Romans, who learned about beer from the Greeks, found the Britons merrily quaffing ale when they arrived with Caesar to conquer the island. So, all you beer-drinkers out there, hold your heads high, walk tall, and be proud of your heritage!

The Pilgrims drank beer aboard the *Mayflower*, and both English and Dutch colonists brought a taste for beer and brewing techniques with them from the Old World. In time,

Americans outdistanced their European forebears in beer production and consumption. Today the land of the free and the brave is the world's number one beer producer: America makes and consumes more than twice as much beer as any other country.

"But is it any good?" the German beer-drinker may snort, and "Is it really beer?" the British ale-quaffer may sniff. Before we get into the question of quality, let's get straight on some definitions. The word *beer* has come to be a generic term for any potable beverage brewed and fermented from malted barley and other starchy grains and flavored with hops; there are a number of different styles of brew that come together under the beer banner. When Americans say *beer*, they mean *lager:* a bright, clear, sparkling, light-bodied beer invented by the Germans in the 1840s. *Lager* in German means "to store": Lagers are set aside for aging, the minimum period being four weeks but several months being better, during which time a slow second fermentation takes place at low temperatures. Most of our lagers are light in color, but there is also dark lager, the color deriving from the addition of roasted barley. Lager's alcoholic content is between 3.0 percent and 3.8 percent, by weight. The term *pilsner* refers to a particularly light-bodied, pale, dry, and mellow style of lager with high carbonation; it derives from the town of Pilsen in Bohemia (modern-day Czechoslovakia). Excellent beer has been brewed in Pilsen since 1292, and Pilsner Urquell today sets the world standard for lagers. Other styles of lager include Munich dark—rich brown in color and malty tasting; Munich light and Dortmunder—both pale, and a bit heavier in taste than pilsners; and Vienna-style—amber in color, strong, and very malty to the taste. Bock beer is a heavy, dark lager with a somewhat sweetish malt flavor; by tradition, it is made in the winter for consumption in the spring.

Ale is an aromatic malt—or malt- and cereal-brew that has a fuller body and more bitter, hoppy flavor than lager beer, along with higher alcoholic content (4 to 5 percent). Stout is a very dark ale with a strong flavor of malt and a sweetish taste. Porter is yet another type of ale; brewed like stout, it has a rich and heavy foam and a less strong flavor.

And then there is light beer, a recent invention, which is essentially lager brewed with a special enzyme that converts a higher portion of the carbohydrates to alcohol, thus lowering the calorie content. Water is added to re-

duce its alcohol level and, alas, its taste.

THE BREWING PROCESS

The process for making beer is really quite simple: You take your malted barley, grind it up, add hot water, and cook it in the mash tub. For many lagers, other high-starch grains—primarily corn and rice—are boiled and then added to the mash. Next, after cooking for the appropriate time and at the appropriate temperature, you filter the mash into the brew kettle, add hops, and boil it. Hops are dried ripe flowers of the hop vine; they contribute flavor, aroma, and the requisite bitterness to the brew. Remove the hops and you're ready to ferment.

Fermentation is accomplished by yeast. Brewers put great store in their specially pedigreed secret strains of the little fungi, which are crucial in determining a beer's taste and must be maintained from one yeast generation to the next in pure and unchanging cultures. Yeasts come in two basic varieties—those that sink to the bottom and those that rise to the top during fermentation—and this decides a beer's style. All lagers are bottom-fermented: The fermentation occurs at relatively low temperatures (45 to 55 degrees F) and may go on for as long as 14 days (5 to 8 is more common in the United States). The more flavorful ales (including porter and stout) are top-fermented at higher temperatures and for shorter periods than lagers.

In both types, once fermentation has taken place the beer is stored in aging tanks, where the yeast and other solids precipitate out and a slow secondary fermentation takes place. In most modern American beer making, the gas released during fermentation is saved and reinjected into the beer at the end of the aging period.

Then comes one more filtration and—for most beers that will be packaged in cans and bottles—pasteurization, which goes on at a temperature of 140 degrees F for 15 minutes. Some brewers (Coors is one) use ultrafine filtration or a sterile technique instead of pasteurization, which they feel harms the hops flavor of the beer.

STORING AND DRINKING

On second thought, maybe the simple part is not the *making* of beer but the *drinking*. Yet even here there are certain refinements. The ideal temperature for lager is 45 degrees F; 50 degrees, for ale; and 55 degrees, for English ale or Irish stout. The average American refrigerator is kept at between 32 degrees and 40 degrees; so leave your beer—especially the ales—out for ten or fifteen minutes before drinking. You want to store your beer bottles upright, away from the light, and in a part of the refrigerator where they won't be jostled around too much. Don't wash beer steins or glasses with soap: It leaves a residue that will break down CO_2 and thus destroy the foam. Use nonsoapy detergent or baking soda and rinse well. If you want a full collar of foam, pour beer straight into the center of the untilted glass. The longer you keep

glass tilted at a 45-degree angle, the smaller the resulting head.

If you treat your beer well, it will treat you well, for beer is nutritionally balanced and healthful. An average 12-ounce bottle contains 150 calories (a third less for light beers), two-thirds of which comes from the alcohol; 4 to 5 percent is carbohydrate, 0.2 to 0.4 percent is protein, and less than 0.02 percent is salt—so it poses no threat even for low-sodium diets. Runners in training drink beer as part of the "carbo-loading" process, and it is recommended for nursing mothers: The alcohol gently relaxes them, so that their milk flows more easily, and it replenishes outgoing body fluids.

CHOICE BREWS

Now, of the thousands of beers available worldwide, which are really special, worth seeking out, traveling great distances for, telling your friends about? The answer, naturally, is that it's a matter of taste. Even taste has its statistical side, however, and this bears looking into when setting up criteria.

The fact is, American beer drinkers have divided into two camps in recent years: There are those who want light—light body, light taste, light color, and light calorie count; and those who want, for lack of a better word, character—fuller body, bracing distinctiveness of taste not masked by overcarbonation, marked differences from brand to brand, and higher alcohol content. As the large domestic brewers respond to the demands of the light-lovers by reducing hop and malt content for milder and blander products, the character-seekers have been turning in greater numbers to imported beers. But a new alternative has appeared on the domestic beer scene. The past few years have seen the resurgence of the regional brewery and the birth of the so-called *microbrewery*, usually a one-family operation that produces a small quantity (less than 10,000 barrels per year) of very fine—and flavorful—beer for local consumption. Outfits like The River City Brewing Company in Sacramento, California, the Boulder Brewing Company in Longmont, Colorado, and the Old New York Beer Company in New York City's Greenwich Village are brewing lagers, ales, stouts, and porters with all the character of the zestiest foreign imports. Their products are usually available only in a few bars and retail outlets near the brewery; but this ensures high quality and freshness. A frequent complaint from beer drinkers familiar with foreign beers on their home grounds is that imported beers taste different in the U.S.A. This may be either because they *are* different, brewed especially for the American market, or because they are too old. Beer has a limited shelf life and becomes stale if allowed to sit around too long.

So we took all these factors into account and came up with the names that follow as the pick of the crop in domestic, light, and imported beers. In the domestic section, the focus is on regional and microbrewery beers. We're not including the big national brands—Budweiser, Miller, Schlitz, Schmidt's, Ballantine, Michelob,

Pabst—because chances are you already know everything you need to about what they're like.

DOMESTIC

REGIONAL BEERS

Anchor Steam Beer: One of the oldest, and finest, of the regional beers. Strong malt flavor, creamy head, a bit sweet. Brewed in San Francisco, now available in limited quantities elsewhere, including East Coast.

Augsburger Old World Bavarian Style: A full-bodied and rich-tasting European style beer. Brewed in Wisconsin, available almost nationwide.

Boulder Beer—Bitter, Porter, and **Stout:** A return to traditional British brewing methods and tastes in the mountains of Colorado. Robust and strong-tasting; highly recommended. The Boulder Brewing Company is one of the few microbreweries not situated on the East Coast or West Coast.

Cold Spring Beer: Sold mostly in Minnesota, Wisconsin, Iowa, Illinois, and the Dakotas, occasionally available in the Northeast. A nice, clean, balanced, and surprisingly fragrant beer, on the sweetish side. Also available: a pricier **Cold Spring Export.**

Coors: No longer technically a regional beer, since it's available nationwide, Coors is *the* beer of the American West. Very light, highly refreshing, clean and easy to drink. Coors tends to taste better in the West because it's fresher and closer to its source in Golden, Colorado.

DeBakker Pale Ale: From Novato,

California (north of San Francisco). A pale, well-malted and -hopped ale with a beautifully balanced taste and big head. No additives or preservatives; unpasteurized. The preferred brand of many in the know. Look for it.

Genessee Beer: Available in upstate New York, Pennsylvania, New Jersey, and New England. More body and malt flavor than most big-selling beers.

Grant Scottish Ale: The pride and joy of the Yakima Brewing and Malting Company, a microbrewery in Yakima, Washington. This ale has all the zest of real Scottish ale, hoppy and full-bodied.

Jax Beer: A New Orleans tradition. Yellow in color, mild and highly carbonated; refreshing, although no overwhelming flavor distinction.

Koehler Beer: Available on tap within a 200-mile radius of Erie, Pennsylvania, where it's brewed, and in bottles even farther away. Tangy flavor, unlike that of most American beers. Worth looking for.

Leinenkugel's Beer: Tastes a whole lot better than its name sounds: light, pale, and flavorful. Sold in Minnesota, Michigan, and Wisconsin.

Lone Star Beer: From—where else?—the Lone Star State. On the dry side, with a nice malt flavor.

McSorley's Cream Ale: A traditional, big, zesty ale, one of the finest in the country.

National Bohemian Light Beer: The "light" refers to the color, not the calorie count. A good and balanced all-around beer made in Baltimore, flavored with imported hops.

New Albion Stout, Ale, and **Porter:** From the oldest of the microbrewers, in Sonoma, California; traditional British beers. Nice brews, but without quite the polish and balance of the Boulder beers.

New Amsterdam Amber Beer: A recent and excellent addition to the microbrewed category offered by New York City's own Old New York Beer Company and available throughout that metropolitan area and suburbs. Heavily hopped, full-bodied, and aromatic.

Newman's Pale Ale: The first-established East Coast microbrewery makes a rich creamy ale of medium density, halfway between British pale ale and American cream ale.

Olympia Beer: Divides the Western beer market with Coors. Very light and clean, it has an extremely pale color. Great with chili!

Pickett's Premium Beer: Brewed in Iowa's sole commercial brewery and available there and in parts of Wisconsin and Illinois. Lightness and balance are keynotes, with a hint of sweetness in aftertaste.

Point Special Beer: Produced in Wisconsin's smallest brewery and named by many as their favorite in taste tests, this one is light, smooth, and European in style. Best when bought closest to brewery in Stevens Point.

Prior Double Light Beer: A flavorful yet light-bodied beer with low carbonation and price, sold in New York, New Jersey, and Pennsylvania. Also available: **Prior Double Dark Beer.**

Rainier Beer: Well-known on the West Coast, especially in Seattle, where it's brewed for lightness. Trace of nutty flavor.

Reading Light Premium Beer: Not a low-cal, but a light-bodied beer with good clean taste and a suggestion of walnuts. Available in the Northeast.

Real Ale: Made by the Real Ale Brewing Company, a microbrewery on the second floor of a clock tower in Chelsea, Michigan. This is the real thing, made with imported hops.

Redhook Ale: From a microbrewery of the same name in Seattle. May soon be marketed in Alaska.

River City Gold: One of the finest of the microbrewery beers, made by a husband-and-wife operation in Sacramento, California. German-style lager with a beautiful tawny color. Also available: **River City Dark.**

Rolling Rock Premium Beer: Pale, pleasing, light malt aroma, almost grassy flavor, trace of hops. Good value, wide availability on East Coast.

Royal Amber: A fine, balanced beer distributed in Kentucky and Ohio. Good hop taste without being overly bitter; deep gold color; light carbonation; slightly nutty flavor. Try it.

Schaefer Beer: Has a big following in New York City, especially among sports fans. Carefully brewed for even taste.

Shiner Premium Beer: You'll have to go to Texas to find this big, malty, highly carbonated brew, but it's got a taste you'll remember.

Stroh Bohemian Style Beer: Very popular on Eastern and Midwestern campuses and sold also in the Carolinas, Stroh is brewed in Detroit. Good beery taste, with pronounced malt and hop flavor.

Sierra Nevada Pale Ale, Porter, and **Stout:** From a California microbrewer. The Pale Ale took first prize at the 1983 Great American Beer Festival in Boulder, Colorado, and the Porter took second. Sold throughout California; expanding into Oregon and soon into Washington state.

Thousand Oaks Premium Lager: Comes from a microbrewer in Berkeley, California. Highly unusual, intense taste.

Tuborg: The first European brand-name beer to be produced in the U.S.A., Tuborg is a Danish product, and the American version follows the original formula. Clean and well-balanced, with a slightly sweet flavor. Some say the Western Tuborg, brewed in Tacoma, Washington, is a bit lighter than the Tuborg brewed in Baltimore, Maryland, and in Michigan.

Walter's: A fine, light-tasting Wisconsin beer, dry without too much effervescence.

Yuengling Premium Beer: One of the more pleasant-tasting American beers: clean, fresh, a touch sweet, but balanced with plenty of character and zest. Strong in eastern Pennsylvania, but turns up occasionally in Maryland, New Jersey, and the District of Columbia.

LIGHT BEERS

People don't drink light beer for its flavor; they drink it because it doesn't make you fat as readily as regular beer do. Some brands are better than others; but by and large light beer lacks distinctiveness. (Calorie content noted here is for 12-ounce bottle or can.)

Amstel Light (95 calories): Imported from Holland. Often rated the best of the lights; certainly has a more assertive taste than most.

Budweiser Light Beer (108 calories): Pretty decent, as light beers go.

Coors Light (110 calories): Goes down easy, but you may not know you're drinking beer.

Erie Light Lager Beer (96 calories): Has a little more *umph* than the run-of-the-mill light beer.

Kalback (110 calories): Imported from Sweden. Manages a worthy denseness and briskness.

Michelob Light (134 calories): Although it's a bit higher in calories than other lights, it's also a bit more satisfying in taste.

Miller's Lite (96 calories): One of the original low-calorie beers and still one of the more respectable offerings.

Olympia Gold (70 calories): Better in the West.

Stroh Light (115 calories): One of the winners in the light category; stands up for itself.

Utica Club Light Beer (96 calories): Has a little more flavor and aroma than the others. Not bad.

FOREIGN BEERS

Here is a round-up, by country, of some of the better foreign beers available in the United States. A growing number of specialty food stores, delis, and small supermarkets are stocking more and more of these labels.

AUSTRALIA

Foster's Lager: Light, fresh, and clean-tasting lager from the largest brewer in the Southern Hemisphere.

Thomas Cooper and Sons Real Ale: Big, rich, creamy head, cloudy gold color, and yeasty flavor. Grab it: This is the real thing in ale. Also look for **Cooper Best Extra Stout** and **Cooper's Real Ale.**

Swan Premium Lager: A good, all-around, balanced lager with a fresh and distinctive aroma.

Toohey's Lager Beer: The traditional favorite of Sydney's Roman Catholic population. Yellow-gold and dry tasting.

Tooth Sheaf Stout: Try it if you like the taste of this dark, rich type of ale.

West End XXX Beer Export: A strong-tasting and aromatic brew, lovely gold tone.

AUSTRIA

Gosser Export Beer: One of the most commonly seen Austrian labels. Highly hopped; 5 percent alcohol.

Ottakringer Bock Malt Liquor: Has high alcohol content and a very big taste to match.

Puntigam Export Beer: Another Austrian label with fairly wide American distribution. On the sour side.

BELGIUM

Belgium makes some of the most unusual, and certainly the most varied, beers in Europe. Some have almost a winey tang, many are quite high in alcohol, and a few of the very best are brewed in monasteries.

Orval: A big, sharp-flavored ale made by Cistercian monks.

Rodenbach Belgium Beer: One of the reddish-colored beers Belgium is known for. Sharp, fruity flavor that may startle at first sip. Many find it superb once they've gotten used to it.

Stella Artois Light Lager: This label is seen all over Europe. A good lager-style brew, but less distinctive than other Belgian offerings.

Westmalle "Triple" Abbey Trappist Beer: One of the finest monastery brews: pale, full-flavored, nicely balanced and 8-to-9 percent alcohol.

St. Sixtus Belgium Abbey Ale: The beer from this monastery is dark brown, zesty, and quite potent—in fact, at about 12 percent, it may be the strongest beer brewed in Belgium.

CANADA

Canadian beer is the import of choice for more and more Americans. Three big breweries—Carling O'Keefe, Molson, and Labatt—dominate in sales; they produce some excellent lagers and ales.

Carling Black Horse Ale: One of the fine Canadian ales; soft, smooth and balanced.

Labatt's 50 Ale: Lighter than most members of the ale family, goes down easy.

Labatt's Crystal Lager Beer: Nice, light, and creamy lager. A Labatt label to look for.

Labatt's Pilsener Blue: Superb beer, light and refreshing.

Molson's Canadian Lager Beer: Highly popular in the U.S.A., and deserves to be. A bit sweeter than most lagers.

Molson Ale (in Canada called **Molson Export**): A truly fine and distinctive Canadian ale; better than Molson Golden Ale.

Moosehead Canadian Beer: A popular Canadian offering, stacks up well against Labatt and Molson.

O'Keefe Ale: A good introduction to the taste of ale: malty and just a touch sweet.

Yukon Gold Premium Lager Beer: Look for this excellent, strong, and unusually flavorful brew, just becoming available in the U.S.A.

CHINA

Tsing-Tao: Slightly sour, but refreshing with highly spiced food.

CZECHOSLOVAKIA

Pilsner Urquell: The original beer from Pilsen: big, full taste and body, sharp and dry, with superb balance. This is beer at its best. Grab it when you see it.

DENMARK

Carlsberg Royal Lager Beer: A well-known label and a fine, light, nicely hopped beer.

Carlsberg Elephant Malt Liquor: Big, strong beer, as its name suggests; highly aromatic, and more alcoholic than most.

FRANCE

Kronenbourg 1664 Imported Beer: Full-bodied; medium gold in color; and growing more popular over here.

Lutèce Bière de Paris: Lives up to its classy name. Expensive but worth it. As delicate and complex as beer gets.

George Killian's Bière Rousse: An excellent red ale.

"33" Export Beer: A lot of American soldiers grew to like this beer in Vietnam. Good flavor, well-balanced, and refreshing.

GERMANY

Germany is to beer what France is to wine. In Germany itself, the variety and quality of the beers is truly impressive. The German beer imported to this country ranges from good to superb, but can't measure up to the product at home, where it is served in a towering tankard and fresh from the brewery.

Augustiner Bräu Munich Export Light Beer: Superb German beer, very light in color, taste, and body.

Beck's Beer: America's number-one German beer import. Light gold; smooth, light taste. **Beck's Dark** may be a bit too dense for most American tastes.

DAB Meister Pils: The classic beer of Dortmund and one of the best-selling beers in Germany. Sharp, dry, and hoppy.

Hacker-Pschorr Light Beer: One of the best anywhere. An excellent, clean, amber-colored beer, with a good malt bite.

Kulmbacher Monkshof Amber Light Beer: A wonderful beer, full-bodied and aromatic. Definitely recommended. Also comes in a dark variety, pretty high in alcohol.

Löwenbräu: Is now also brewed in the U.S.A. The Munich variety is superior, but, unfortunately, it's only available in Canada.

Pinkus Ale: Lovely dark gold color; strong hop flavor. A German classic. Highly recommended.

Pinkus Pils: Another winner. Lovely gold color; bracing hops taste.

Pinkus Weizen: One of the better wheat beers (brewed with a mixture of 30 percent wheat, 70 percent malted barley). Light-bodied and easy to drink. Try serving with a wedge of lemon.

Spaten Munich Light: A big, hearty, robust beer from the famous Munich brewery. Worth looking for.

St. Pauli Girl Beer: Mild, balanced, but not especially distinguished German beer. Also comes in a dark version.

GREAT BRITAIN

The traditional British brew is ale, which is identified as *mild* or *bitter* when it's ordered in a pub and pulled on draft. The Brits prefer bitter, which is pasteurized but unfiltered and served at cellar temperature. The British ale we get over here is bottled, but still quite good. In general, the British ales are rather low in alcohol and carbonation and have a mildly hoppy taste.

Bass Pale Ale I.P.A.: The I.P.A. stands for *India Pale Ale*, a British classic, often imitated but brought to perfection by Bass. Many give credit to the famous chalky water of Burton-on-Trent for the superiority of this ale.

John Courage Export: Available here on draft in certain bars and restaurants. Nice malty character.

MacEwan's Scotch Ale: Dark amber, rich and malty. Unbeatable for heartiness.

MacEwan's Edinburgh Ale: A more subtle and lighter-bodied brew than the Scotch Ale. Also highly recommended.

Mackeson Stout: The big rival to Ireland's Guinness. Not everyone can stomach this ultradark, thick-and-heavy style of brew; but those who like stout must try this one.

Ind Coope Double Diamond Bur-

ton Pale Ale: A light-tasting, dry, and pleasant ale. The top seller in Britain.

Newcastle Brown Ale: Nutty brown color; rich and pleasing malt taste. Extremely popular and highly regarded in Britain.

Theakston Old Peculier Yorkshire Ale: Harks back to the traditional, old-style English brews, with a recipe supposedly unchanged since 1837.

HOLLAND

Heineken Lager Beer: America's most popular imported beer. Widely available, even better on draft.

Grolsch Natural Holland Beer: First-rate, clean, balanced, and lively tasting. Now getting wider distribution.

IRELAND

Guinness Extra Stout: The real thing, as found in Ireland and Britain, is superior to the exported product; but if you go for stout, this is the classic. Even better on draft.

Harp Lager: A splendid, firm, and pungent lager beer with beautiful tawny color. High recommendation.

ITALY

Dreher Export Beer: Unusual tasting, dry beer.

Peroni Premium Beer: Dark amber color; light-bodied, with nice hop fragrance and taste. Surprisingly good, since one doesn't usually associate Italy with beer.

JAPAN

Kirin Beer: This excellent brew is the best, and most popular, of Japan's beers. Bitter, hoppy, almost astringent.

Sapporo Lager Beer: Another interesting offering from Japan. Not quite as sharp and bracing as Kirin.

MEXICO

Dos Equis XX Beer: A superior Mexican beer in the dark, malty Viennese style. Other labels by the same company include Dos Equis XX Light Beer and an interesting Dos Equis Special Lager.

Tecate Cerveza: Pale and light and easy-drinking beer.

NEW ZEALAND

Steinlager New Zealand Lager Beer: Recommended, if you can find it, for a full-tasting and balanced brew.

Leopard Lager: Unusual and slightly sweet taste. One of the better-known New Zealand labels.

NORWAY

Aass Bok Beer: Interesting name and interesting taste: big, yeasty, and strong.

Rignes Special Beer: Excellent, and often quite reasonably priced, for an imported beer. It has a kick but not a bite.

PHILIPPINES

San Miguel Beer: Golden in color; pure, clean, light in taste; well-carbonated, with a slightly bitter tang. Definitely a superior beer.

SWITZERLAND

Cardinal Lager Beer: An excellent beer, with a superb balance of hops and malt. Look for it.

Feldschlossen Hopenperle: You

shouldn't have much trouble finding this high-quality beer. Strong-flavored and deep in color, it is not a dark beer but it has some of that robust quality.

Löwenbräu Zurich Export Light: Not to be confused with Munich's Löwenbräu. This Swiss product is lighter, paler, and more subtle. It's also unpasteurized, which is quite unusual in a bottled beer.

Beer and Ale Recipes

See section One for information on barware, mixing supplies, and mixing tips. For conversion to metric or other measurements, refer to tables on pages 11 and 22.

FOXTAIL
Pour beer over ice in beer stein or collins glass. Add twist of lemon.

MOUNT SAINT HELENS
Pour Pinkus Weizen beer over ice in beer stein or collins glass. Add a dash of raspberry syrup.

SHANDYGAFF
With left hand pour 6 ounces ale into collins glass, while at the same time pouring 6 ounces ginger beer with right hand. Stir.

RADLER
This is what it's called in Germany; the Irish call it a Shandy. Pour beer into stein, leaving room for about an inch of lemonade at the top; pour in lemonade.

LIME SHANDY
As above, but substitute lime juice for the lemonade.

BEER THE MEXICAN WAY
Pour 12 ounces beer into stein, add a pinch of coarse salt, then squeeze the juice from a small wedge of lemon or lime over drink; discard fruit. Serve unstirred.

BLACK VELVET
Pour 4 ounces chilled stout into highball glass, then add 4 ounces dry sparkling wine.

CALCUTTA CUP
Pour 4 ounces chilled stout into highball glass; add 3-to-4 ounces tonic water.

SHANDY STOUT
With one hand pour 6 ounces stout into collins glass, while at the same time pouring in 6 ounces lemon-lime soda with other hand. Stir.

TWO-LANE BLACKTOP
Pour 4 ounces stout into highball glass; add 3 to 4 ounces ginger ale.

ARF AND ARF
Fill beer stein to the top with ice. Pour in equal parts stout and lager beer.

TROJAN HORSE
Pour 4 ounces stout into highball glass, then add 3 to 4 ounces cola.

WILD BREW YONDER
Pour 1 ounce vodka and 2 teaspoonfuls blue curaçao into highball glass. Stir. Fill to top with cold beer.

LOADED PISTOL
Fill highball glass with ice. Pour in 1½ ounces tequila, and top with beer. Sprinkle surface with coarse-ground salt.

FAITH, HOPE, AND GARRITY

Stir 1 ounce Irish whiskey, 4 ounces V-8 juice, 1 teaspoonful barbecue sauce (preferably the smoky style), and 1 teaspoonful lemon juice with ice in mixing glass. Strain into collins glass, and top with beer.

BLEARY MARY

Stir 1½ ounces whiskey (preferably canadian), 3 ounces tomato juice, 1 teaspoonful Worcestershire sauce, and ½ teaspoonful Tabasco sauce with ice in mixing glass. Strain into collins glass. Slowly stir in beer to top. Sprinkle salt and freshly ground pepper on surface of drink.

SCHNAPPS SHOOTER

Pour 1½ ounces peppermint schnapps into shot glass. Pour 6 ounces beer into highball glass. Throw back the schnapps and chase with beer.

MULLED SPICED ALE

Dissolve 1 teaspoonful sugar and 1 pinch cinnamon in a little dark ale in bottom of metal tankard. Fill to top with ale, and heat by inserting a hot poker.

2

WATERS
AND MIXERS

Back in the old days before 1977, when people talked about "meeting for drinks" or a waiter asked for "drink orders," it was taken for granted that the drinks in question would contain some form of alcohol. Then along came Perrier with its $3-million ad campaign, which fed neatly into the new health consciousness of the American public. Suddenly, sophisticated American drinkers were raising glasses containing nothing more potent than sparkling mineral water, ice, and perhaps a twist of lime. No excuses needed to be made about being "on the wagon" or "under the weather" or whatever: Perrier was respectable, even chic. The American taste for lightness in beverages had reached its logical conclusion.

Perrier opened the floodgates to bottled water: Per capita consumption of bottled water more than doubled from 1970 to 1980. Natural spring waters, natural mineral waters, sparkling mineral waters, spring-fresh carbonated waters, club sodas, and seltzers poured onto the American market, swamping the consumer who only wanted a nice refreshing, healthy drink. Brands and styles of bottled waters have proliferated; price and flavors vary widely, and often with no relation to one another; domestic and foreign brands compete by means of healthy-sounding names and fancy labels that impart little or no information about the mineral and salt content. The beleagured consumer needs some light shed over the waters.

CLEARING UP WATERS

The basic distinctions in bottled water are between carbonated and noncarbonated, natural and processed. Carbonated water is impregnated with CO_2: When you pour it into a glass it fizzes, when you drink it, it tingles in your mouth and tickles your nose. Carbonated waters come in three basic varieties: sparkling mineral water; club soda, which is treated tap water to which minerals, salt, and carbonation have been added; and seltzer, which is carbonated tap water without the salt. Obviously, neither seltzer nor club soda bubbles naturally out of the earth. Sparkling mineral water, however, may either have natural carbonation, like Perrier, or have the carbonation added artificially. Bottled-water connoisseurs agree that nature does it better: The natural effervescence is lighter, lasts longer in the glass, and doesn't add an unpleasant harshness or bitterness to the taste. Most brands that have natural effervescence will say so right in their names; for example, Peters Val—Naturally Sparkling Mineral Water, from West Germany; or Saratoga—Naturally Sparkling Mineral Water.

Seltzer, which used to be an ethnic specialty of New York's Lower East Side and come from the seltzer man in old-fashioned syphon bottles, is currently enjoying a fad. In fact, seltzer is the fastest-growing beverage in the country; and it's not difficult to see why. Seltzer is healthier than club soda because it contains no added salt, and it's much cheaper than most sparkling mineral waters. Although waiters in posh places may look askance if you order seltzer-with-a-twist, many people are serving just that in their homes, and the Perrier diehards never seem to know the difference. Seltzer is also being substituted for club soda in many traditional mixed drinks such as scotch and soda.

The natural-versus-processed distinction also holds true for noncarbonated bottled water, but beyond that definitions grow a little fuzzy. In fact,

any bottled water can call itself *mineral water* unless it's distilled—which means that all the minerals have been processed out. As with carbonated waters, the naturals in the noncarbonated category will usually have the words *natural* or *spring* in their names, as in Great Bear Natural Spring or Hinckley and Schmitt Natural Spring waters. These natural mineral waters are bottled just as they flow from the ground. The processed waters are usually purified of their mineral content and then get certain minerals restored. Oddly, some so-called *mineral* waters have a lower mineral content than ordinary tap water. No Federal regulations yet exist for bottled waters, and information about mineral content is seldom printed on the label. So one must be governed, to a large extent, by taste.

Not long ago, *Consumer Reports* rated a whole slew of bottled waters, and they found that the best-tasting of all was New York City tap water! Their tasters' criteria reflected the preferences of most Americans for light, soft, and neutral waters. But unless you live in New York City, you probably want to have some bottled spring water on hand for splashing into whiskey, especially bourbon (this is what Kentuckians mean when they speak of "Bourbon and branch").

At the opposite end of the flavor spectrum are the highly alkaline, hard waters—Vichy Célestins is the best-known example—which many find "soapy" or "medicinal" tasting. Europeans down these waters as aids to digestion after rich, heavy meals; if you want to acquire a taste for them, this might be the best time to try. Europeans also claim a variety of medical benefits derived from their mineral waters, but science has never documented any of these.

When using bottled sparkling waters as mixers, stick with the nonalkaline brands (see listings below), club soda, and seltzer. Scotch-and-soda is an old favorite, and the bubbly mixer can be any form of sparkling water. The same goes for vodka and rum, both of which react well to a little effervescence. More recently, sparkling water has been used to enliven dry white or red wine in "spritzers."

Other carbonated beverages that are suitable for mixing with alcohol include tonic water (also called *quinine water*) and various soft drinks. The drier the better is a good rule of thumb in deciding on tonic waters, which mix well with vodka, gin, and rum. Some companies offer sugar-free brands. Soft-drink mixers have been going out of style for several years now, and we say good riddance. This custom is a holdover from Prohibition, when something strong and sweet was needed to mask the awful taste of the bootleg stuff. Now that perfectly good rum and bourbon and blended whiskey are available here, why ruin it by pouring in soda pop? However, if you must, the traditional mixes are: rum and cola (try it with a squeeze of lemon), bourbon or blended whiskey (please, never scotch) and ginger ale and blended whiskey and 7-Up (as with Seagram's 7 Crown in the 7 & 7). According to the Pepsi Co., vodka and Mountain Dew is fast becoming a classic.

CHOOSING THE WATERS

The following listings of bottled waters are far from complete, or even comprehensive. Instead, we have tried to seek out the best and most widely available brands. As far as club soda and seltzers go, you're on your own: there are national brands and local supermarket brands—taste variations are not that great, anyway; so try a few until you find one you're happy with.

NONCARBONATED

Caddo Valley Spring Water: Comes from the Ouachita Mountain Range in the Ozarks, bottled in Texas.

Calistoga: Natural geyser water from California's Napa Valley. Nice, clean, and pleasant tasting.

Deep Rock Artesian Fresh Drinking Water: A fine natural water from an 850-foot artesian well, sold in seven Western states.

Deer Park 100% Spring: Sold in bulk sizes. A good drinking water, widely available.

Evian Natural Spring: Very popular in France, where it originates.

Fiuggi Natural Mineral Water: Noticeable, but not overpowering, mineral taste. From the valley of the River Sacco in central Italy.

Great Bear Natural Spring: A good domestic brand, number one in the Northeast.

Mountain Valley Water: From a natural spring in Hot Springs, Arkansas, and available nationwide. Superb water, highly recommended.

Hinckley and Schmitt Natural Spring: Light, natural, and slightly sweet. Available in the Midwest.

211

Poland Spring Pure Natural Mineral Water: A Maine spring water of fine quality and wide availability. Company has been owned by Perrier since 1980.

Silver Springs Drinking Water: One of the better processed domestic waters. From Florida.

CARBONATED

Apollinaris Natural Mineral Water: Rather high in sodium, but nice natural effervescence. On the alkaline side. From Bad Neuenahr, West Germany.

Badoît Naturally Sparkling Mineral Water: Low on bubbles, high on minerals. From France.

Calistoga Sparkling Mineral Water: Naturally carbonated geyser water from the Napa Valley. One of the higher-rated American brands.

Ferrarelle Naturally Sparkling Mineral Water: Low salt content, but highly alkaline. From Italy.

Gerolsteiner Sprudel Natural Mineral Water: A sharp-tasting and moderately effervescent water from West Germany. Recommended.

Jagger's Sparkling Scottish Water A lovely light water that runs off the moors of Scotland. Mix it with Scotch, what else?

Montclair Sparkling Natural Mineral Water: Nice, light, low-salt, and balanced water from Canada, with good effervescence. Highly recommended.

Perrier Naturally Sparkling Mineral Water: The marketing miracle of the '70s, from the source in Vergeze, France. Can't knock success—it's good.

Peters Val Naturally Sparkling Mineral Water: A bit stronger taste than most, with moderate fizz. From West Germany.

Poland Spring Natural Spring Water: The bubbly version of this Maine water is light, clean, and soft. Nice for mixing.

Ramlösa Sparkling Mineral Water: A very light-tasting and lightly sparkling water from Sweden. Iron- and lime-free. Good for drinking and mixing.

San Pellegrino Mineral Table Water: An Italian water with a strong alkaline flavor; the bubbles are added artificially. Reputed to be a laxative.

Saratoga Naturally Sparkling Mineral Water: A good introduction to the alkaline waters: It's got the taste, but not overwhelmingly.

Vichy Célestins: One of the saltiest and most alkaline of waters, with very light carbonation. Definitely an acquired taste. From France.

CHEERS!

Drink has always smoothed the way of social intercourse, and throwing a party should be the natural outcome of your education in wines and spirits. Whether you want to invite five or fifty, this section will prepare you with party punches, party plans, party food, and party toasts. After that, you're on your own, ready to greet your guests with aplomb. Here's to you, the best of hosts!

1

PUNCHES

Back in the days when men wore lace at their throats and swords at their sides and swaggered about in breeches and stockings, punch was all the rage. Colonial squires and English gentlemen would mix them up hot or cold, winter or summer, and present the flowing bowl at social gatherings in the spirit of convivial hospitality. Punches were (and are still) often curious drinks with odd ingredients; but the informing principle continues to be: Pour on the alcohol and don't stint. The name itself is rather curious, deriving from the Hindi word *pac*, meaning "five," a reference to the five traditional ingredients: liquor, water, sugar, lemon, and spice. These days punches may be light or robust, cold or hot, liquory or winey or fruity or milky, spiced or bland. So long as it's mixed, liquid, alcoholic, and in a bowl, it qualifies as punch.

Punch consumption went into a decline after its peak in the middle of the 19th century. From then until fairly recently, punches were largely relegated to such formal social events as weddings, Christmas celebrations, New Year's parties, garden parties, and proms. But the popularity of sangría and similar wine drinks has prompted something of a revival. People are finding out how easy it is to mix these concoctions and how enjoyable the results can be.

Punch is a party natural because it can be prepared in advance and in large quantity, freeing the host from the bother of constantly refilling drinks requests. Some punches can also be prepared in individual servings, so that one can sample the recipe before inflicting it on everyone one knows—or relive that party spirit all by oneself. You may feel foolish drinking out of the cutesey little cups, known as *knuckletraps*, that usually come with punch bowls; these can be dispensed with in favor of Delmonico glasses, rocks glasses, or plain old tumblers.

CHOOSING
THE RIGHT PUNCH

There are various schools of thought concerning the proper punch, each convinced that it alone has the secret of success. The rum school maintains that without this cane spirit the beverage is not entitled to the honorable name of *punch*. The no-rum school shudders at the very idea of dispersing good rum among so many contaminants. Then there are those who hold with the attraction of opposites as the guiding principle behind punch mixing—they insist that punch must unite sweet and sour, dark and light, strong and weak. For example: sweet sugar, sour lemon juice; dark rum, white wine; strong brandy, weak soda.

Champagne punch is traditional at weddings, hot buttered rum on cold wintry nights, and the time-honored Philadelphia Fish House Punch when you want the strong stuff our Founding Fathers drank. A bowle is a wonderful way the Europeans have devised to turn fresh fruit into a refreshing drink—the fruits change with the season. A mint julep can be punched up to served a group, and milk punch is guaranteed to wake you up, put you to sleep, wipe out a cold, take care of a hangover or get a new one started—depending on your whim of the moment. Swedish Punsch is not really a punch at all but an aged liqueur combining the intense Indonesian rum known as *Batavia arak*, neutral spirits, and wine; the Swedes drink it hot in the winter as an accompaniment to pea soup.

One neat serving touch is to float an island of ice in the middle of the punch bowl. If the recipe calls for fruit garnish, try freezing the fruit into the island in the following way:

Secure a large plastic container, pour in water to about halfway and freeze. Now lay on the orange slices, mint leaves, strawberries, or whatever; cover with water and return to freezer. Finally, fill container to top with water and freeze the whole thing solid. When it's time to serve, submerge in warm water for a few seconds before dislodging the fruited island into the punch bowl.

For each gallon of punch, you'll want a two-quart block of ice. As a general rule in preparing cold punches, have all the liquid ingredients chilled before pouring over the ice. Champagne punches are usually served with the ice on the outside, in a kind of ice-bed in which the punch bowl nestles.

If you have a flair for hostly pyrotechnics, you might want to wow your guests with this Old New England method of heating up hot drinks: Get a clean poker, hold it in a roaring blaze until it's nice and hot, then plunge it into a mug of hot buttered rum or whatever; remove and serve.

Punch Recipes

See Section One for information on barware, mixing supplies, and mixing tips. For conversion to metric or other measurements, refer to tables on pages 11 and 22.

COLD PUNCHES

NOTE: Remember to chill all ingredients before mixing cold punches.

PRIMAVERA CHAMPAGNE PUNCH

Pour into punch bowl 4 ounces brandy, 2 ounces curaçao, 1 ounce Grand Marnier, and 1 ounce maraschino liqueur. Stir well. If bowl is not nestled in ice to keep punch cold, add small block of ice. Just before serving, pour in a bottleful of champagne, slices of orange, chunks of pineapple, and sprigs of mint.

SPARKLING SEA-BREEZE PUNCH

Pour into punch bowl 16 ounces cranberry juice, 6 ounces grapefruit juice, 8 ounces gin, the juice of ½ lime, and superfine sugar to taste. Stir well. Float a fruit isle (see p. 218) in the bowl if desired—if not, no ice is necessary if all liquids have been well chilled beforehand. Finally, pour in 1 bottle of champagne and garnish with cherries and orange peel.

SOCIETY HILL CHAMPAGNE PUNCH

In a bowl or pitcher that can be covered and refrigerated, mix 8 ounces Jamaica rum, 2 ounces triple sec, 2 ounces kirsch, 2 ounces grenadine; also 3 sectioned tangerines, 1 sectioned grapefruit, and 2 cups fresh pineapple cubes. Cover, and refrigerate several hours. Just before serving, add 2 bottles champagne and garnish with mint leaves.

FRAMBOISE PUNCH SORBET

Pour 4 ounces framboise and 2 ounces orange curaçao into punch bowl. Then scoop in 1 quart raspberry sorbet. Mix well. Just before serving, pour in 2 bottles champagne. Garnish with fresh raspberries.

GREEN EYES PUNCH

Pour into punch bowl 3 quarts California Emerald Riesling, 6 ounces brandy, 6 ounces apricot brandy, and 20 ounces apple juice. Place block of ice in bowl. Float 3 or 4 thin cucumber slices on top.

ORANGE CUP PUNCH

Pour into punch bowl 6 ounces orange juice, 16 ounces white wine, 1 bottle rosé wine, and sugar to taste. Stir until sugar is dissolved; add small block of ice. Float a few thin orange slices on top.

STRAWBERRY BOWLE

Pour into punch bowl 4 bottles white wine and 8 ounces crème de cassis. Stir. Add block of ice and stir again.

Float 2 cups hulled strawberries and thin slices of orange on surface.

STRAWBERRY BOWLE II

Pour 2 cups dry red wine into mixing bowl, add ½ cup superfine sugar, and stir until sugar dissolves; add 2 quarts fresh strawberries. Refrigerate at least 1 hour. Just before serving, put small block of ice in punch bowl and pour over it wine mixture from refrigerator. Add 2 bottles sparkling wine, and stir gently.

PEACH BOWLE

Follow recipe for Strawberry Bowle II, except use peeled, sliced peaches instead of strawberries.

SPARKLING PUNCH WITH CURLS

Pour in punch bowl a "fifth" (750 ml bottle) of brandy, 4 ounces curaçao, 6 ounces orange juice, 4 ounces lemon juice, and 4 ounces grenadine. Stir well. Add superfine sugar to taste, and stir again until sugar is dissolved. Put a small block of ice into bowl, then pour in bottle of sparkling dry white wine. Carefully peel an orange so that the peel comes off in one thick spiral, and drop 3 or 4 curls into punch bowl.

SPECIAL HOUSE PUNCH

Pour into punch bowl over large block of ice 3½ bottles wine, 4 ounces amaretto, 4 ounces brandy and 4 ounces cherry brandy. Stir; then refrigerate for 1 hour. Just before serving, add 16 ounces ginger ale.

DRAGOON PUNCH BOWL

Slice 2 lemons very thin and toss in bottom of punch bowl; cover with 3 tablespoonfuls sugar. Bruise lemons with muddler or tip of wooden spoon. Pour in 6 ounces cognac, 6 ounces sherry, 1 quart ale, and 1 quart Guinness stout. Stir well. Place a block of ice in bowl and, finally, pour in champagne.

CLARET CUP

Pour into large pitcher 1 bottle red wine, 2 ounces each brandy and Cointreau, and 1 tablespoonful sugar. Stir until sugar dissolves. Just before serving, add 1 lemon and 1 lime sliced thin, a few slices fresh pineapple, and a generous splash of club soda.

SANGRÍA

Pour into large pitcher 1 bottle red wine. Add thin slices of orange, lemon, and lime, and chunks of pineapple. Pour in ¼ cup sugar, and stir to dissolve. Refrigerate overnight. Just before serving, taste to adjust sweetness and pour in 1 pint club soda. Stir again gently.

For white sangría, substitute white wine.

ARTILLERY PUNCH

The night before: Into an 8-quart container that can be covered and refrigerated pour a purée of 1 quart strawberries, 12 ounces unsweetened pineapple juice, and 1 quart orange juice. Stir well. Add 1 bottle bourbon, 1 bottle dark rum, 4 quarts hard cider. Stir again briefly, cover and refrigerate overnight. Just before serving, place a large block of ice in a 6-or-7-gallon tub.

Pour mixture over ice. Pour in 10 bottles sparkling white wine. If you prefer to serve punch in a smaller bowl and replenish as necessary, pour in a little more than 1 bottle of the wine for every quart of refrigerated mixture.

PEACH BRANDY PUNCH

Peel and slice 1 pound peaches and toss with 6 tablespoonfuls sugar. Pour in 3 bottles white wine, then let mixture stand at room temperature for at least an hour. Just before serving, pour in 1 quart club soda, 2 ounces cognac, and 2 ounces triple sec. Stir gently. Place a block of ice in punch bowl.

PAPAYA PUNCH

Put into blender chunks from 1 large papaya, 2 ripe bananas, and a pound of apricots peeled, pitted, and halved. Blend until smooth and pour into punch bowl. Add 1 quart orange juice, ½ cup lime juice, 1 bottle light blended whiskey, and 1 quart club soda. Stir gently, and garnish with 2 limes sliced thin.

BARBADOS BOWLE

Put into blender 6 bananas, 1 cup lime juice, and 1 cup sugar. Blend until smooth. Pour over block of ice in punch bowl. Add 12 ounces each light and dark rum, 12 ounces mango nectar, and 44 ounces pineapple juice; stir well. Let mixture stand in refrigerator for an hour. Before serving, garnish with 1 banana and 1 lime, sliced thin.

INTERPLANETARY PUNCH

Pour into punch bowl 24 ounces light rum, 4 ounces dark rum, 8 ounces peppermint schnapps, 1 quart mango nectar, 12 ounces cream, and 1 quart orange juice. Stir. Add large block of ice. Float on surface of punch leaves picked from 8 mint sprigs, thin slices of 1 orange, and 1 large fresh mango cut into small pieces.

FISH HOUSE PUNCH

Stir in punch bowl ½ pound sugar and 2 quarts water until sugar dissolves. Add 1 quart lemon juice, 2 quarts rum, 1 quart cognac, and 4 ounces peach brandy. Put large block of ice in bowl, and let mixture sit at least 2 hours—ice will dissolve to dilute mixture. (In a very warm room, use less water—1½ quarts—because more ice will dissolve.) Stir and taste. Adjust sweetness as necessary.

NAVY PUNCH

Pour half a bottle (or 12 ounces) each dark rum, brandy, and Southern Comfort into punch bowl. Add 2 cupfuls pineapple chunks, 3 ounces lemon juice, and 1½ teaspoonfuls superfine sugar. Stir well to dissolve sugar; add block of ice. Just before serving, pour in 4 bottles white sparkling wine and stir gently.

PENNSYLVANIA PUNCH

Pour into punch bowl 2 pints water, 1 scant cup sugar, 1 bottle each bourbon and brandy, ½ bottle peach brandy, and 6 ounces lemon juice. Stir well. Add block of ice. Garnish with very thin orange and lemon slices.

CAPTAIN'S TEA PUNCH

In punch bowl, stir 4 bottles dry white

wine, 12 ounces gin, 1 cup chilled brewed green tea, 1 cup light rum. Add 2
lemons, sliced very thin. Complete
with block of ice.

SHAKESPEARE'S BOWL

Stir in punch bowl 24 ounces gin, 4
ounces Cointreau, 2 ounces brandy, 6
ounces lemon juice, and 1 heaping teaspoonful superfine sugar. Stir well to
dissolve sugar. Add one bottle lemon
soda. Drop in small block of ice. On
top, float thin slices from 1 lemon.

LIQUORICE PUNCH

In large container that can be covered
and refrigerated, put 12 ounces sambuca, 1 quart orange juice, 1 ounce
lemon juice. Cover and refrigerate.
Just before serving, put block of ice in a
punch bowl, pour in refrigerated mixture, add 1 pint bitter lemon, and stir.
Garnish with lemon slices.

BOURBON FOG

Brew 2 pints strong black coffee, then
refrigerate until well chilled. Pour the
coffee into punch bowl, and add 2
pints Bourbon and 2 pints French vanilla ice cream. Stir until smooth and
creamy. Sprinkle nutmeg on top.
Serve in mugs, and garnish with cinnamon stick.

NOGS

RAPPAHANNOCK EGGNOG

Beat yolks of 12 eggs with electric
mixer for about 30 minutes. Then,
with mixer on low, slowly and constantly add 12 level tablespoonfuls

sugar. Shot by shot add 3 pints bourbon, 8 ounces rum, and 12 ounces
brandy; then pour in 3 pints milk. Just
before serving, stir in 1 pint whipped
cream.

COGNAC NOG

Separate 12 eggs. Beat yolks until
light. Slowly and constantly add $1\frac{1}{2}$
cups sugar, and beat until mixture is
thick and pale. Chill at least 2 hours.
Beat the egg whites to stiff peaks and
reserve. Lightly whip heavy cream to
make 4 cupfuls, and reserve. Into
chilled yolk-and-sugar mixture, slowly
beat 6 cupfuls Cognac and 2 cupfuls
dark rum. With wire whisk, blend in 4
cupfuls milk and the whipped cream.
Fold in the beaten egg whites. Sprinkle
surface of punch with freshly grated
nutmeg when it is served.

HOT PUNCHES

MULLED BURGUNDY

Slice 3 lemons thin. Put in $2\frac{1}{2}$-quart
pot with 1 cupful sugar and 1 teaspoonful ginger. Add 1 bottle red burgundy,
4 ounces dry sherry, 1 small bottle
black currant cordial, and 2 cups
water. Heat, but do not let it boil. Add
a few whole cloves; stir. Strain into
mugs.

NEGUS

Over low heat, warm 1 bottle sherry in
cooking pot. Add 1 thin-sliced lemon.
Pour in 4 cups boiling water. Add nutmeg, and sugar to taste. Pour in 1 small
bottle (6.8 ounces) brandy. Stir, and
serve in mugs.

MULLED CLARET

Simmer rind of half a lemon, 12 whole cloves, and pinch of nutmeg in 2 cups water about 30 minutes in a saucepan. Strain into bowl and cover. Pour 1 bottle claret into saucepan, add 4 ounces port and 1 tablespoonful sugar, and heat. Pour spiced water from bowl into saucepan and bring to near-boil, then reduce heat. Serve in mugs garnished with lemon peel.

GLÜHWEIN

Heat 1 bottle of madeira in large saucepan. Add peels from 1 lemon and 1 orange, 3 cinnamon sticks (broken), 3 whole cloves, and 1 whole nutmeg (cracked). Add 1 tablespoonful honey, and stir to dissolve; taste; add more if desired, again stirring to dissolve. Let simmer at least 10 minutes. Strain into mugs, and stir with cinnamon sticks.

HOT SPICED KIR

Combine in large saucepan 2 cups Beaujolais, ½ cup crème de cassis, 4 strips lemon peel, 4 whole allspice, a pinch of cinnamon. Stir; let simmer 10 minutes. Strain mixture into warmed wine glasses. Serves 4.

HOT PORT BISHOP

Stick 12 cloves into an orange, put in baking dish, bake until brown. Cut browned orange into quarters and place in large saucepan. Pour in 1 bottle port and heat slowly—do not allow to boil. Stir in 2 cups rum, 12 whole allspice, 12 more cloves, 4 strips lemon peel, and pinch of cinnamon. Simmer 10 minutes. Remove from heat and ad-

just sweetness with brown sugar if necessary. Strain into mugs.

SMUGGLER'S NOTCH HOT BUTTERED RUM

Simmer for an hour in 2 gallons water: 1 dozen broken cinnamon sticks, 3 dozen cloves, 1 pound brown sugar. Strain into preheated mugs to fill to three-quarter level. Add rum to fill, and float 1 pat butter atop each mug. Use cinnamon stick to stir.

COGNAC GLOGG

In a heavy saucepan, heat 1 bottle Cognac, ½ cup sugar, 12 whole cloves, and 1 stick cinnamon to near-boil. Reduce heat; add 2 cups sherry, then 1 cup raisins. Pour into preheated mugs.

APPLE RUM PUNCH

Put in baking dish 6 oranges stuck with 12 cloves each. Bake until brown. Put oranges in warmed punch bowl, and pour over them 1 bottle rum and ½ bottle brandy. Stir well. Set top of mixture alight, then pour on 3 quarts apple juice to extinguish. Sprinkle with ground cinnamon and nutmeg; serve in warm mugs.

WASSAIL BOWL

Put ½ cup raisins in small bowl and pour on 1 ounce calvados. Let stand 2 hours. Meanwhile, core 6 baking apples to within 1 inch of bottoms; put 1 tablespoonful dark brown sugar in each cavity. Butter a baking dish and arrange apples in single layer. Bake them 45 minutes at 300 degrees, then transfer to warmed punch bowl with slotted spoon. While they are baking, combine in a saucepan 4 cups sweet sherry, 3 tablespoonfuls grated lemon rind, 1 large pinch each cinnamon, nutmeg, ground cloves, and ground cardamom. Simmer 5 minutes. Meanwhile, in large bowl beat 6 egg whites (reserve yolks in separate bowl) with a pinch each of salt and cream of tartar, until egg whites hold soft peaks. Slowly add ¼ cup sugar, and continue to beat until whites hold stiff peaks; set aside. Take bowl of egg yolks and beat until they are thick, then stir in hot sherry mixture slowly with a whisk until well combined. Fold egg whites into yolk-and-sherry mixture; pour over apples in punch bowl, then sprinkle with nutmeg and the brandied raisins.

A YARD OF FLANNEL

Separate 4 eggs. Set aside two of the whites in a bowl. In another bowl, beat all 4 yolks; add 4 tablespoonfuls brown sugar and ½ tablespoonful nutmeg. Stir. Beat the 2 egg whites and fold them into yolk mixture. Boil 1 quart ale and gradually stir egg mixture into it. Pour all into another saucepan, then back into first pan, and continue back and forth until mixture is smooth and frothy. Serve hot.

2

PARTY PLANNING

When is the last time your host greeted you at the door dressed in a smoking jacket and red bow tie, handed you a freshly mixed manhattan (his own secret recipe) before you had time to entrust your hat to the maid, and told you, as he sailed off to the next guest, to help yourself to the cigarettes tastefully stacked in silver boxes? Parties, clearly, are not what they used to be.

These days a host can set out a few bottles of good white wine, stock the refrigerator with beer and seltzer, tell the assembled to serve themselves—and not one guest will go home disappointed. Then again, one can lay in a case of French Champagne and watch even the stodgiest guests pop their corks. Imaginative hosts can declare it Tropical Fiesta and serve mai tais, zombies, and piña colada to folks who can't even guess the ingredients, and be talked about for days. The point is: Anything goes, so long as you match the liquid ingredients to the people you've invited. All it takes is a little planning and an acquaintance with certain basic rules of thumb.

Above all, whatever kind of party you're throwing, remember: Don't run out, don't skimp, and don't panic.

PEOPLE

The foremost element of a successful cocktail party is, obviously, the people. While there's no hard-and-fast rule governing how to make up a guest list, the best parties do often seem to bring together the widest variety of characters. Ever been to a party where there's one clown and 29 quiet, sensitive souls? Even worse may be 29 clowns and one sensitive soul. Think about who will get along, and make sure every guest knows at least one other person. Don't necessarily assume that more is better. A huge loud smoky crush is no fun for anyone. If possible, try to get an accurate count of the number of guests planning to attend. It will make your life easier.

DRINKS

Now that you've made up your guest list, think about what the invited drink. Maybe *you* would like to show off your new skill in mixing pitchers of perfect martinis; but if your friends never touch hard liquor there may be some bad feelings. On the other hand, those who ask for bourbon-on-the-rocks out of habit will probably be delighted to try a mint julep if you let them know it's a specialty of the house. Even if you don't feel up to mastering a bartender's repertory of drink recipes, you may want to pick out a few from these pages that could become trademarks of your party style. And if you take a minute to ponder it, you can probably figure out which friends are likely to take you up on specially mixed drinks and which will stick forever to beer, white wine, or whatever.

Now for the rules of thumb governing how to stock up on liquor supplies.

Liquor bottles have gone metric: What used to be termed a *fifth* (of a U.S. gallon, that is: four fifths of a quart, 25.6 fluid ounces) is now 750 milliliters (see Table of Bottle Measures in Section One). This is the standard size for liquor and wine bottles, and when we say *bottle*, this is what we mean.

For all spirits, figure 17 drinks per bottle when pouring jigger (1½-ounce) drinks, and 12 drinks per bottle for generous 2-ounce drinks. For table wines and sparkling wines, figure 6 servings to a bottle; 8 from a bottle of fortified or aperitif wine; 25 from a bottle of brandy; 17 from a bottle of most liqueurs.

Standard soft-drink bottle size is 32 ounces; you can mix 8 drinks with this amount.

If you're throwing a "typical" cocktail party, it will go on for about two hours, during which time the typical guest will consume three drinks. Figure between three-quarters and one pound of ice per person, and don't worry if a lot of it goes down the drain. A bowl of party punch disappears at a faster rate than individually mixed drinks do. Intriguingly, seasoned hosts have noted that the older the crowd, the more liquor it consumes.

Take all these factors into account when planning your party, but don't get hung up on the calculations. The charts below will help in determining exactly how many bottles of spirits, wines, and aperitif wines to stock for parties of various sizes. When buying for bigger groups, you'll save money if you go for the liter size rather than the 750 milliliter one. You know your friends and their drinking tastes; because few hosts are willing (or able) to stock every type of wine and liquor, buy the bottles that will be in most demand.

The element of risk enters in when you don't know the drinking tastes of your invited guests. Always get too much rather than too little. You will probably be able to use the leftovers on another occasion; if not, many liquor stores will accept returns if you make such an arrangement with them beforehand.

Wine is almost always served at a

For spirits and wines, we assume each guest will have 3 drinks during the course of the party; for aperitifs, fortified wines and after-dinner brandies and liqueurs, 2 drinks per person seems to be the usual maximum. Bottles figured at 750-milliliter size.

BOTTLES OF SPIRITS FOR COCKTAIL PARTIES

2-ounce servings

Number of guests	Number of bottles
6	2
10	3
15	4
20	5
30	8
40	10

BOTTLES OF APERITIFS AND FORTIFIED WINES FOR COCKTAIL PARTIES

3-ounce servings

Number of guests	Number of bottles
6	2
10	3
15	4
20	5
30	8
40	10

BOTTLES OF WINE AND SPARKLING WINE FOR COCKTAIL PARTIES

4-ounce servings

Number of guests	Number of bottles
6	3
10	6
15	7
20	10
30	15
40	20

"typical" cocktail party today. In fact, if you've been following the trends in drinking habits you know that nearly half the guests will opt for wine over spirits these days. Therefore, if you don't know your crowd well assume you will need more wine than liquor.

Another factor is regional preference. A cocktail party in the South, for instance, will most likely turn up more bourbon than scotch drinkers, but in New York City stock up on scotch.

One popular party ploy is to have a main selection, such as a punch, a featured wine, margaritas, or mulled cider. Offer this first to your guests, but remind them that you also have other drinks. Most people will enjoy getting into the swing by choosing the specialty of the house, and some beer, whiskey, juice, and soda should take care of the rest.

Those who do not drink alcohol will always feel more welcome if you have taken care to provide something in addition to club soda. Apple cider, nonalcoholic beer, a sparkling grape juice or cider, or a good mineral water will be much appreciated. A good host never pushes alcohol—or any other substance, for that matter—on a guest. If he or she declines, simply ask what they would prefer. If you don't know your guests well, it's a good idea to give them an option of a nonalcoholic beverage in your opening offer. While drinking alcohol is one of the pleasures of a cocktail party, it is not an end in itself. Your main goal as a host is to get people together and make them feel comfortable.

COCKTAIL FARE

Even more than drink, cocktail-party food has become a matter of personal preference and individual style. Modernist hosts hold that less is more and restrict their offerings to peanuts; health-minded hosts serve bowls of what they call *crudités* (which used to be called "raw vegetables"); galloping gourmets heap platters with stuffed mushroom caps, puff pastries, miniature quiches, and homemade pâté; financially well-endowed hosts dispense with such frippery and stick to caviar. You, too, can follow your own instincts.

Whatever you plan to serve, it's important not to run out of it in the first half hour. For that "typical" two-hour cocktail party, figure that your guests will reach for food ten or twelve times. If you're serving cheese, nuts, and hors d'oeuvres, for instance, plan on a quarter pound of cheese, two ounces of nuts, and six-to-eight hors d'oeuvres per guest.

A boon to today's host is the ready availability of prepared foods in specialty shops or delicatessens. Smoked fish, freshly made pâtés, marinated mushrooms, seafood salad, and caviar spreads are just a few of the delicious party foods you can buy at the last minute—along with hams, cheeses, breads, crackers, nuts, olives, and so on. You needn't spend hours in the kitchen to offer your guests unusual and tasty hors d'oeuvres. At the end of this chapter we've appended a few of our favorite recipes easy to prepare at home. Shop around beforehand. Know what you want to buy and what you'd like to make—if anything—and be sure you have enough trays or platters for easy serving.

During the party, check to replenish dips or canapés or add crackers to the cheese tray and remove any picked-over platters. For a big party where the food table is not easily accessible to most of the guests, be sure to pass the hors d'oeuvres.

OTHER PARTIES

When you're hosting a dinner party with wine, you can pretty much figure one bottle for every two people. Often hosts find that, when they serve two different wines, the guests drink more—of both. Therefore, at a dinner for six with two different wines, better have four bottles—two of each wine. Have seven bottles total on hand for ten guests; five bottles of *each* wine for fifteen guests; a total of thirteen bottles for twenty guests; and a caterer, bartender, and maid for any more than that.

If you are serving brandy and liqueurs after dinner, stock up according to the formulas below. Another nice occasion to consider: a lateish evening party, say at nine, or after the theater, for dessert, coffee, and liqueurs.

Beer is the thing at beach parties, barbecues, and TV football parties. Unless your pals resemble the cast of *Animal House,* plan on three brews per body. You'd be surprised at how many fellows who insist that Miller is good enough for them will notice the difference when you serve your favorite regional, microbrewery, or imported beer.

If you know some people who enjoy sampling different wines, think about hosting a wine-tasting party. Decide on a theme, for example: German whites of the Rheingau, or rosés of the world for a summer party; nouveau Beaujolais in the late fall when it first arrives from France; sparkling wines to pick you up in midwinter; or California and French wines made from the same grape variety. A reputable wine dealer will help you in selecting the specific bottles. Customary food for such tastings is nothing more than cubes of mild, hard cheese and small

BOTTLES OF BRANDY AND LIQUEURS FOR AFTER-DINNER DRINKS

1-ounce servings from 750-milliliter bottles

Number of guests	Number of bottles
6	½
10	1
15	2
20	2
30	3
40	4

slices of French or Italian bread. The idea is to cleanse, rather than cloy, the palate between the different wines. Perrier, seltzer, bottled spring water, or tap water (if yours is clean tasting) will also help guests refresh their taste buds. Make sure you have plenty of the appropriate type of glassware.

Easy Hors d'Oeuvres

See Section One for information on barware, mixing supplies, and mixing tips. For conversion to metric or other measurements, refer to tables on pages 11 and 22.

VEGETABLE DIP

1 pint cottage cheese
1 cup yogurt
½ cup chopped fresh dill
½ cup chopped scallions
2 dashes Tabasco sauce
Salt and freshly ground black pepper, to taste.

Mix all ingredients in a blender; taste; add more seasoning if necessary. This dip is better if covered and refrigerated overnight. Serve in bowl surrounded by an assortment of fresh raw vegetables: green beans, cauliflower or broccoli florets, zucchini rounds, green or red pepper strips, peeled and sliced turnips, carrots, celery, etc.

CHEESE TOAST

Toast white or whole wheat bread lightly on both sides. (Several slices can be done quickly under the broiler.) Place pieces of toast on baking sheet. Put slices of Cheddar or gouda cheese on toast. Top with thin slices of top-quality smoked ham. (Optional further topping: slice of canned pineapple.) Just before serving, heat the toast under preheated broiler until cheese melts and puffs. Cut in quarters and serve.

CREAM CHEESE SPREADS

Soften an 8-ounce hunk of cream cheese, and you have the beginnings of any number of delicious cocktail spreads. One of the simplest is to fold either chopped chutney or a small jar of red caviar into the cream cheese. Serve with thin-sliced pumpernickel bread or crackers. Another variation follows.

BOURSIN AU POIVRE

8 ounces cream cheese, softened
1 clove garlic, crushed
1 teaspoonful caraway seed
1 teaspoonful basil, dried or fresh
1 teaspoonful dill weed, dried or fresh
1 teaspoonful chopped chives
Lemon pepper.

Blend cheese with other ingredients, except pepper. Form a slightly flattened ball, and roll it in pepper. Refrigerate until ready to serve.

HUMMUS AND PITA

1 20-ounce can chick peas (garbonzo beans), drained
½ cup water
½ teaspoonful ground cumin
⅓ cup lemon juice, or to taste
⅓ cup tahini (sesame seed paste)
2 cloves garlic, crushed.

Purée chick peas with remaining ingredients in a blender. Add salt and freshly ground pepper to taste. Add more lemon juice or garlic, if desired. Put in serving bowl, sprinkle lightly with 1 tablespoonful olive oil, and garnish with lots of fresh chopped parsley. Serve with pieces of pita bread, or with raw vegetables.

DANISH CHEESE STACKS

½ pound butter, softened
½ pound Danish blue cheese
6 tablespoonfuls cognac
20 thin slices pumpernickel.

Cream the butter, add blue cheese, mix until smooth. Add cognac. Spread 16 of the slices of bread with mixture, then make four stacks of four slices; top each with an unspread slice. Refrigerate stacks until firm. Cut into eighths —either rectangles or triangles. These (and other) sandwiches can be kept fresh in the refrigerator for a couple of hours if you cover the platter with a clean, damp dish towel.

SHRIMP WITH CURRY MAYONNAISE

For Shrimp:

2 pounds shrimp, medium or large size
2 bottles or cans of beer (12-ounce size)
1 clove garlic, peeled
2 teaspoonfuls salt

½ teaspoonful thyme
2 bay leaves
1 teaspoonful celery seed
1 tablespoonful chopped parsley
⅛ teaspoonful cayenne pepper, or dash Tabasco sauce
Juice of half a lemon.

For Mayonnaise:

1 cup mayonnaise
2 tablespoonfuls curry powder, or to taste.

(1) Rinse shrimp. Combine other shrimp ingredients in saucepan and bring to boil. Add shrimp, bring to boil again. Reduce heat; simmer about 2 minutes, or until shrimp are pink. Take pot off heat and let shrimp cool in the liquid; then remove shells. (2) Mix the mayonnaise with curry powder to taste. (3) Arrange shrimp on lettuce-lined platter with bowl of the curried mayonnaise in the center. Cover and chill until ready to serve.

MELON AND PROSCIUTTO

An old classic, and perfect for summer parties. You'll need a melon baller, if you don't already own one. Roll a thin slice of paper-thin sliced ham around each melon ball and secure with a toothpick.

3

THE ART
OF TOASTING

Some people enjoy nothing better than to be called upon to set the seal on a festive occasion with an appropriate toast. They rise manfully, glass in hand, and in a few easy phrases express the sentiment that all are feeling and none could put into words. Others would sooner leap from an airplane without a parachute than be forced to deliver an impromptu toast. They rack their brains but come up with nothing more imaginative than "Here's how!" or "Down the hatch!" As dread deepens into despair, they weigh the advantages of fainting, fleeing, or feigning temporary insanity.

If you are one of these, read on.

First of all, there's no reason to make up your own feeble toast when you can just as easily steal someone else's. The custom of proposing toasts over alcoholic drinks dates back to the late 17th century, and scores of pithy, witty, amusing, and solemn toasts have been spoken and recorded since then. Lucky indeed were the first toasters, for the original toasts consisted simply of the name of some lovely lady, the speaking of which was supposed to have the same flavor-enhancing effect on the drink as a slice of spiced toast (once considered a very special treat). By the middle of the 18th century, men were toasting the health not only of ladies but also of friends, politicians, and monarchs. And so evolved our practice of toasting couples at weddings, sons and daughters at christenings, bosses at testimonial dinners, and just about anyone else on any occasion that seems to merit it.

If you're attending some function where you think it's likely you'll be singled out for toast-making, go prepared. Take down the Bartlett's or get your hands on some toastmaster's treasury; select an appropriate quotation or tag and memorize it. Most people will never know that Ben Jonson or Ambrose Bierce wrote your toast, and those who do will be impressed by your erudition and powers of recall.

If, however, you think this is cheating and insist on inventing an original

233

toast, keep these tips in mind: Match the toast to the occasion; be personal when toasting people (for example, throw in some anecdote that shows you're familiar with their quirks or some incident in their past); be warm and lively but not gushing; never insult the person you're toasting unless it's that kind of function—and even then, think twice; speak up and speak slowly, so that you can be heard and understood; and, above all, be brief. "To the happy pair!" is clearly not adequate if you're the best man or the maid or matron of honor at a wedding; but a half-hour discourse on the nature of love, sex, and commitment just won't work unless you're Richard Pryor. Stay reasonably sober so that you won't make a fool of yourself.

It doesn't hurt to rehearse before a mirror and, if you really don't trust your memory, bring along a card with the toast written out on it. There are more dignified ways of silencing a crowd than clearing one's throat into a microphone or asking everyone to "please be quiet." It's usually enough to stand up, smile, and look as though you have something wonderful to say. If you can't be witty, be sincere: A heartfelt toast, no matter how awkward, says more than the most polished phrases glibly prattled.

There follow some of our favorite toasts from around the world and across the centuries.

Cheers!

Keep your head cool and your feet warm,
and a glass of good whiskey will do you no harm.

Absent friends, though out of sight,
we recognize them with our glasses.

Gin by pailfuls, wine in rivers,
Dash the window glass to shivers!
                              ——*Sir Walter Scott*

Let us have wine and women, mirth and laughter,
Sermons and soda water the day after.
                              ——*Lord Byron*

Drink today and drown all sorrow,
You shall perhaps not do't tomorrow
Best while you have it, use your breath;
There is no drinking after death.
                              ——*Beaumont and Fletcher*

Drink! for you know not whence you come, nor why:
Drink! for you know not why you go, nor where.
                              ——*Omar Khayyam*

Fill the cup and let it come,
I'll pledge you a mile to the bottom.
                              ——*William Shakespeare*

Let us wet our whistles.
                              ——*Petronius*

There's many a toast I'd like to say,
If I could only think it;
So fill your glass to anything,
And thank the Lord, I'll drink it!
                              ——*Wallace Irwin*

Mingle with the friendly bowl,
The feast of reason and the flow of soul.

——*Alexander Pope*

There are two things that will be
believed of any man whatsoever,
and one of them is that he has taken to drink.

——*Booth Tarkington*

Let us eat and drink, for tomorrow we die.

——*New Testament*

Candy is dandy, but liquor is quicker.

——*Ogden Nash*

I drink when I have occasion
and sometimes when I have no occasion.

——*Miguel de Cervantes Saavedra*

But fill me with the old familiar juice.
Methinks I might recover by and by.

——*Omar Khayyam*

I drink as the fates ordain it.
Come fill it and have done with rhymes.
Fill up the lovely glass and drain it
In memory of dear old times.

——*William Makepeace Thackeray*

Were I to prescribe a rule for drinking,
It should be formed upon a saying
quoted by Sir William Temple:
the first glass for myself,
the second for my friends,
the third for good humor,
and the fourth for mine enemies.

——*Joseph Addison*

Claret is the liquor for boys, port for men;
but he who aspires to be a hero must drink brandy.

——*Samuel Johnson*

Here's to the crook; here's to the cheat,
Here's to the mob and here's to the gang,
Here's to the sniper; and here's to the thief,
Low they all grovel and high they all hang.

Let the toast pass
Drink to the lass,
I'll warrant she'll prove
an excuse for the glass.
                    ——Richard Brinsley Sheridan

Let us toast the fools, but for them
the rest of us could not succeed.
                              ——Mark Twain

Here's to old Adam's crystal ale,
Clear, sparkling and divine,
Fair H$_2$O, long may you flow,
We drink your health (in wine).
                              ——Oliver Herford

Here's to your good health,
and your family's good health,
and may you all live long and prosper.
                              ——Joseph Jefferson

Here's to the land we love and the love we land.

Here's a health to every one;
Peace on earth, and heaven won.

May the flower of love never be nipped by the frost of dis-
     appointment,
nor shadow of grief fall among a member of this circle.

May the hinges of friendship never rust,
nor the wings of love lose a feather.
                              ——Dean Ramsay

Here's a health to all those that we love,
Here's a health to all those that love us,
Here's a health to all those that love them that love
     those
That love them that love those that love us.

Were't the last drop in the well,
As I gasp'd upon the brink,
'Ere my fainting spirit fell,
'Tis to thee that I would drink.

—Lord Byron

Here's Champagne to our real friends,
And real pain to our sham friends.

Here's to you, as good as you are,
And here's to me, as bad as I am;
And as bad as I am, and as good as you are,
I'm as good as you are, as bad as I am.

Drink to me only with thine eyes,
And I will pledge with mine:
Or leave a kiss but in the cup,
And I'll not ask for wine.

—Ben Jonson

Drink to the man who keeps his head,
though he loses his heart.

Old wood to burn, old wine to drink,
and friends in trust,
and old authors to read.

—Francis Bacon

Good luck till we are tired of it.

As we meet upon the level,
May we part upon the square.

To each and all a fair good night,
And pleasing dreams and slumber bright.

—Sir Walter Scott

Here's to the times we might have had,
Here's to the girls we might have won.
Here's that we do the thing next time,
That last time we should have done.

CHEERS!

To the old, long life and treasure
To the young, all health and pleasure.

—*Ben Jonson*

Good day, good health, good cheer, good night!

Finally, here are the equivalents in other languages of "To your health!"

Prosit!	German, from Latin
Salud!	Spanish
A vôtre santé!	French
Na Zdrowie! Vivat!	Polish
Na Zdorovia!	Russian
Kippis!	Finnish
Skål!	Swedish
L'chaim!	Hebrew
Salute!	Italian

INDEX

241

Augustiner Braü Munich Export Light
Beer, 203
Auld Man's Milk, 62
Auld New York, 61
Aunt Agatha, 83
Aunt Jemima, 173
Australian beer and ale, 201
Austrian beer, 201
Auslese wines, 121
Avignonesi, 116
Ayl village, 122

B

Bacardi Cocktail, 84
Baden wines, 120
Bad Kreuznach, 123
Badoît Naturally Sparkling Mineral Water,
212
Bahama Mama, 86
Bailey's B-52, 185
Bailey's Original Irish Cream, 167, 170
Bajan Snap, 93
Bal Harbour, 181
Ballantine beer, 198
Balmoral, 61
Baltimore Oriole, 67
Banana Boat, 75
Banana Frappé, 178
Banana Peel, 88
B&B, 168, 175
B&G Fonset-Lacours, 107
Bannockburn, 62
Bar at home, 7–11
Barbados Bowle, 221
Barbarella, 177
Barbaresco wine, 114
Barbary Coast, 61, 97
Barbecues, 229
Barbera grape, 114, 126
Barbican, 61
Bardolino wine, 115
Bar knife, 14
Barolo wine, 114
Baronial, 157–58
Barsac parish, 106
Barware and bar tips, 13–22
  barware, 13–16
  glassware, 16–19
  mixing supplies, 19–21
Bass Pale Ale I.P.A., 203

Bassermann-Jordan, Dr. von, 122
Beach parties, 229
Beaujolais-Villages wines, 109
Beaulieu Vineyards, 127
Beaulieu Vineyards Burgundy, 127
Beaulieu Vineyards champagne, 133
Beaulieu Vineyards Georges de Latour Private Reserve, 127
Beck's Beer, 203
Bedtime, 66
Beer and ale, 195–207
  brewing process for, 196–97
  choice brews, 197–98
  domestic, 198–201
  foreign, 201–205
  history of, 195
  recipes, 206–207
  storing and drinking, 197
  types of, 195–96
Beerenauslese wines, 121
Beer The Mexican Way, 206
Beer vessels, 18
Bee-Stung Lips, 92
Before The Revolution, 90
Belgian beer and ale, 201–202
Bellini, 138
Bénédictine, 168
Benmarl winery, 129
Benson Collins, 59
Bentley, 157
Bent Nail, 57
Berberana, 117
Bereich Bernkastel, 122
Bereich Johannisberg village, 122
Beringer/Los Hermanos, 127
Bermuda Dream, 87
Bernkasteler Doktor vineyard, 122
Bernkastel village, 122
Berry Bubbly, 181
Berryetto, 183
Betsy Ross, 173
Betsy Rosso, 173
Between The Sheets, 177
Big Bertha, 76
Big Boy Now, 67
Biondi-Santi, 116
Birthday Cooler, 43
Birthday Party, The, 187
Bit-O-Honey, 187
Bitter Bikini, 156
Bitter Blossom, 46